PICTORIAL EDINBURGH SERIES

EDINBURGH'S OLD TOWN
AND ITS ENVIRONS

PICTORIAL EDINBURGH SERIES

Malcolm Cant

EDINBURGH'S OLD TOWN

AND ITS ENVIRONS

MODERN PHOTOGRAPHY BY

Peter Stubbs FRPS

MALCOLM CANT PUBLICATIONS

To
Archie in Australia,
my second grandson

First published in 2008 by
Malcolm Cant Publications
13 Greenbank Row
Edinburgh EH10 5SY

ISBN 10: 0 9552487 1 X
ISBN 13: 978 0 9552487 1 9

British Library Cataloguing-in-Publication Data

A catalogue record for this book is available on request

Book and cover design by Mark Blackadder

Printed and bound by
The Cromwell Press, Trowbridge, Wiltshire, UK

CONTENTS

BY THE SAME AUTHOR

Marchmont in Edinburgh 1984
Villages of Edinburgh Volume 1 (North) 1986
Villages of Edinburgh Volume 2 (South) 1987
Edinburgh: Sciennes and the Grange 1990
Yerbury: A Photographic Collection 1850-1993 1994
Edinburgh: Gorgie and Dalry 1995
Villages of Edinburgh: An Illustrated Guide Volume 1 (North) 1997
The District of Greenbank in Edinburgh 1998
Villages of Edinburgh: An Illustrated Guide Volume 2 (South) 1999
Old Tollcross, Morningside and Swanston 2001
Marchmont, Sciennes and the Grange 2001
Old Dalry in Edinburgh 2002
Old Gorgie 2002
Edinburgh from the Air: 70 Years of Aerial Photography 2003
Old Dean and Stockbridge 2004
Knowing Your Grandfather 2004
Edinburgh Shops Past and Present 2005
Edinburgh People at Work and Leisure 2006
South Edinburgh 2007

INTRODUCTION AND ACKNOWLEDGEMENTS

When I first started to write about Edinburgh several years ago, it tended to be about the suburbs, especially in my series *Villages of Edinburgh*. At the time I was greatly encouraged by the work already done by the late Charles J. Smith. In recent years, however, my own collection of material on the city centre has grown sufficiently to enable me to tackle *Edinburgh's Old Town and its Environs* as part of my Pictorial Edinburgh Series.

The book is divided into four parts with black and white images, separated by three short colour sections depicting the work of the well-known Edinburgh photographer, Peter Stubbs. Part 1 begins, appropriately, with Edinburgh Castle, photographed by the late Norward Inglis, whose daughter, Barbara Simpson, has again allowed me to reproduce items from her father's wide collection of Edinburgh material. My script on the castle has been greatly strengthened by the assistance of Peter Yeoman of Historic Scotland. The remainder of Part 1 deals with the public buildings and closes of Castlehill and the Lawnmarket, concluding with a short account of the Bank of Scotland's presence in various Old Town locations over its long history.

Part 2 then takes up the story from St Giles Cathedral to Holyrood Palace, an area which encapsulates much of Edinburgh's ancient history. There are photographs of the churches, St Giles, the Tron and Canongate, and many other historic buildings and closes. Norward Inglis' mid-1950s picture of New Street and the Canongate is particularly poignant in view of the impending Caltongate development. This part of the book concludes with three pages on Holyrood Palace. I am grateful to Chris Tabraham of Historic Scotland for his helpful suggestions on my various captions.

Part 3 begins with the Scottish Parliament and runs westwards along Holyrood Road, the Cowgate, the Grassmarket, and then up Victoria Street to George IV Bridge. In the last decade, Holyrood Road (previously named South Back of the Canongate) has been transformed by clearing away many of the old industrial sites and replacing them with modern architecture. By contrast, the Cowgate, the Grassmarket and Victoria Street have retained much of their old-world charm. Part 3 concludes with pictures of the North Bridge and South Bridge, including Edinburgh University, the Royal College of Surgeons Edinburgh and the old Empire Theatre.

Part 4 deals with the Old Town environs to the south, namely the area around Bristo, Lauriston Place (just outside the old Flodden Wall), Tollcross and Lothian Road. The topics covered are Parker's Stores, the McEwan Hall, the Royal Infirmary, George Heriot's School, Central Hall, the Usher Hall and several excellent transport scenes, again contributed by Alan Brotchie.

Several of the photographs in the book come from my own collection but many others have been contributed by individuals whose names appear throughout the text.

I am also indebted to many people for advice and information. In alphabetical order they are: Margaret and Derek Allan; George Baird; Ian Belford; Kate Blackadder; Mary Brockington; Alan Brotchie; Hamish Coghill; Graeme Cruickshank; Colin Dale; David Easton; Dr Andrew Fraser; Douglas Glass; Brian Green; Phil Greenan; Jimmy Hogg; Peter Holmes; Andrew Holmes; Isabell Huggins; Louise Jenkins; Anne Kinnear; Roger Legge; Gordon McKean; Duncan McMillan; John Martin; Rev. Charles Robertson; Brian D. Smith; Daniel Sneddon; Dr Walter Stephen; Chris Tabraham; Debbie Tait; Mrs Sheila Wilkie; Pat and Tony Winkle; and Peter Yeoman. The staff of several organisations, archives and regiments also assisted: The Argyll and Sutherland Highlanders; Augustine United Church; The Bank of Scotland; The Black Watch; John Donald, China Merchants; Edinburgh City Archives; Edinburgh Room of the Central Library; George Heriot's School; Historic Scotland; Macdonald Hotel; Museum on the Mound; National Museums of Scotland, including the National Museum of Flight and the National War Museum of Scotland; Royal College of Surgeons Edinburgh; Royal Commission on the Ancient and Historical Monuments of Scotland; The Royal Scots; the Salvation Army; Scottish Borders Art Glass; and the Victoria League in Scotland.

As with all my previous books, I received assistance from a small group of professional people without whose commitment I could not publish my own books: Nicola Wood edited the script to her usual exacting standards; Mark Blackadder designed the book and the jacket with artistic flair; and Oula Jones made everything accessible with her comprehensive index.

As always, I thank my wife, Phyllis, and the members of our extended family, including several grandchildren who are now old enough to be involved.

Malcolm Cant 2008

PART 1

EDINBURGH CASTLE

JOHNSTON TERRACE

CASTLEHILL

LAWNMARKET

BANK STREET

THE MOUND

Part 1 deals with the comparatively short section of the Royal Mile, beginning, appropriately, with Edinburgh Castle and running downhill by Castlehill and the Lawnmarket to the junction with Bank Street and George IV Bridge. The Lawnmarket continues as far as St Giles Street but on its north side there is only one building of major significance and that is the High Court, built in 1937 as the Sheriff Court.

There are 30 illustrations which include most of the main places of historical importance. The area, however, is so steeped in national and local history that it would require a much wider selection of pictures to include everything. In this Introduction there are two interesting photographs from very different times: one is of the unveiling of the war memorial to the Gordon Highlanders on the Castle Esplanade; and the other, dating from the early 1950s, shows a typical tramway scene at Melbourne Place (part of George IV Bridge) where would-be passengers were required to walk to an island in the middle of the road.

There are six pages devoted to Edinburgh Castle, starting with two very traditional views by Edinburgh photographers in the 1950s. In the first picture, the outline of the Castle has altered very little since the picture was taken, but, in the foreground, there is no sign of the Weston Link at the Art Galleries and there does not appear to be any restriction on car parking around the two buildings. The second view is from the same period and shows the castle from the Caledonian Hotel. Edinburgh Castle is equally photogenic from its south side with the Half Moon Battery towering above Johnston Terrace. The 1960s picture with the line of tour buses contrasts well with the similar view in 1874 by Archibald Burns.

In and around Castlehill there are several places of great antiquity. In 1672, Edinburgh's first piped water supply from Comiston Springs entered the city at the head of Castlehill and fell, by gravity, to several public wells in the streets below. The cannonball embedded in

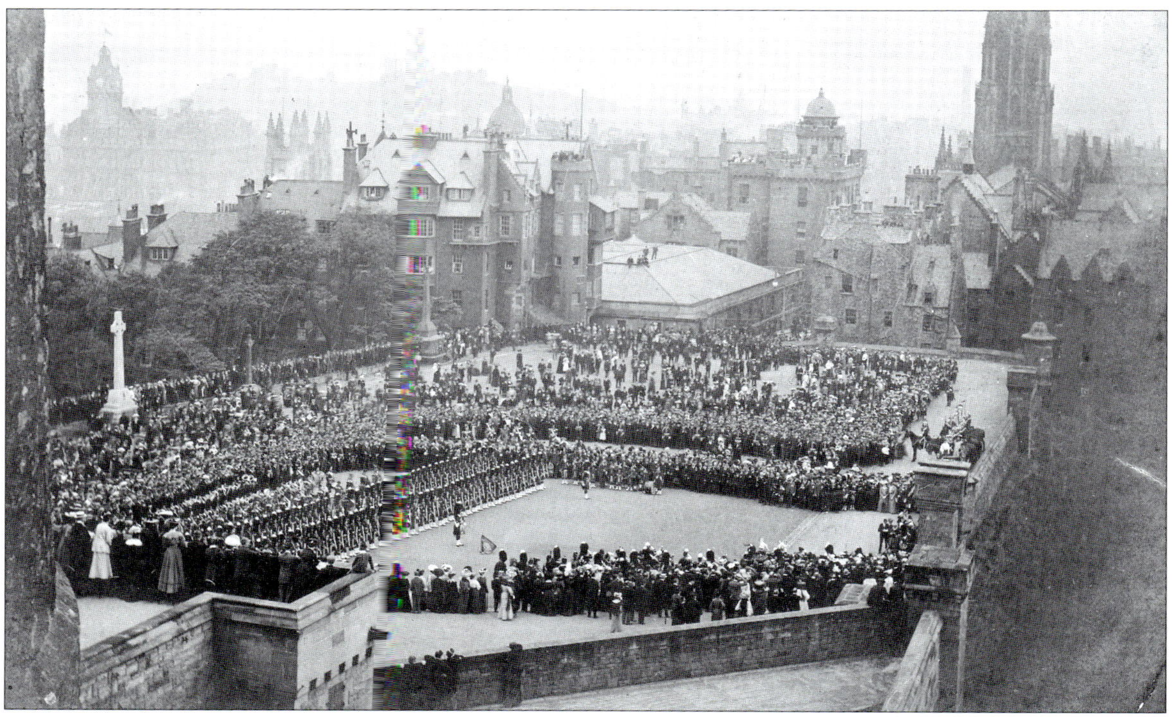

Troops drawn up in formation on the castle esplanade for the unveiling of the memorial to the officers and men of the Gordon Highlanders who died in the South African War, 1899–1902. *Malcolm Cant Collection.*

the wall of nearby Cannonball House is said to mark the height of the spring water at Comiston. By far the most dominant building is, however, the former Tolbooth St John's Church, which in recent years has found a new lease of life as The Hub, the headquarters of the Edinburgh International Festival.

The first of the Lawnmarket pictures is the Bowhead which stood at the corner with Upper Bow. It was demolished in 1878 despite very vocal opposition from the conservationists of the day. Other views of the Lawnmarket show its transition through the ages, culminating in a modern view of the Queen's Own Highlanders (Seaforth and Camerons) as they march for the last time in 1994. Three closes have also been included: Riddle's Court where Baillie John McMorran resided before his untimely death at the hand of a local schoolboy: Brodie's Close where the notorious Deacon Brodie lived and worked; and Lady Stair's Close.

There are several views of the Bank of Scotland which was established in 1695 in Myln Square before moving only one year later to Parliament Close. The third move, to Old Bank Close, was much more enduring, from 1700 until 1806. Thereafter the bank moved to its present-day position on the Mound, but it was not until 1870 that the site was fully exploited by David Bryce, the architect. At the present day, the Mound building is the headquarters of HBOS, formed in 2001. It also houses the Museum on the Mound (open to the public) which tells the story of the bank since 1695.

The last page of Part 1 shows New College and the Assembly Hall, home of the Scottish Parliament between 1999 and 2004. After Holyrood was built, the Assembly Hall reverted to its principal use as the meeting place of the General Assembly of the Church of Scotland. Part 1 then leads into the first short colour section depicting various modern scenes of the Old Town by the photographer, Peter Stubbs, whose work appears in other parts of the book.

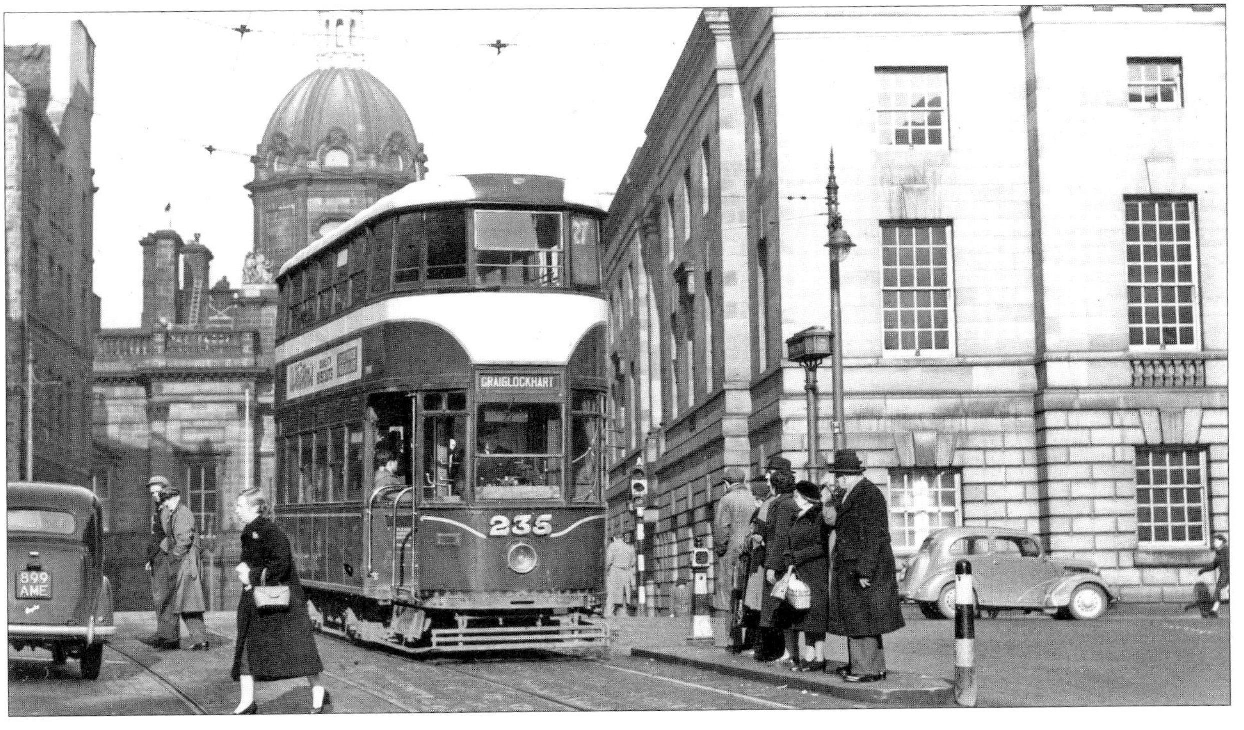

Car 235 is on service No. 27 in Melbourne Place (part of George IV Bridge), en route for Craiglockhart. The tram is approaching a passenger island in the middle of the road, an arrangement that was already beginning to be dangerous when the trams stopped in 1956. Hopefully, our civic leaders are not about to repeat the folly! *Courtesy of A. W. Brotchie.*

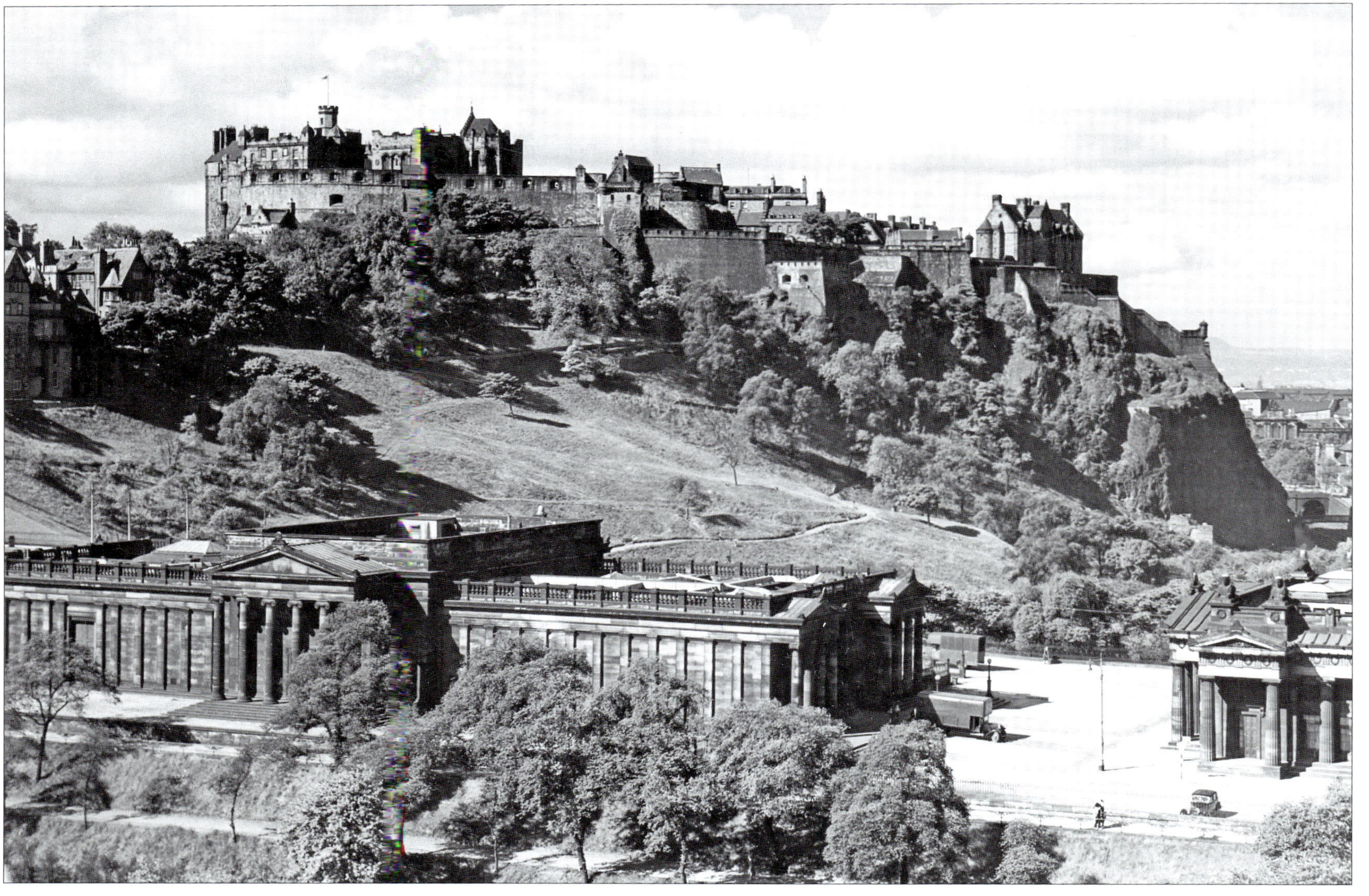

This 1950s, traditional view of the castle from the Scott Monument is sufficiently detailed to identify many of the principal features of this ancient fortress. On the extreme left is the Half Moon Battery (built between 1573 and 1575) and, to its right, the Forewall Battery dating from the same period. Immediately behind the Half Moon Battery is the Royal Palace (with the flag pole), Crown Square and the Scottish National War Memorial, designed by the architect, Robert S. Lorimer, completed in 1927 on the highest point of the castle rock. The Royal Palace, with origins in the fifteenth century, now houses the Honours of Scotland and the Stone of Destiny that was returned from Westminster in 1996. In the centre of the picture, the slightly lower fortification is the Argyle Battery, built in the 1730s, and Mills Mount Battery from where the One O'Clock Gun is now fired. The Argyle Tower is on the left of Mills Mount Battery, and the largest building, on the right, is the late nineteenth-century military hospital.

In the foreground, on the left, is the National Gallery of Scotland, completed in 1854 from drawings by William H. Playfair. The other gallery is the Royal Scottish Academy, also by Playfair, first built 1822–6 and then later from 1831 to 1836 to create a much longer and more elegant building. Originally, the building was the home of the Royal Society, the Institution for the Encouragement of the Fine Arts, the Society of Antiquaries, and the Board of Trustees for Manufactures and Fisheries.
Photograph by Norward Inglis.

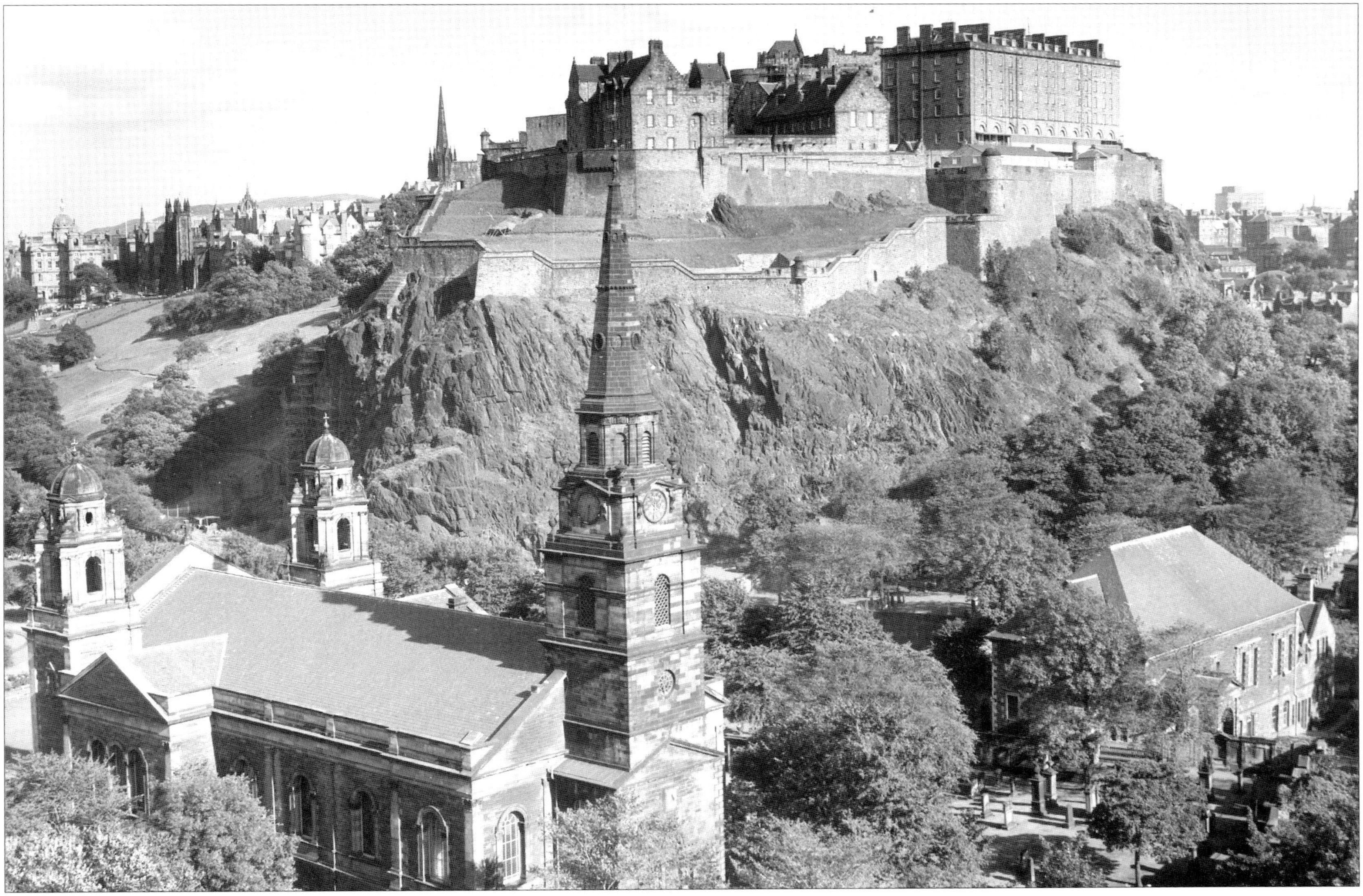

The castle's double line of defences on its west side can be seen clearly in this photograph taken from the Caledonian Hotel. Three main buildings are evident. On the left (in line with the spire of St Cuthbert's Parish Church) is the military hospital, to the right of which is a slightly smaller building, originally used as an ordnance storehouse, but now housing the National War Museum of Scotland. The National War Museum, opened in 1933 as the Scottish Naval and Military Museum, has a collection of items pertaining to Scotland's military history from the seventeenth century to the present day. The third building is the largest, on the extreme right, the seven-storey New Barracks begun in 1796 and finished in 1799 at a time when Napoleon was consolidating his position in Europe. The barracks are large enough to house an entire infantry battalion of 600 officers and men. When it was first built it was heavily criticised for being out of keeping with the remainder of the castle, mainly because of its great bulk.

In the foreground are the steeple and twin towers of St Cuthbert's Parish Church. There has been some form of ecclesiastical presence on this site since at least the twelfth century but the present-day appearance is largely the work of the architect, Hippolyte Blanc, in the 1890s. The previous church building had again become ruinous and was almost completely rebuilt, but retaining the spire of 1790. The church hall, on the right of the picture, entered from King's Stables Road, is now in secular use. *Photograph by John K. Wilkie.*

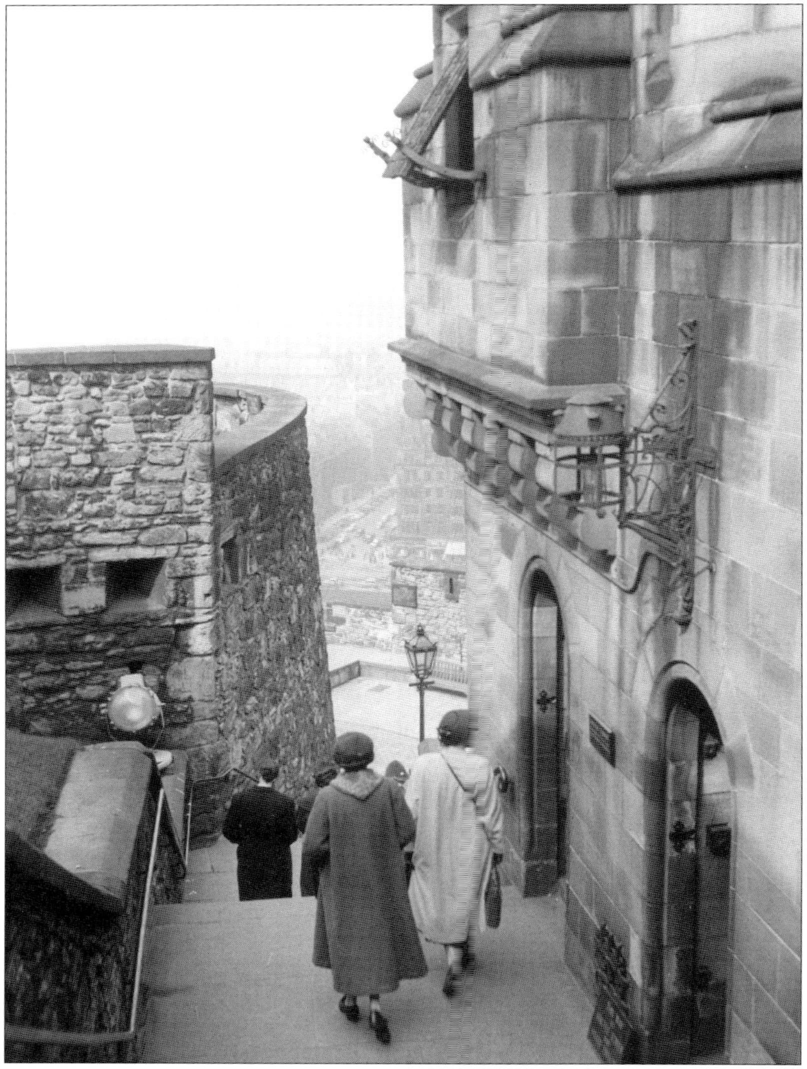

The photograph above shows visitors going down the Lang Stairs with the Argyle Tower on the right. The flight of steps was relaid by prisoners of war, held in the castle in the 1780s during the War of American Independence. Despite its almost medieval appearance, the Argyle Tower is relatively 'modern', being the work of Hippolyte Blanc in 1887. It is, in effect, a second and third storey to the Portcullis Gate below, which dates from immediately after the Lang Siege of 1571–3. At the top of the picture, the timber shutter swivels on two supporting brackets to close an opening in the parapet wall. If it was designed as some form of machicolation (i.e. for dropping burning oil on the enemy) the practice had almost certainly been discontinued by the time that Blanc was working on his plans.

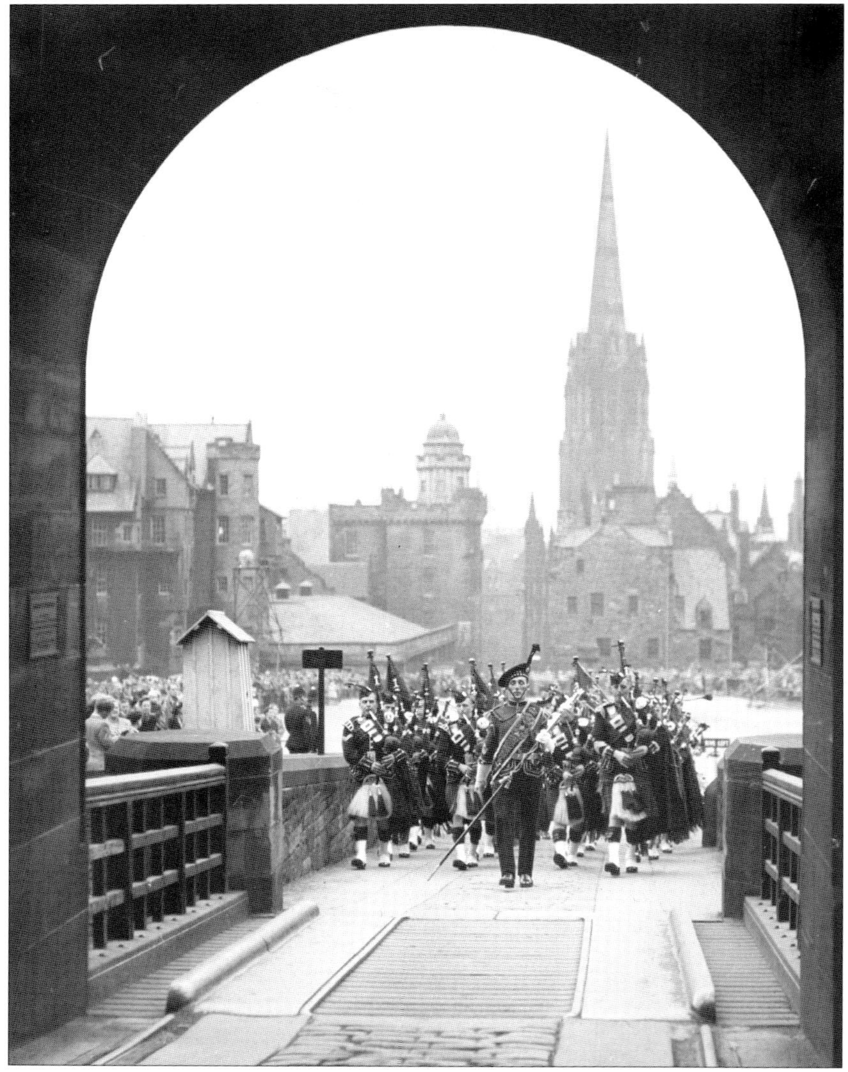

The Pipes and Drums of The 1st Battalion The Royal Scots (The Royal Regiment) are led by their drum major across the drawbridge of the castle. The photograph is undated but the Edinburgh City Police, seen on the left, stopped wearing helmets in 1950. The Royal Scots regiment was raised in 1633 when Sir John Hepburn, under a royal warrant from King Charles I, recruited 1,200 men in Scotland. The first battle honour awarded to The Royal Scots was at Tangier in 1680, since when a further 148 were gained in a history which involved them in almost every campaign the British Army has fought. On 28 March 2006, 373 years to the day after their formation, they became part of The Royal Regiment of Scotland. They merged with the King's Own Scottish Borderers on 1 August 2006 to form the 1st Battalion of the new Regiment. *Both photographs by Norward Inglis.*

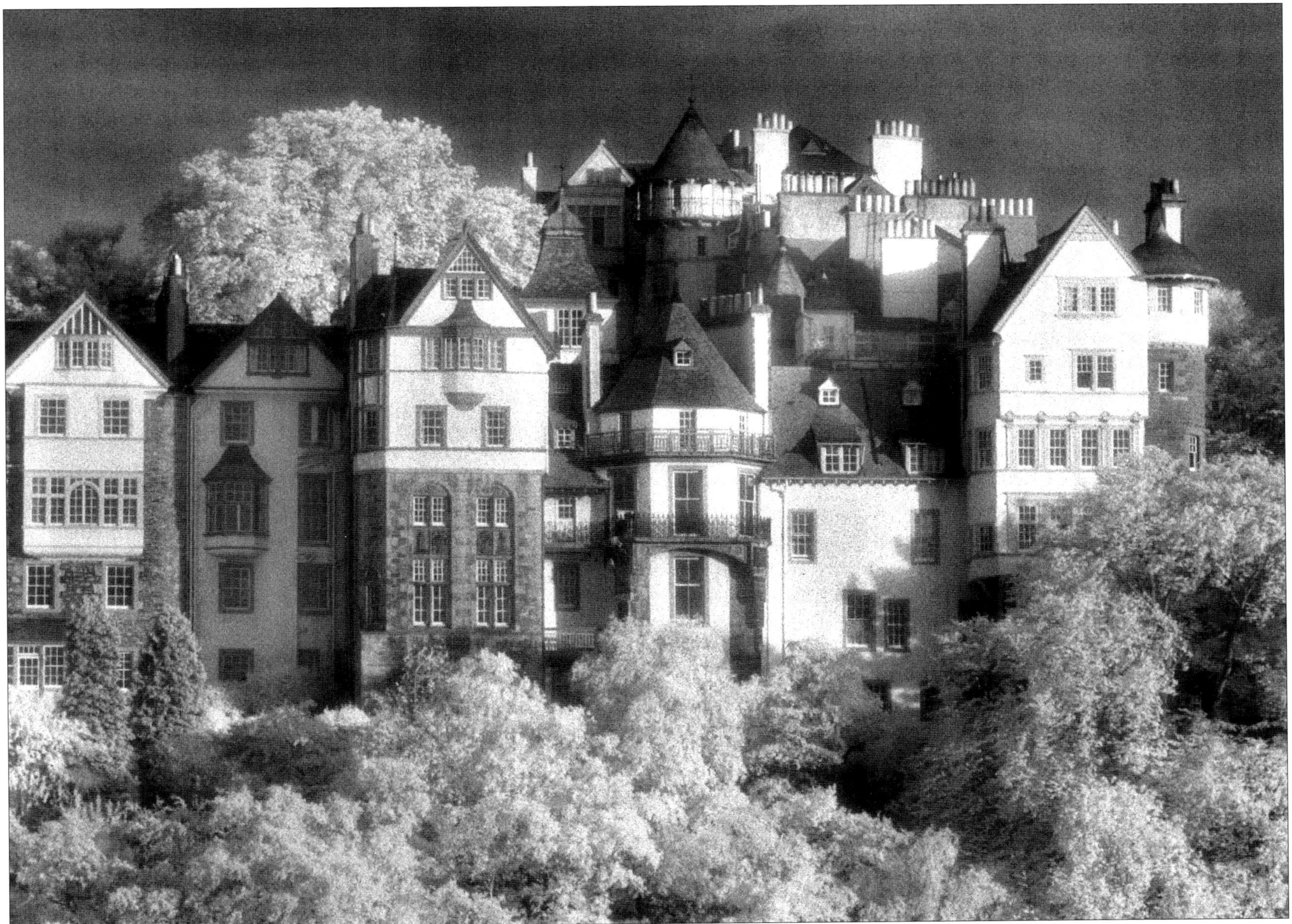

Ramsay Garden, photographed from the north, presents a most picturesque group of buildings, which takes full advantage of the precipitous site beside the castle esplanade. The central, octagonal-shaped building, known as 'the Goose Pie' was built for Allan Ramsay, the poet, in 1733, and was enlarged by his grandson, General John Ramsay, in 1798. A century later, Patrick Geddes, who pioneered much of the revival of the Old Town, extended Ramsay Garden as a range of high quality flats in three phases, the architects being S. Henbest Capper in 1892 and Sydney Mitchell in 1893 and 1894. *Photograph by Peter Stubbs.*

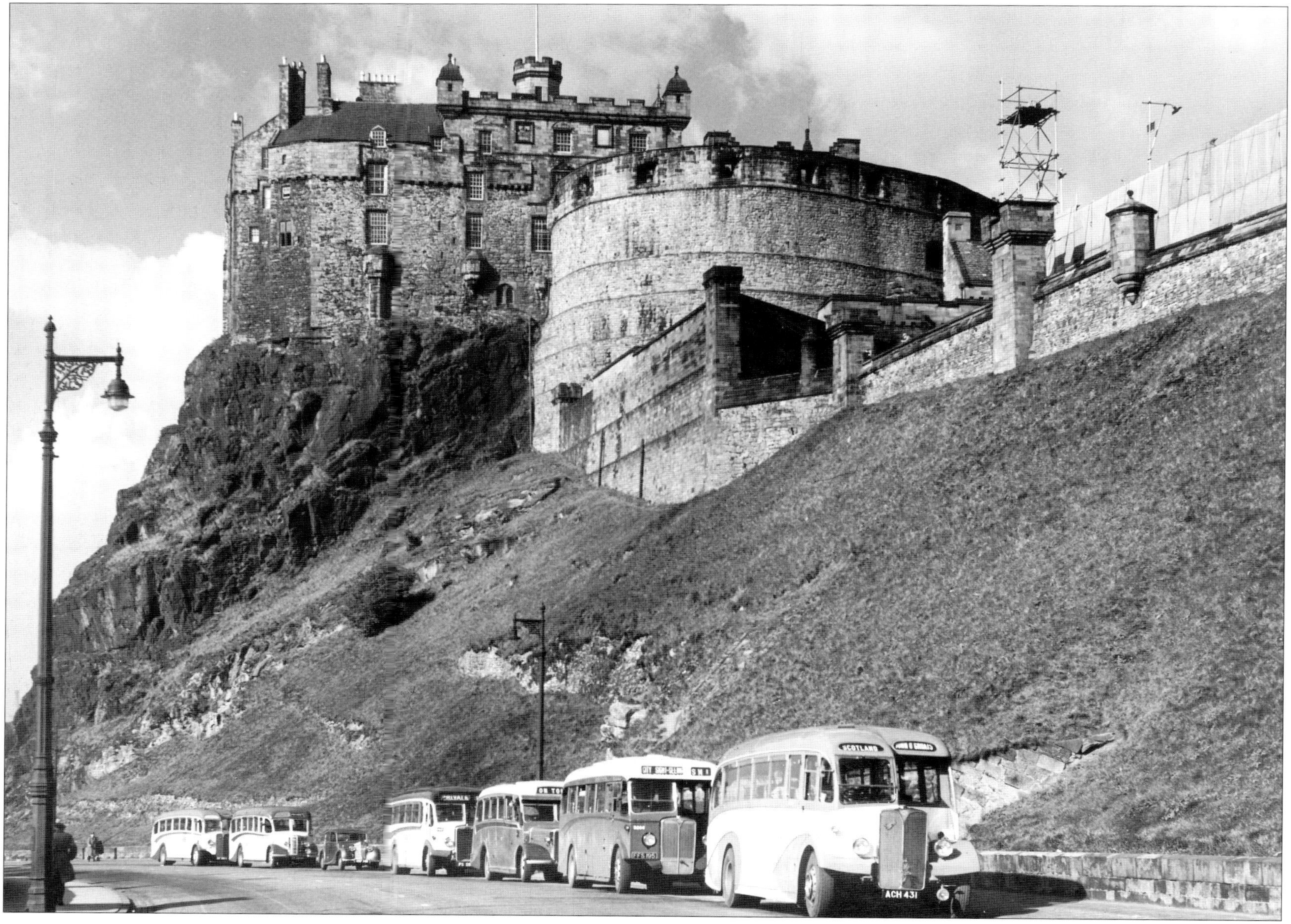

The huge mass of the Half Moon Battery dominates the centre of the picture. It was built after the Long Siege of 1571–3 around the remnants of David's Tower that had been badly damaged in hostilities. The battery is almost devoid of vulnerable openings and is topped by a row of deep embrasures, or gun loops. To the left of the battery is the east wall of the royal palace showing the tall clock tower that faces into Crown Square. The last monarch to sleep in the palace was Charles I, in 1633, the night before his coronation. Much earlier, in 1566, Mary Queen of Scots gave birth here to her son, James, the future James VI of Scotland and I of England. At the present day, many apartments in the palace are open to the public, including the Crown Room that houses the Honours of Scotland and the Stone of Destiny. Part of the east wall of the Great Hall, completed in 1511, can be seen on the extreme left of the picture. Johnston Terrace was a very convenient spot for tour buses to park while their passengers visited the castle. *Photograph by Norward Inglis.*

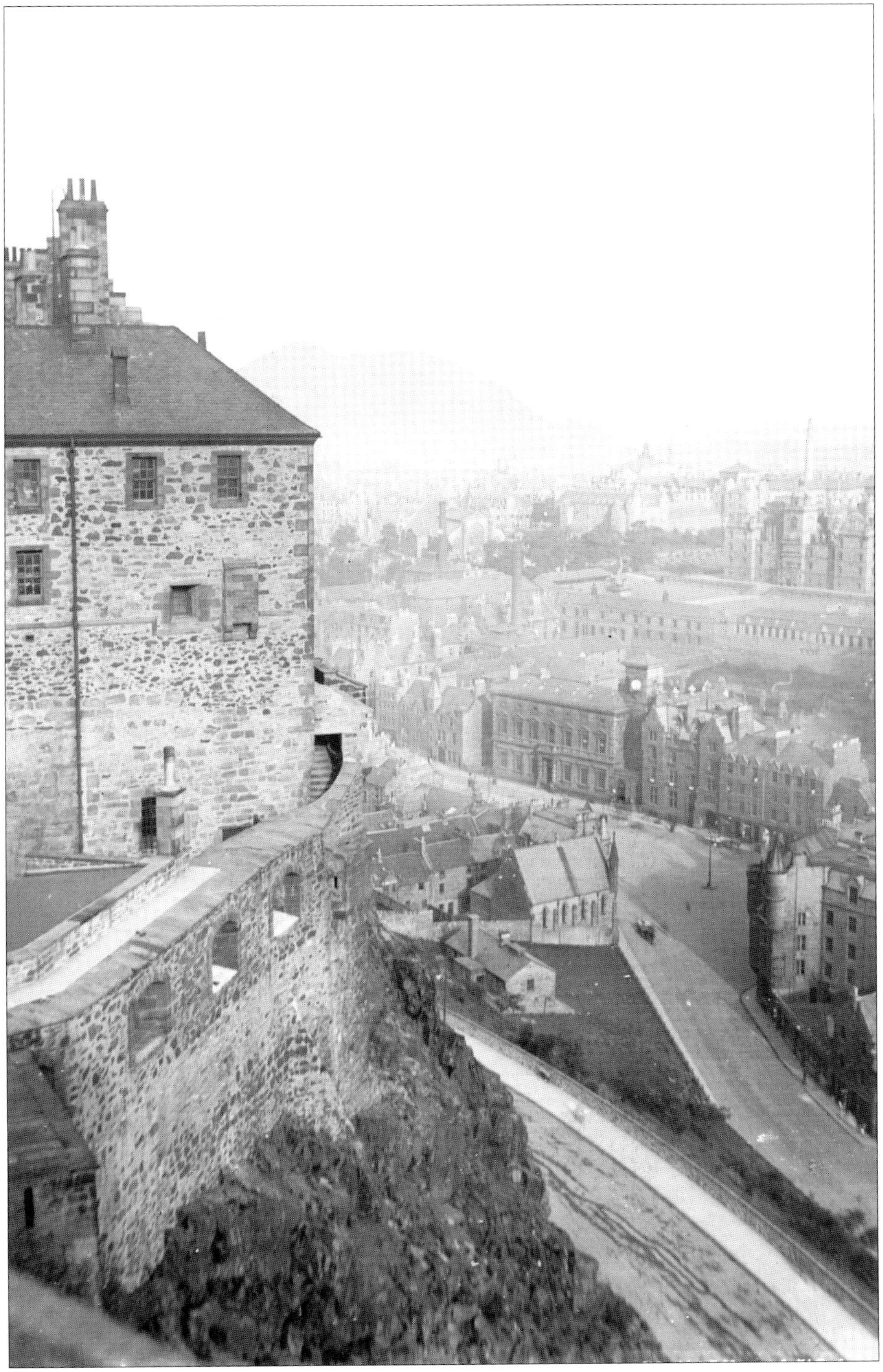

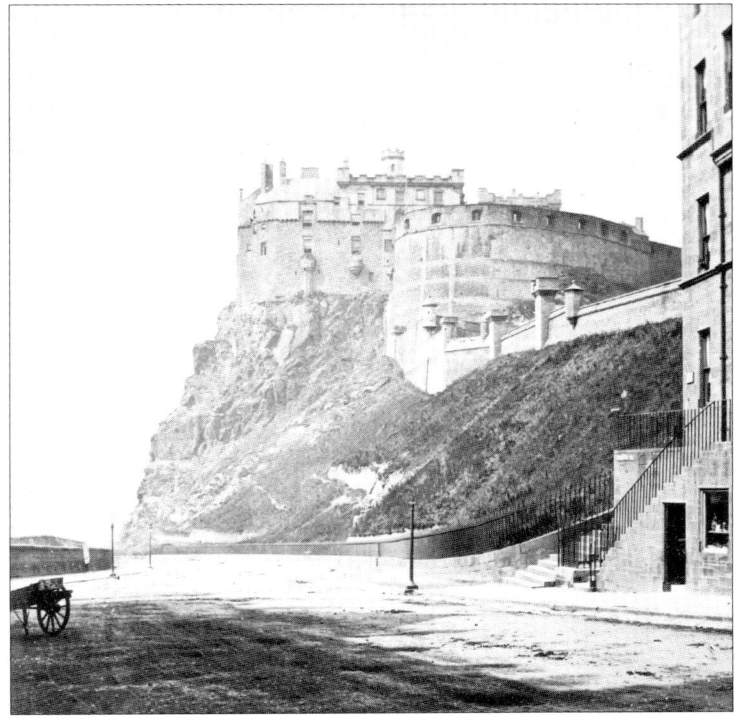

Left. The photograph is taken along the line of Dury's Battery, part of the castle's western defences. It is named after its designer, Captain Theodore Dury, and was built following the Jacobite Rising of 1708. The structure on the left is the Queen Anne Building, erected, at the same time as the battery, as a barracks for officers and gunners during the reign of Queen Anne (1702–14). It was built up on two levels of late medieval vaults and now houses the Prisons of War exhibition. The steps at the end of the battery give access to the Devil's Elbow with more vaults, and a precarious drop to Johnston Terrace.

Johnston Terrace, King's Stables Road and the Grassmarket are on the right of the picture. The church on the corner of King's Stables Road, designed by the architects Hardy & Wight in 1884, was opened as the Robertson Memorial Church. On the south side of the Grassmarket the building with the clock tower is the Corn Exchange. *Malcolm Cant Collection.*

Above. This 1874 photograph by Archibald Burns is an interesting contrast with the similar view on the opposite page. The principal parts of the castle are almost unaltered but the street scene below is very different. The mock turrets and defences along the south side of the esplanade were erected in 1816. The flight of steps known as Castle Wynd can be seen on the right. *Malcolm Cant Collection.*

Right. This unusual view of Ramsay Lodge was probably taken around the time of the First World War when the lodge was occupied as the 'King Edward and Queen Mary Victoria League Club'. Surviving correspondence, dated 13 January 1917, carrying the lodge address includes a letter from 'G. M. Shrum' in which he alludes to food shortages: 'no cream … can hardly buy chocolate … only one piece of bread at a meal … if you have soup, you can't get dessert'. *Courtesy of Margeorie Meke.*

Below left. This lady is making her way down Castlehill. Ahead of her is the snow-covered ornate archway to Castle Hill School now used as the Scotch Whisky Heritage Centre. On the opposite side of the road, the low, flat-topped building is Castlehill Reservoir dating from 1850. There were, of course, earlier water tanks at Castlehill dating from Edinburgh's first water supply from Comiston in 1672. Further downhill, the taller building, with the castellated tower, is the Outlook Tower, acquired by Patrick Geddes in 1892, and turned by him into 'the world's first sociological laboratory'. Geddes, born in Ballater in 1854, has been described as 'the Father of British Townplanning'. *Malcolm Cant Collection.*

Below right. The gusset of land formed by Castlehill and Johnston Terrace has been dominated by the huge tower and steeple of the Tolbooth Church since the middle of the nineteenth century. It was designed, with a 245-foot spire, in the Gothic style by James Gillespie Graham and A. W. N. Pugin, and built between 1839 and 1844. From the beginning, it was intended to have a dual role, both as a church for the immediate area and as a meeting hall of the General Assembly of the Church of Scotland, until it moved to the Mound after the 1929 union with the Free Church. Over the years the church has changed its name on numerous occasions in response to various congregational unions: it became Tolbooth St John's in 1940; Highland Church Tolbooth St John's in 1956; and Greyfriars, Tolbooth and Highland in 1979. For a while after the 1979 union, services were held at both Greyfriars and Tolbooth. After a period of uncertainty in the 1980s, the building was taken over by the Edinburgh International Festival and beautifully renovated as their headquarters, known as The Hub.
Malcolm Cant Collection.

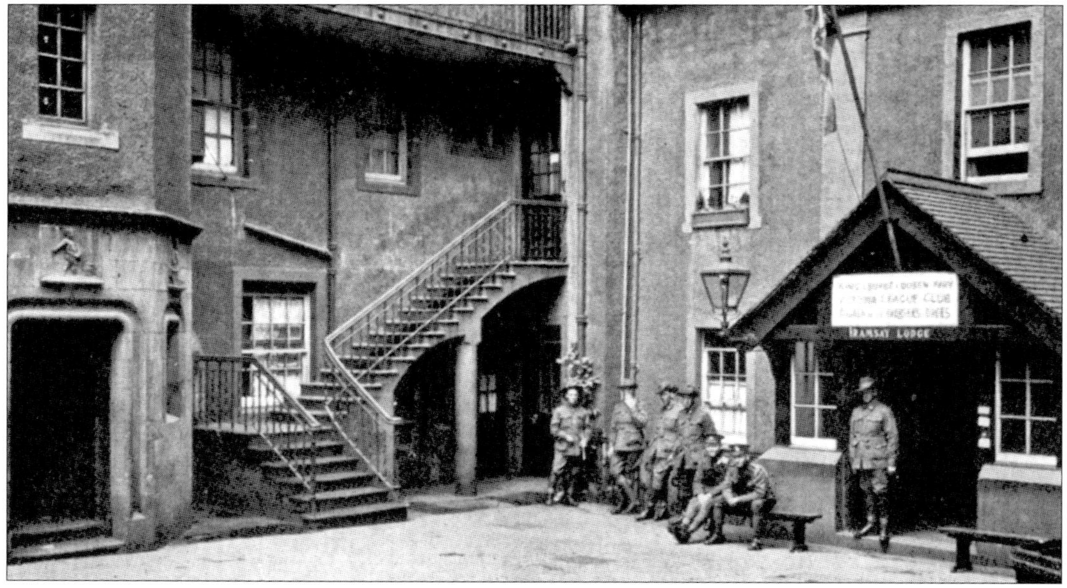

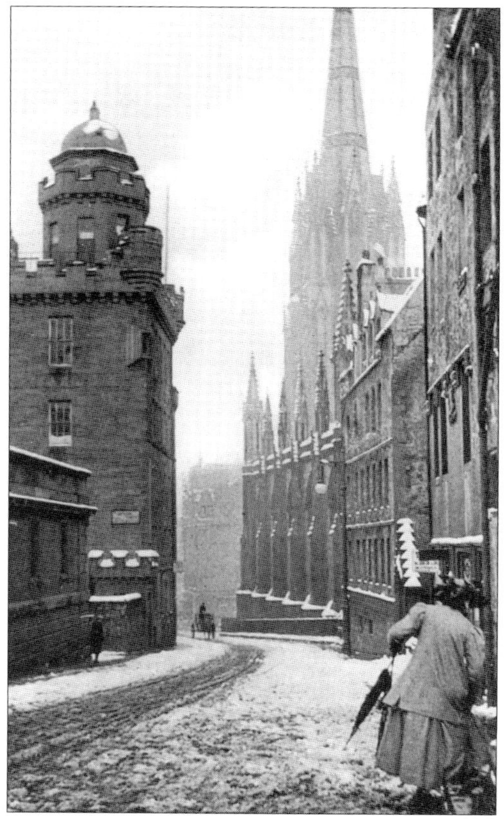

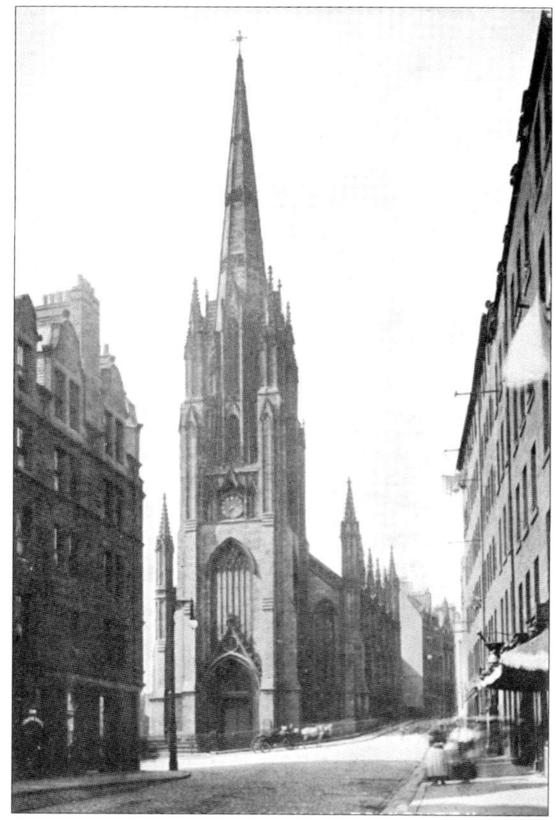

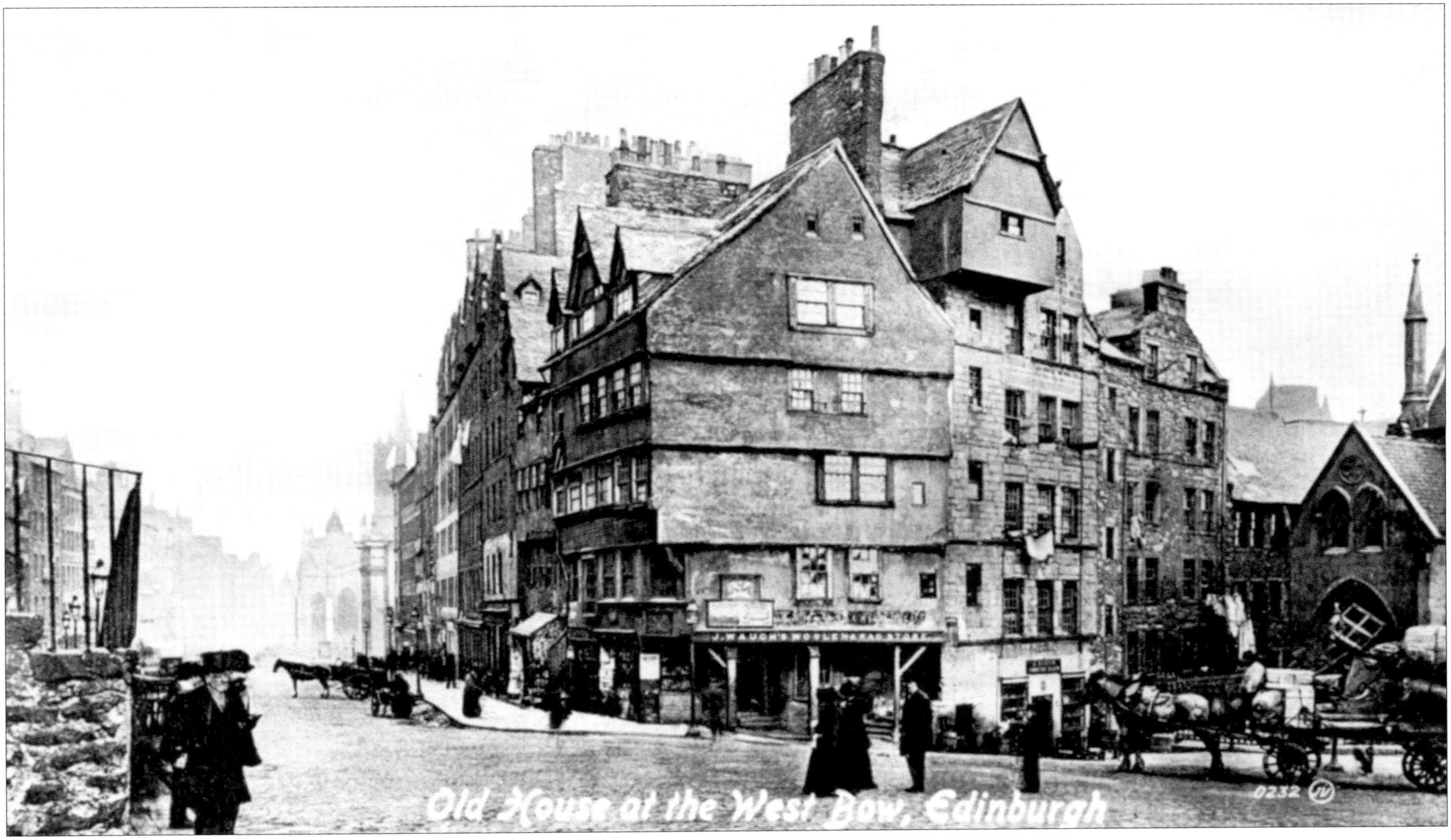

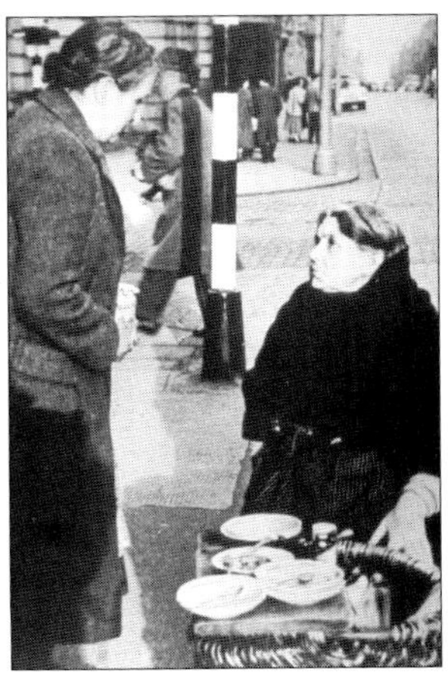

The buckie seller deals with a customer at her pitch outside Deacon Brodie's Tavern in the Lawnmarket in 1957. *Photograph by Hamish Coghill.*

This picturesque building stood for many years at the corner of the Lawnmarket and Upper Bow until 1878 when it was demolished before the end of its useful lifetime. Over the years, the ground floor of the tenement was occupied by various tenants. In this picture it is J. Waugh's Woollen and Rag Store, but previously the same type of business was run by Thomas Sword. The group of buildings was known as the Bowhead, being the top end of the old West Bow before it was truncated by the construction of Victoria Street. The West Bow is believed to date from at least the fourteenth century, and was the principal entrance to the city when Queen Anne returned to Scotland in 1561. Had the Bowhead survived to the present day it would have been a magnificent example of Edinburgh's earliest architecture. Bruce J. Home, author of *Old Houses in Edinburgh* published by William J. Hay, *c.* 1909, said: 'It cannot be estimated as less than a calamity that these venerable tenements, which had weathered the storms of centuries, were wantonly demolished in 1878 by the vandalistic action of the then existing civic authorities'. Little has changed. *Courtesy of Robin Sherman.*

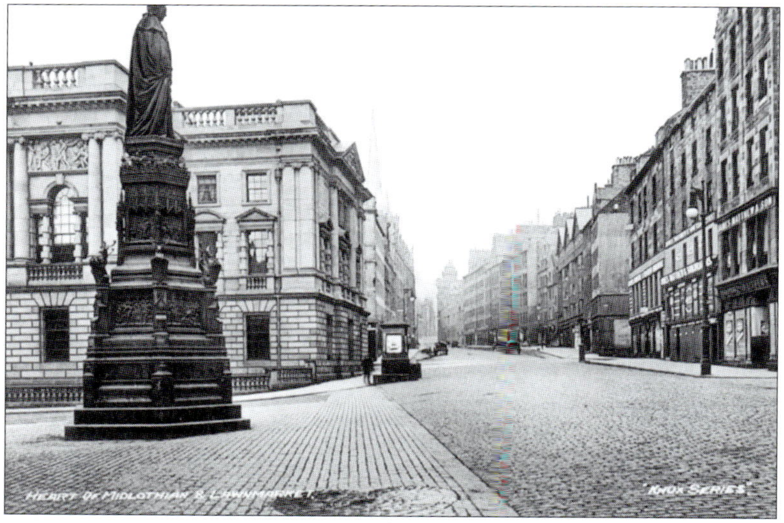

Above. The Heart of Midlothian, seen in the foreground of the picture, is a few yards south of the position of the Old Tolbooth which was demolished in 1817, and which during its lifetime had been used as a civic meeting place, a parliament, a court and a prison. On the left is the statue of the 5th Duke of Buccleuch.

Below. This undated view of the south side of the Lawnmarket shows many of the businesses that traded from fairly small premises. From left to right, they include: a map mounter; a stationer & tobacconist; a money loan office; an ices and confections business, and several others.

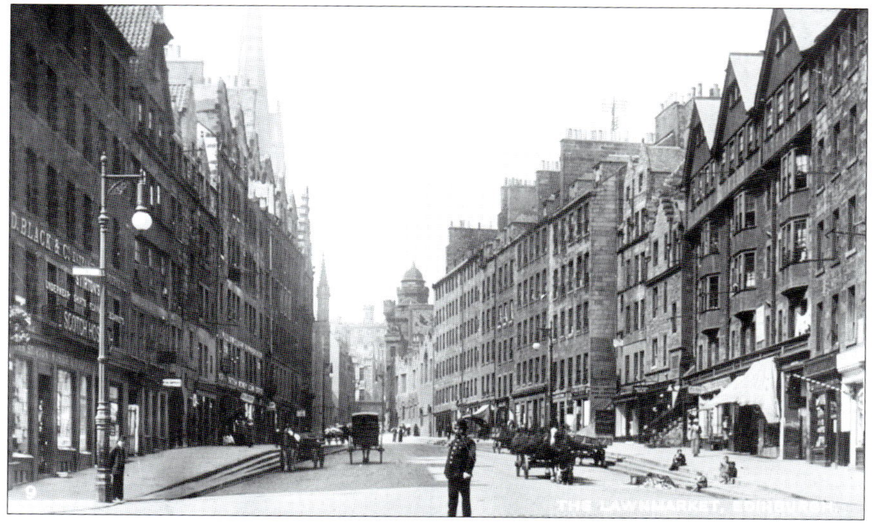

Above. The photograph shows the Lawnmarket at a time when the police authorities presumably had the manpower to devote to traffic control. The corner block, on the extreme left, is occupied by D. Black & Company, famous for Scotch Hosiery.

Below. Amateur and professional photographers gather on the Lawnmarket to record the last parade of the Queen's Own Highlanders (Seaforth and Camerons) on 22 July 1994, before they were amalgamated in September 1994 with the Gordon Highlanders to form The Highlanders (Seaforth, Gordons and Camerons). On the formation of The Royal Regiment of Scotland on 28 March 2006, the name changed to The Highlanders, 4th Battalion Royal Regiment of Scotland. *All Malcolm Cant Collection.*

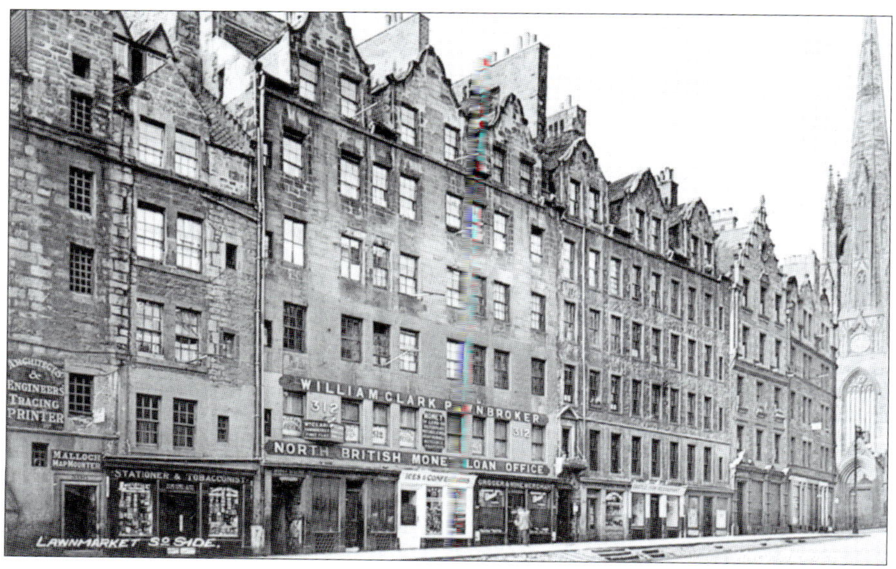

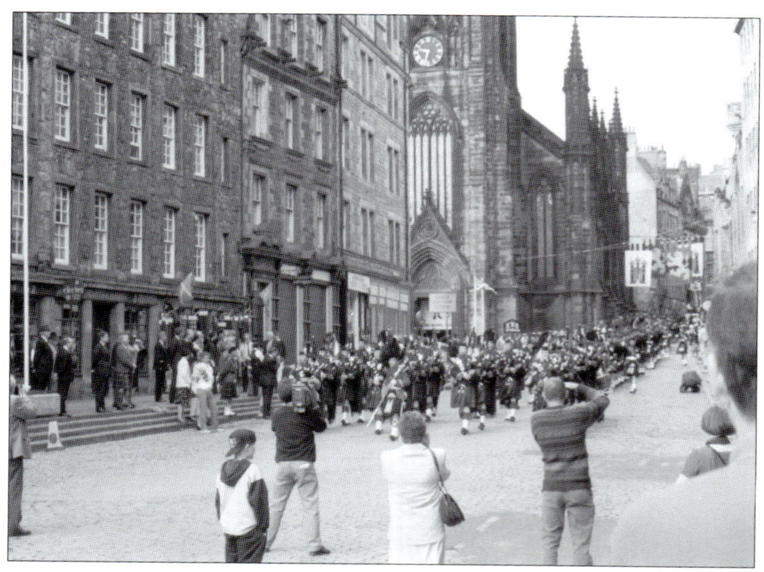

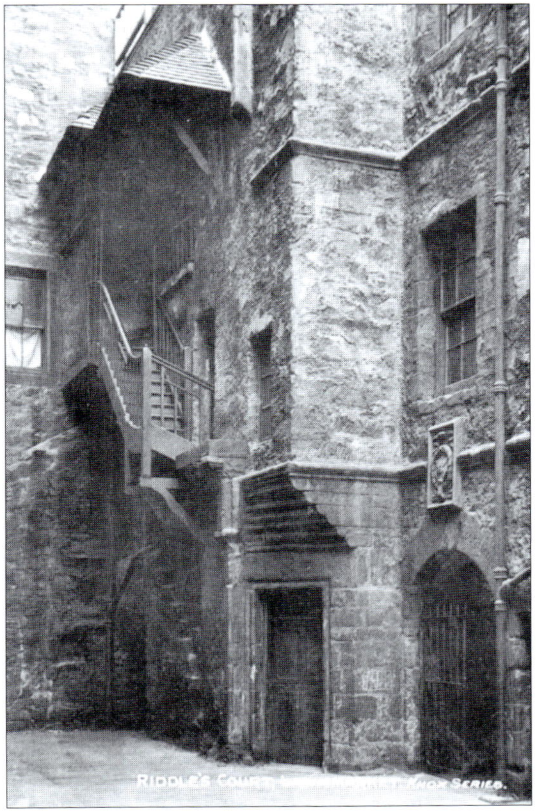

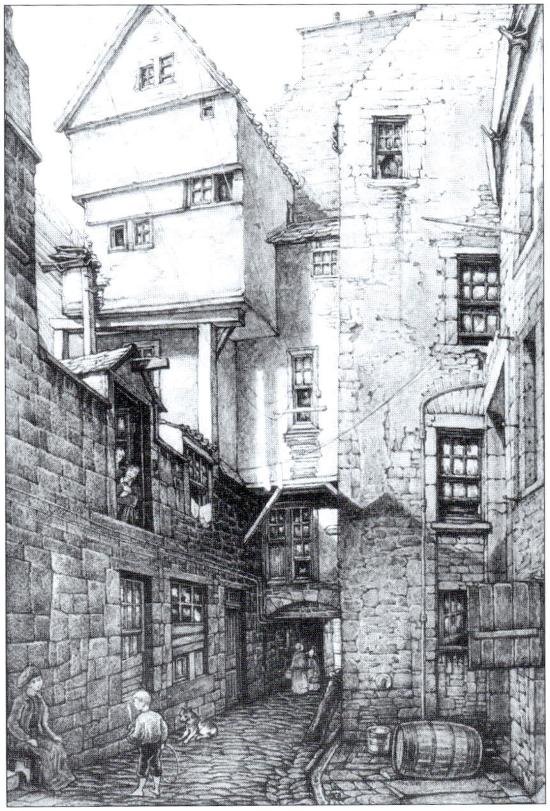

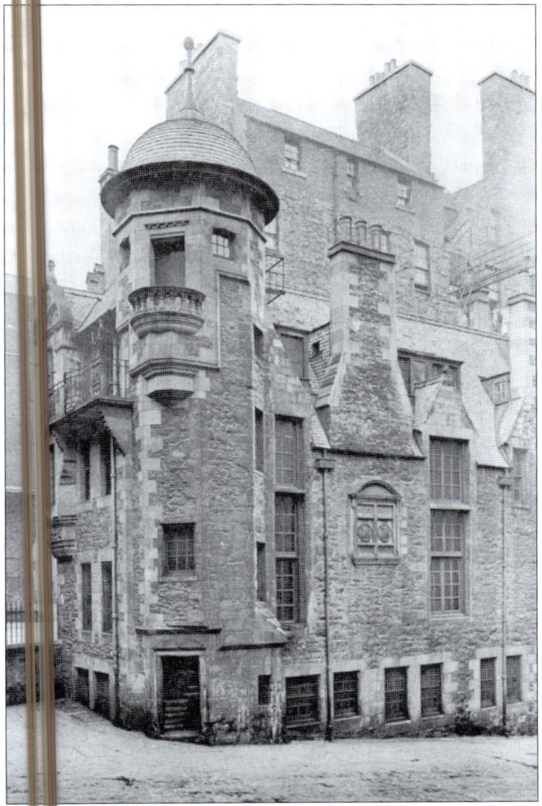

Above. Access to Riddle's Court is by Riddle's Close on the south side of the Lawnmarket. The name is derived from George Riddell an Edinburgh burgess. Its most famous resident was, however, Baillie John McMorran, City Treasurer from 1589 to 1591. His business as a grain exporter brought him great wealth but little admiration from the poor people who could not afford his high prices during times of shortage. His house was considered to be the last word in modern comfort with good security, glass in the windows, painted ceilings and a garderobe. For all his wealth and influence, he met an untimely death at the hands of boys from the High School who had staged a sit-in in support of longer holidays. McMorran arrived and ordered the Town Guard to break down the door, whereupon one of the boys fired a shot from a classroom window and brought McMorran to the ground.
Malcolm Cant Collection.

Above. The illustration shows the lower portion, long since demolished, of Brodie's Close. It ran between the Lawnmarket and the Cowgate and was also truncated when Victoria Street was built. At the present day, Brodie's Close is entered from the south side of the Lawnmarket. The name is derived from the infamous William Brodie, the inspiration for Robert Louis Stevenson's epic tale, *Dr Jekyll and Mr Hyde*. By day, Brodie was a respectable citizen but by night he gambled, drank and associated with prostitutes. To finance this lifestyle he took wax impressions of his friends' door keys and got an accomplice to make duplicates so that he could gain illegal access. He was eventually caught and hanged on 1 October 1788. It is said that the hangman took three attempts to complete the job because Brodie had been fitted with a steel collar round his neck in the hope of saving himself. *From* Old Houses in Edinburgh *by Bruce J. Home.*

Above. Lady Stair's Close runs northwards from the Lawnmarket to Bank Street and was once the main thoroughfare before the upper section of the Mound and Bank Street was completed. The principal building in the close is Lady Stair's House which bears the date 1622 and the monogram of Sir William Gray of Pittendrum and his wife Egidia Smith who was the sister of Sir John Smith, Lord Provost of Edinburgh from 1643 to 1645. The house, however, takes its name from the early eighteenth century when it was the property of Eleanor, Countess of Stair, whose second husband was Lord Stair. Towards the end of the nineteenth century the house was restored by the 5th Earl of Rosebery who, gifted it to the city in 1907. At the present day, it is occupied as the Writers' Museum, specialising in relics pertaining to Robert Burns, Sir Walter Scott and Robert Louis Stevenson.
Malcolm Cant Collection.

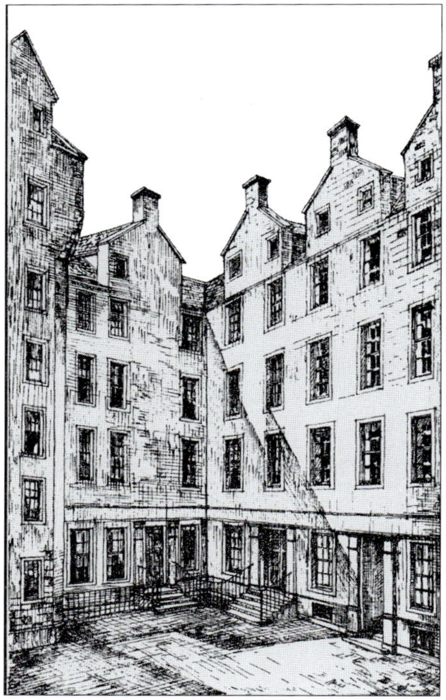

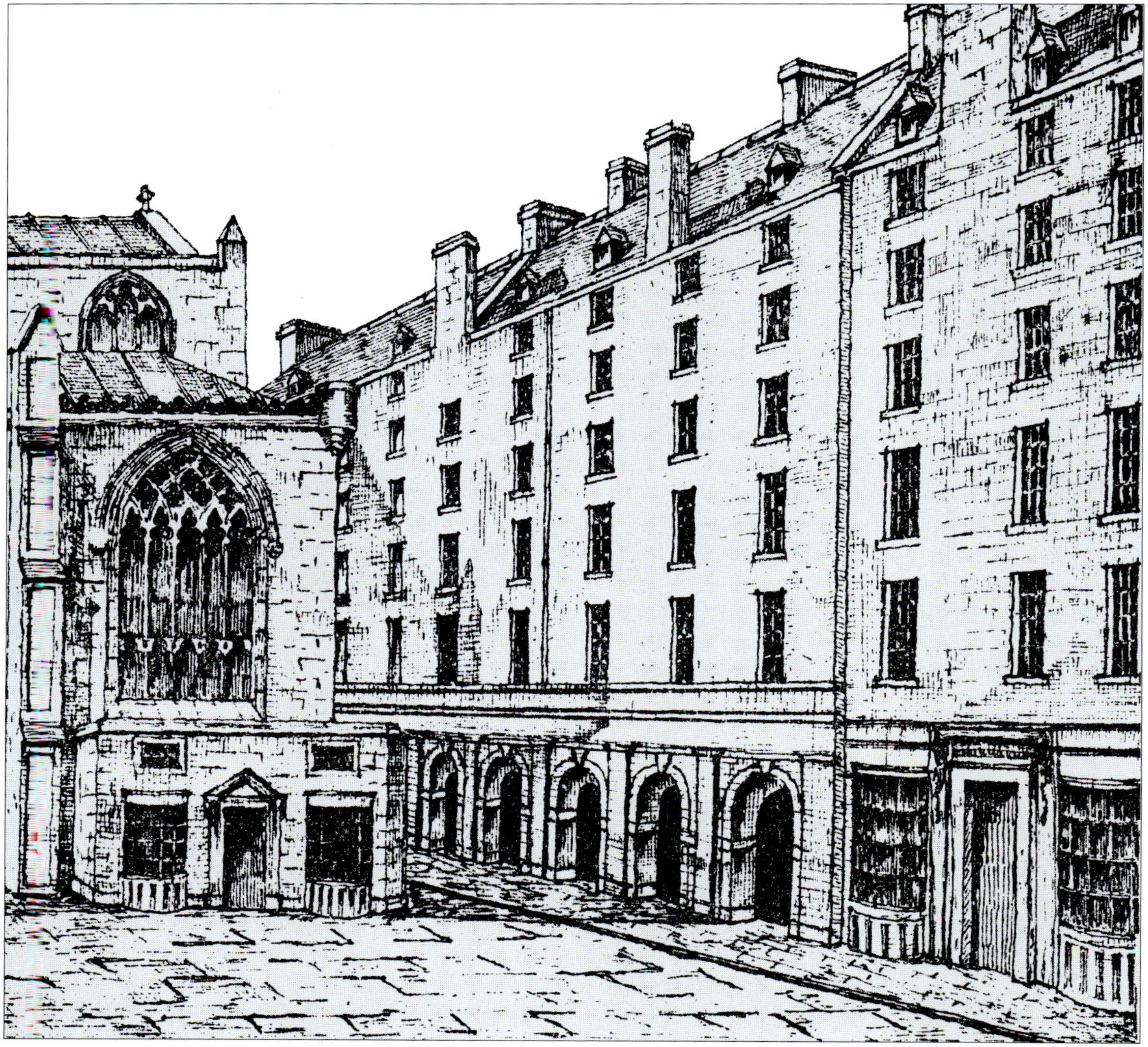

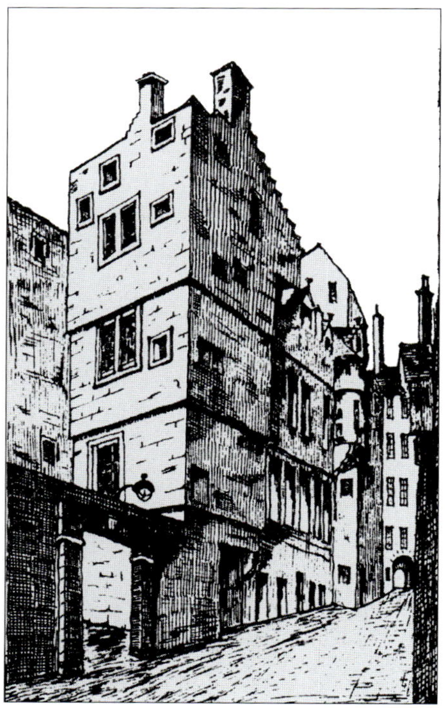

Above left. The Bank of Scotland was established in 1695 in Mylne Square in part of a flat tenanted by James Sympson, and built for Alexander Simson by Robert Mylne, Master Mason for Scotland. Mylne Square stood about the position of the Scotsman Hotel but was demolished for the construction of North Bridge.

Above. In 1696 the bank purchased premises in Parliament Close from Sir Alexander Seton of Pitmedden, and moved into 'that great new building or tenement of land lately built by Alexander Paterson of Caverhill'. Unfortunately, the property was destroyed by fire on 3 February 1700. It stood to the east of St Giles Cathedral.

Left. The bank's third move was to Old Bank Close on the south side of the Lawnmarket where it remained until 1806.

All from The Bank of Scotland 1695–1945, *by Charles A. Malcolm, produced to commemorate the two hundred and fiftieth anniversary of the bank.*

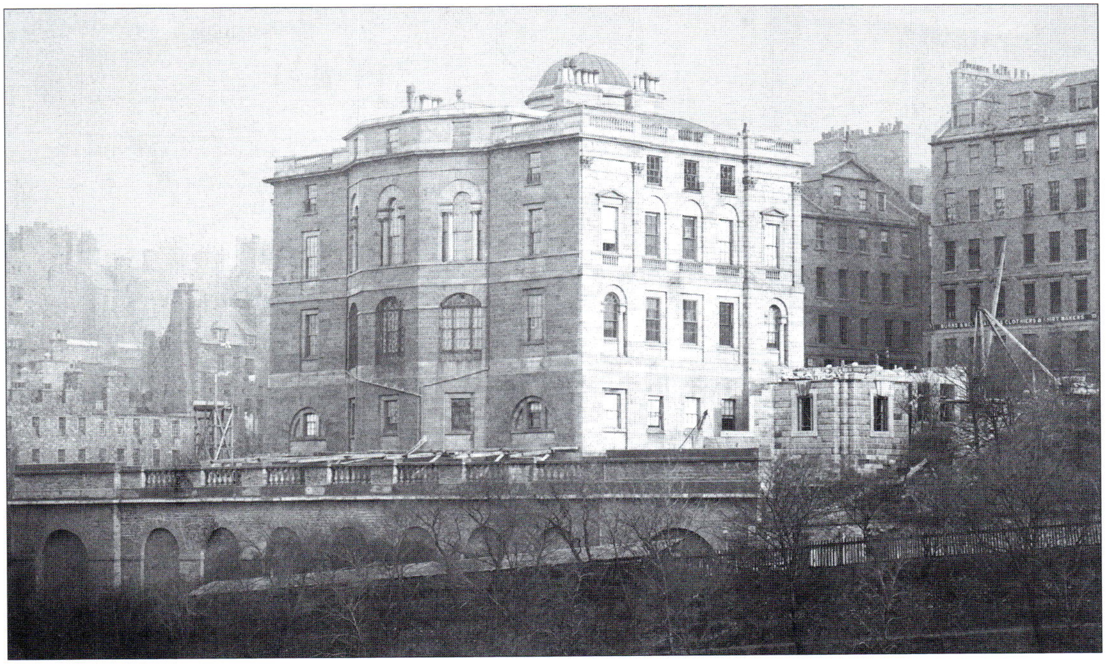

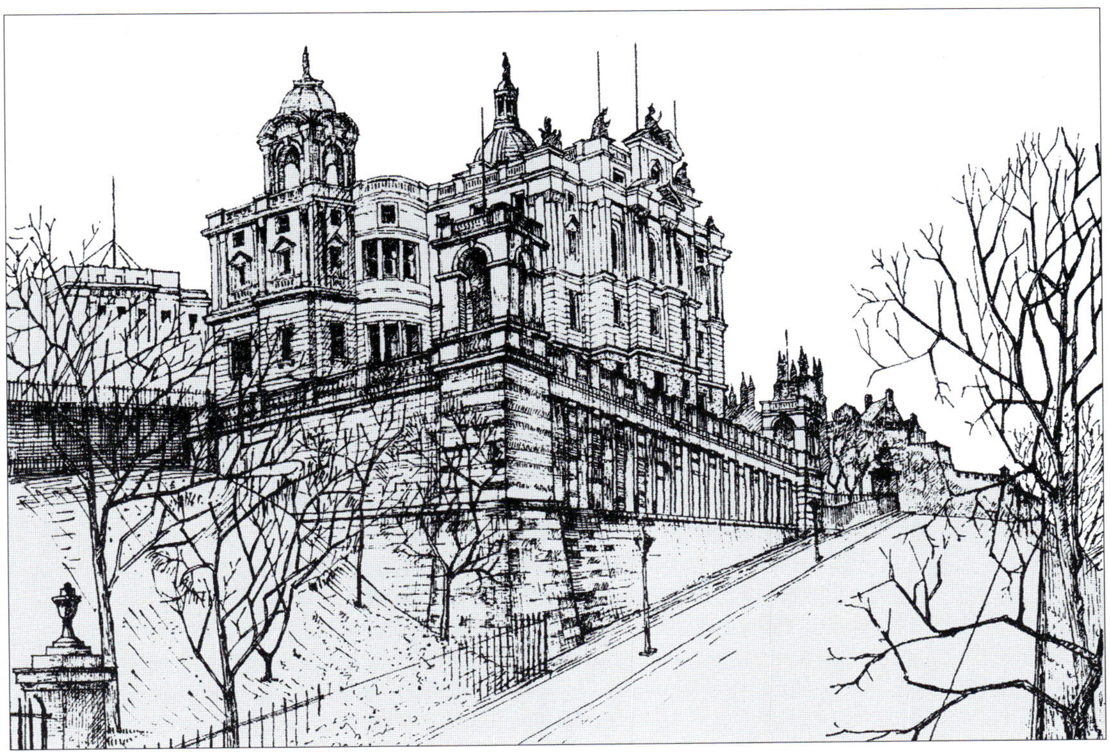

Below. After more than a century at Old Bank Close, the directors of the bank were again looking for larger premises. The site chosen, on the corner of the Mound and Market Street, turned out to be one of the most impressive in Edinburgh. The first building, designed by Robert Reid and Richard Crichton in 1801, was built by William Sibbald Jnr. between 1802 and 1806. As seen from the top of the Mound it was a bold construction of two main storeys, a heavy balustrade and a somewhat squat dome. *From* Modern Athens *by Thomas H. Shepherd.*

Left. In 1863 the architect, David Bryce, was commissioned to extend and enhance the original building. The photograph shows work in progress on the north-west tower by Wm. Beattie & Son who completely transformed the building between 1864 and 1870. During this work, the original dome was replaced by a much grander one, elevated by an octagonal drum, and crowned by a statue of Fame. *Courtesy of Bank of Scotland plc.*

Below left. This is the view of the bank with which most people in Edinburgh identify. As seen from Princes Street, it has a spectacular appearance especially when flood-lit at night. The drawing shows David Bryce's completed building from the north-east. The screen wall, abutting Market Street, was completed by the architects, Peddie & Kinnear, in 1878, very shortly after the death of David Bryce. *From* The Bank of Scotland 1695–1945.

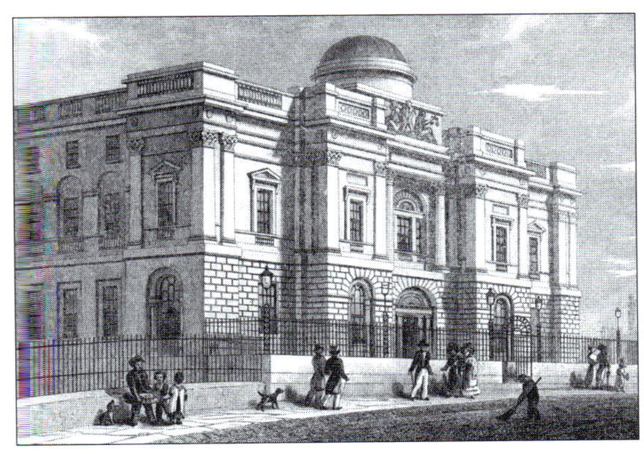

Right. New College and the Assembly Hall on the Mound were designed by William H. Playfair and built between 1845 and 1850 as a church and theological college for the Free Church which had come into being at the time of the Disruption in 1843. Seen from Hanover Street, the twin entrance towers frame the spire of the Tolbooth Church in Castlehill, giving the impression, in low sunlight, that the two buildings are as one. The General Assembly of the Church of Scotland is held annually in May in the Assembly Hall. *Photograph by Norward Inglis.*

Below. The corner of Market Street and the Mound is dominated by the memorial to the officers and men of the Black Watch who died or were injured in the South African War 1899–1902. The bronze statue of a soldier leaning on his rifle, by Birnie Rhind, stands on top of a pedestal of pink marble, which shows the names of the fallen. There is also a large bronze relief of the Black Watch in action. The statue was unveiled on 25 May 1910. *Malcolm Cant Collection.*

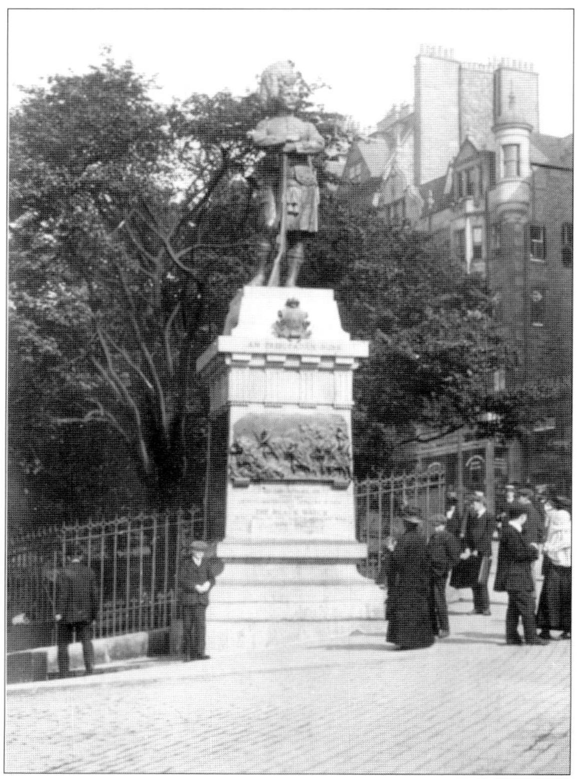

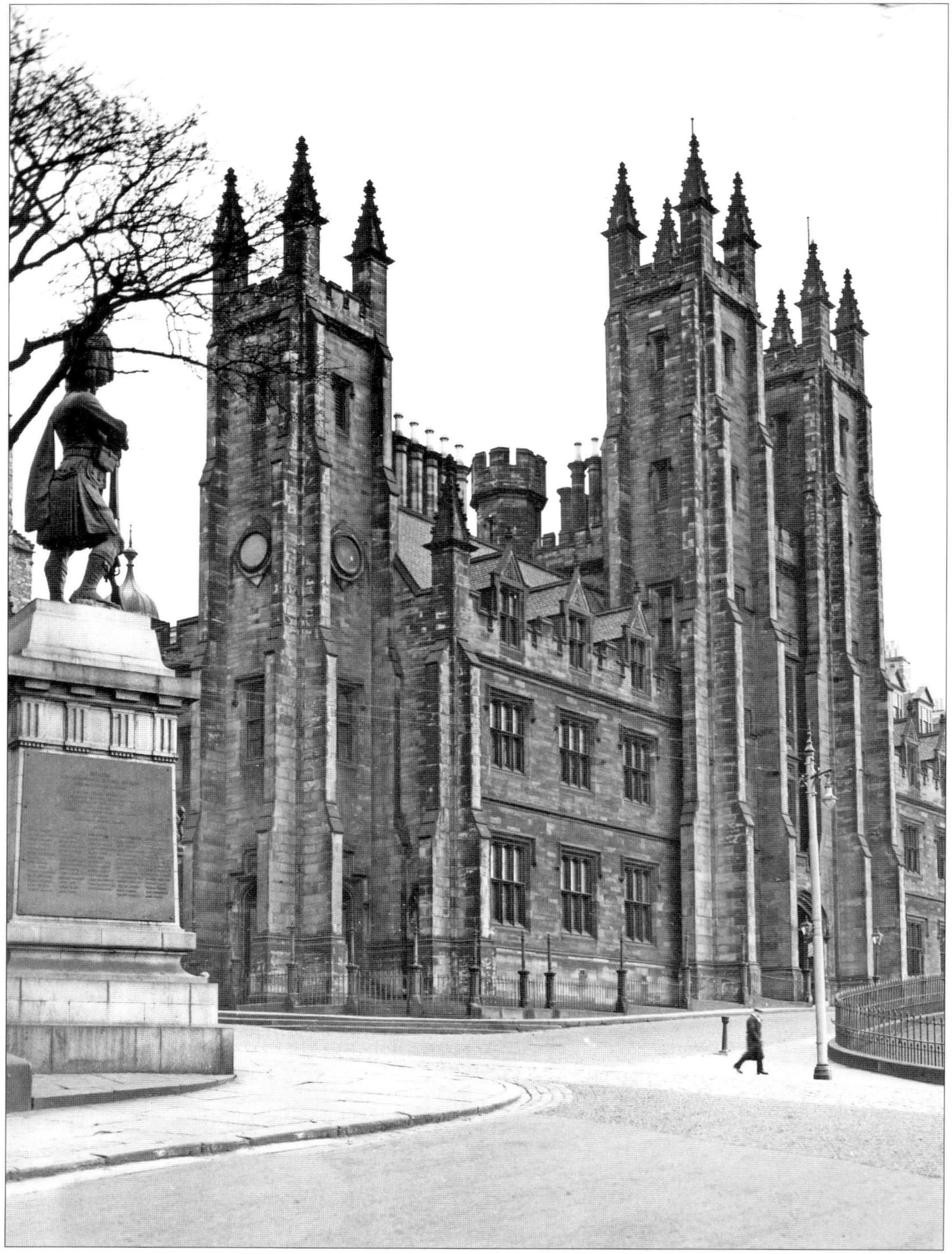

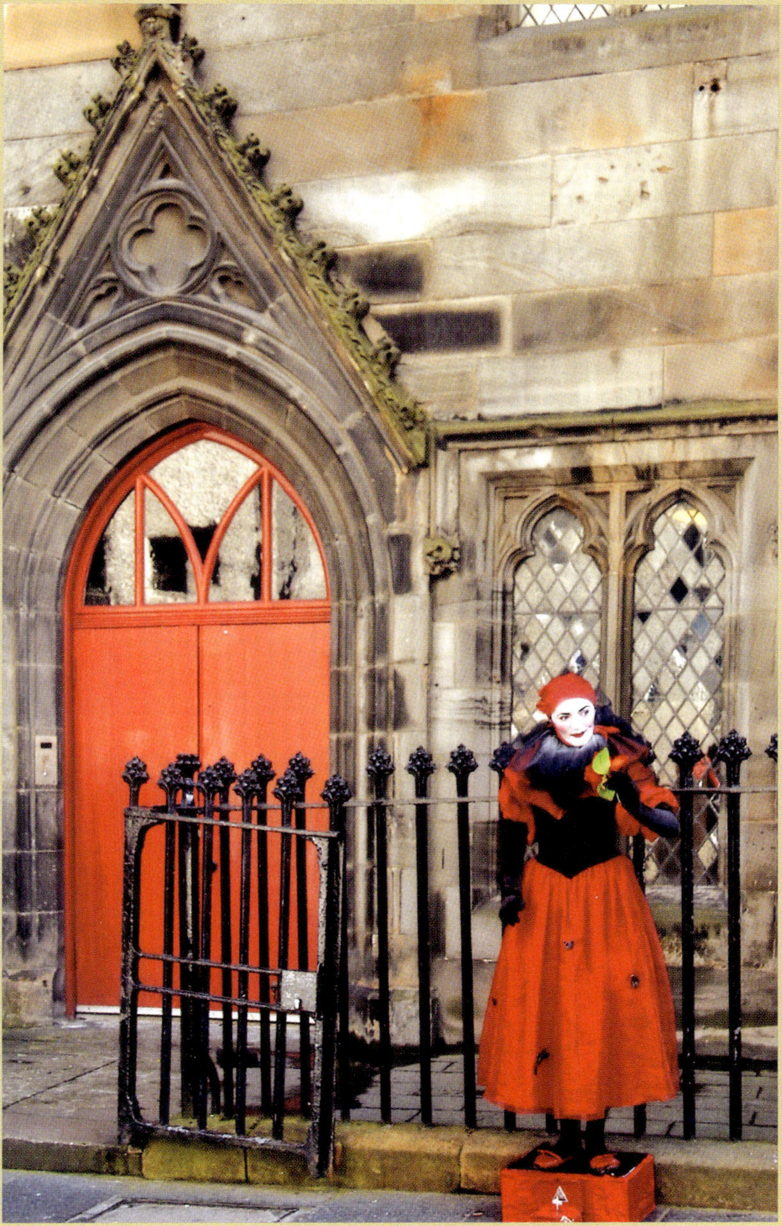

The lady in red has chosen her stance well for a silent vigil at the side door of The Hub in Castlehill.

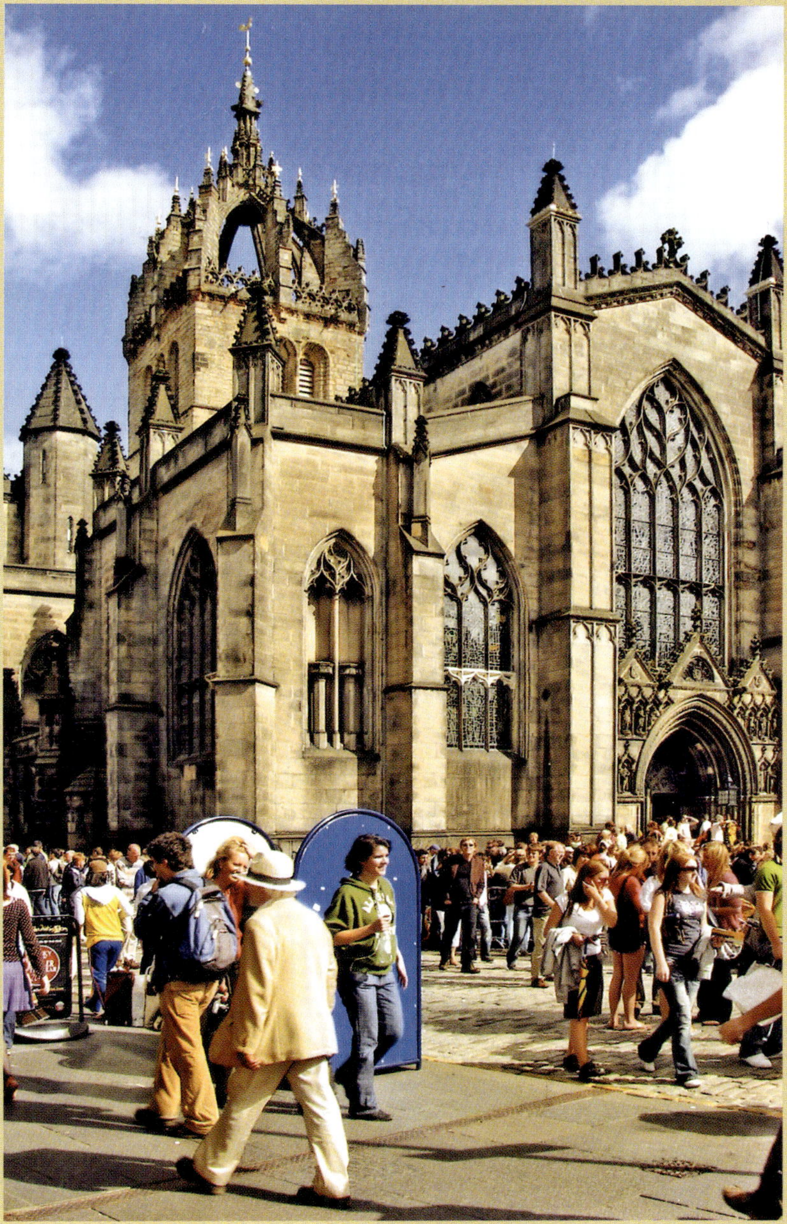

Festival crowds mingle in the sunshine outside St Giles Cathedral in the High Street. *Photographs by Peter Stubbs.*

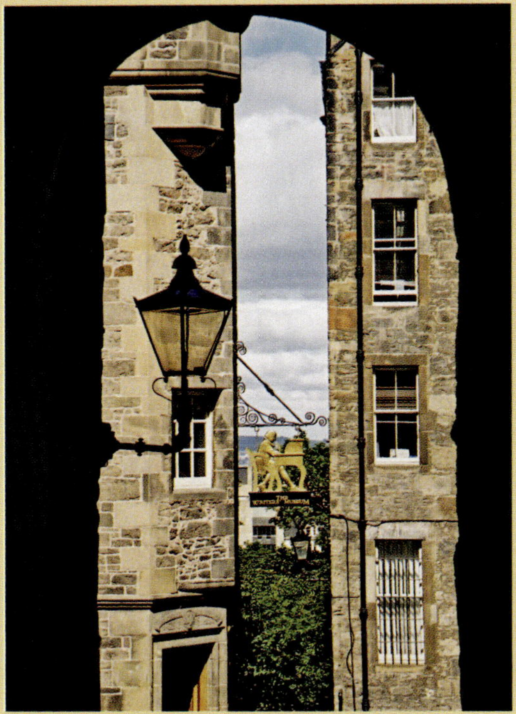

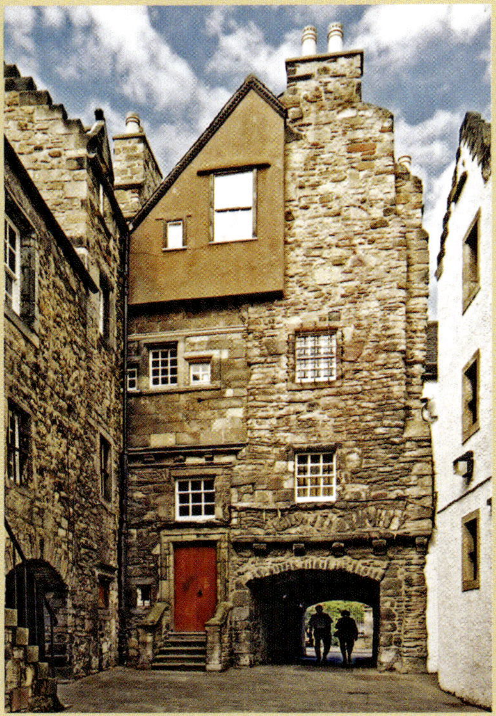

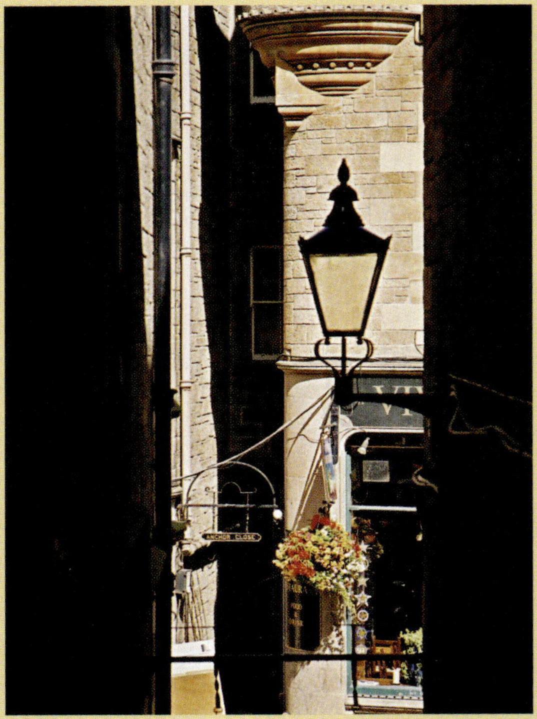

Above left. The sign of the Writers' Museum is framed in the arch of Lady Stair's Close on the north side of the Lawnmarket.

Above centre. Bakehouse Close, on the south side of the Canongate, takes its name from the Incorporation of Bakers which was established there in the late eighteenth century.

Above right. Anchor Close with the projecting lantern, originally lit by gas, is on the north side of the High Street. The works of Burns and *Encyclopaedia Britannica* were printed there by William Smellie.

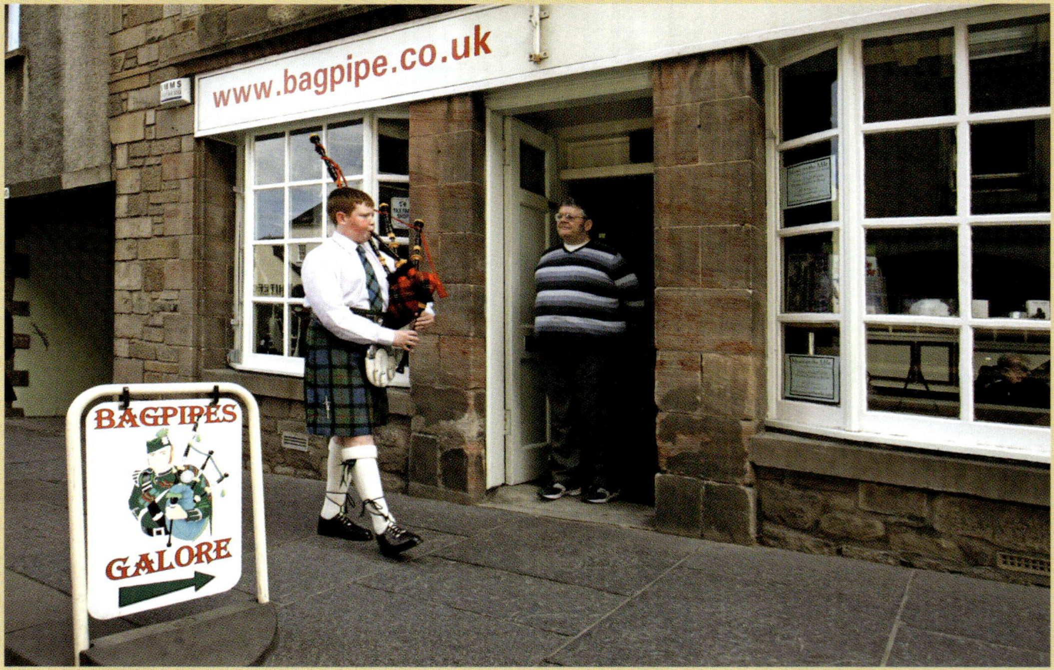

Right. Marc Jones, aged 13, of Firrhill High School, is in full swing on the Highland bagpipes watched by Tom, his grandfather and tutor – and where better to learn than at Bagpipes Galore in the Canongate with their wide selection of music, recordings, chanters and pipes. *Photographs by Peter Stubbs.*

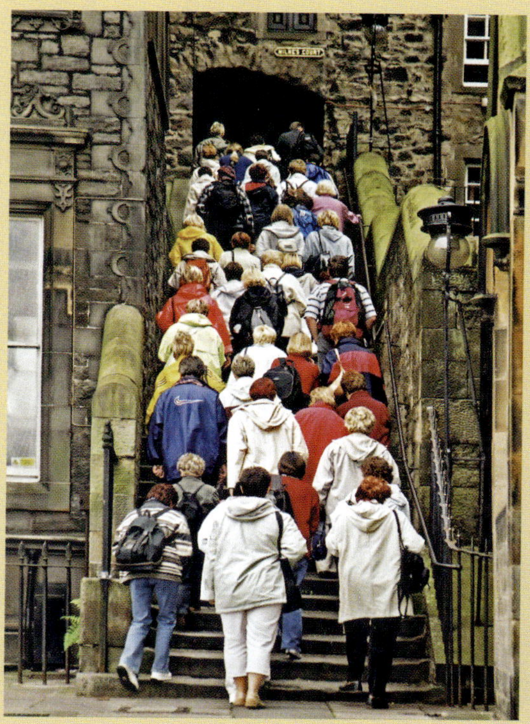

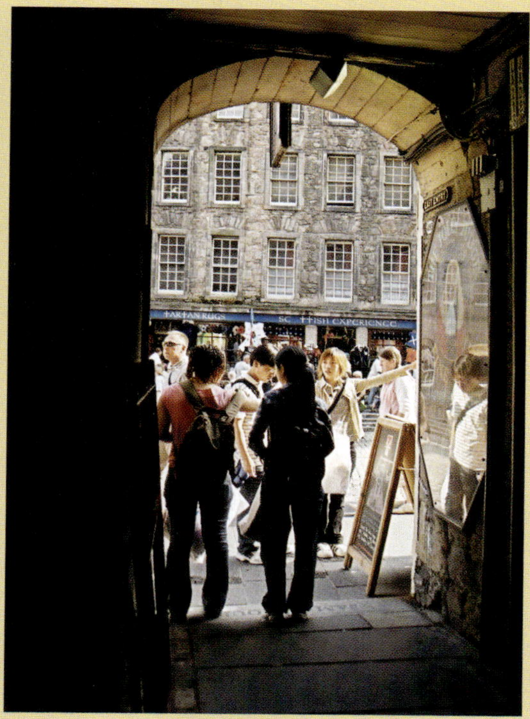

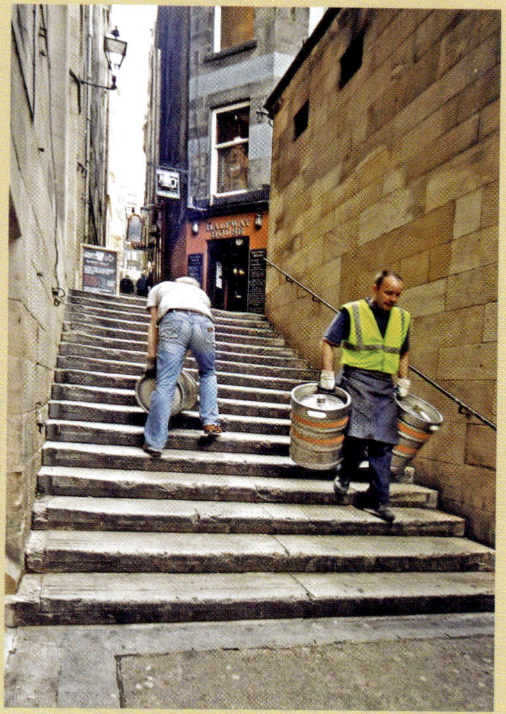

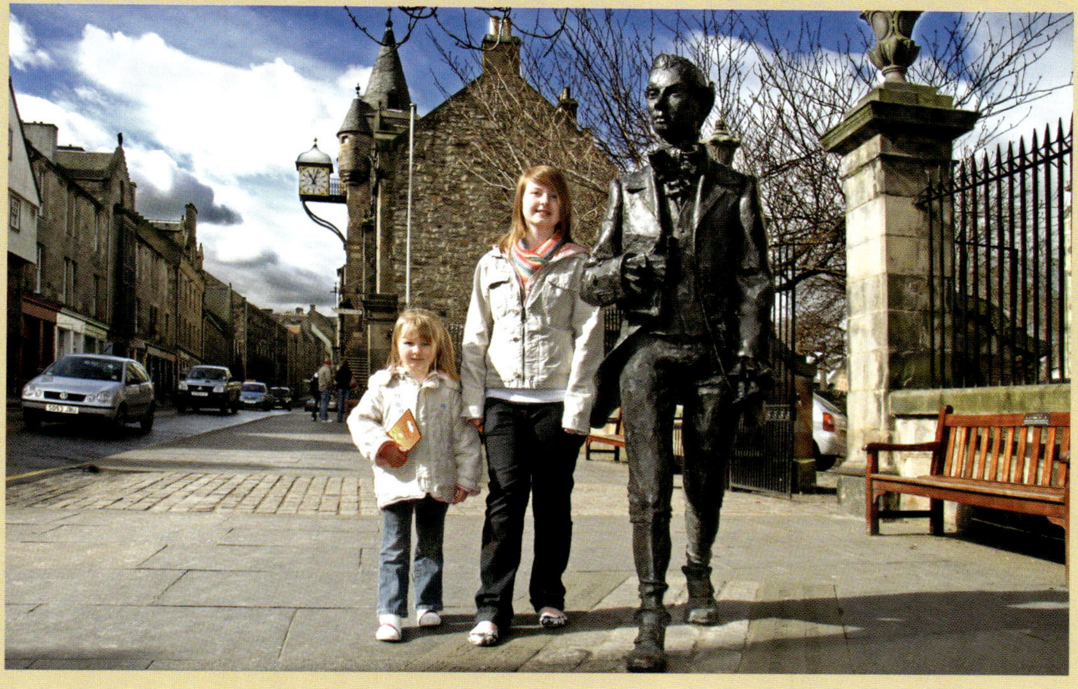

Above left. A large group of festival visitors tackle one of the Old Town's many flights of steps – this one at Milne's Court running between the Mound and the Lawnmarket.

Above centre. A bustling scene in the Lawnmarket is reflected off the advertising board for the Jolly Judge pub in James Court.

Above. Half way up or half way down – either way it is an arduous task supplying beer to Halfway House in Fleshmarket Close, off Cockburn Street.

Left. Sisters Joanna (*right*) and Naomi O'Brien accompany the poet, Robert Fergusson, on a stroll down the Canongate, past the Canongate Kirk. *Photographs by Peter Stubbs.*

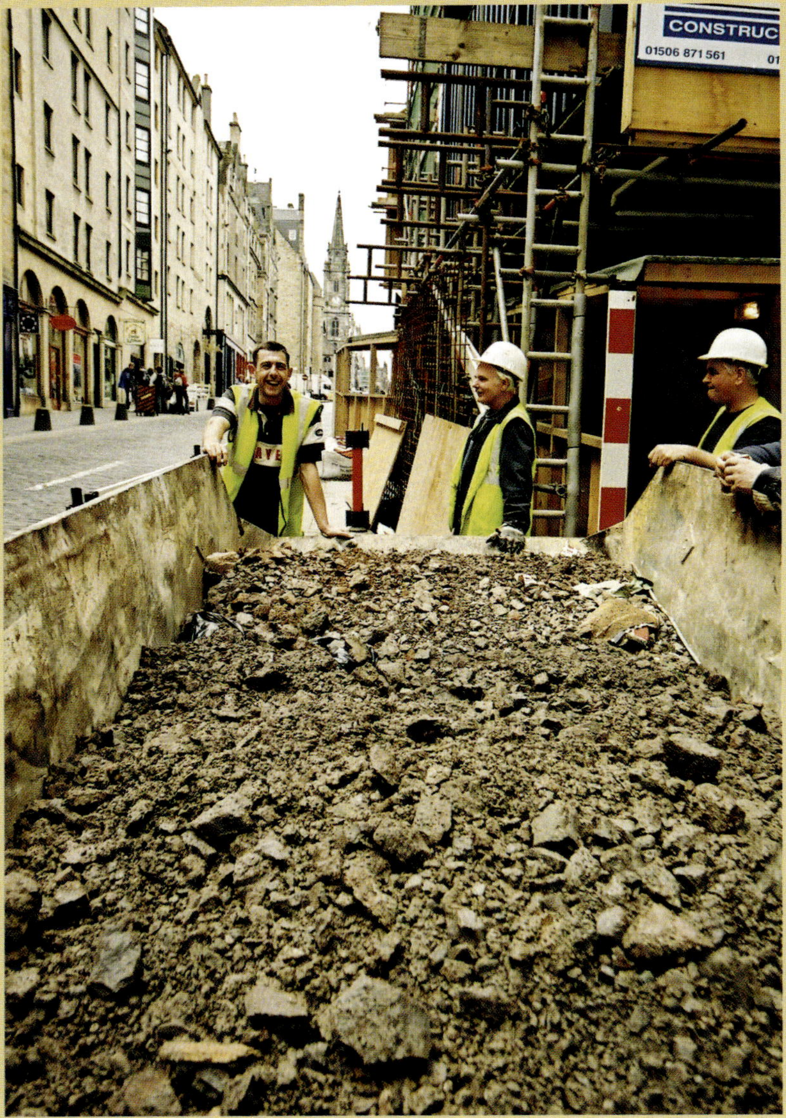

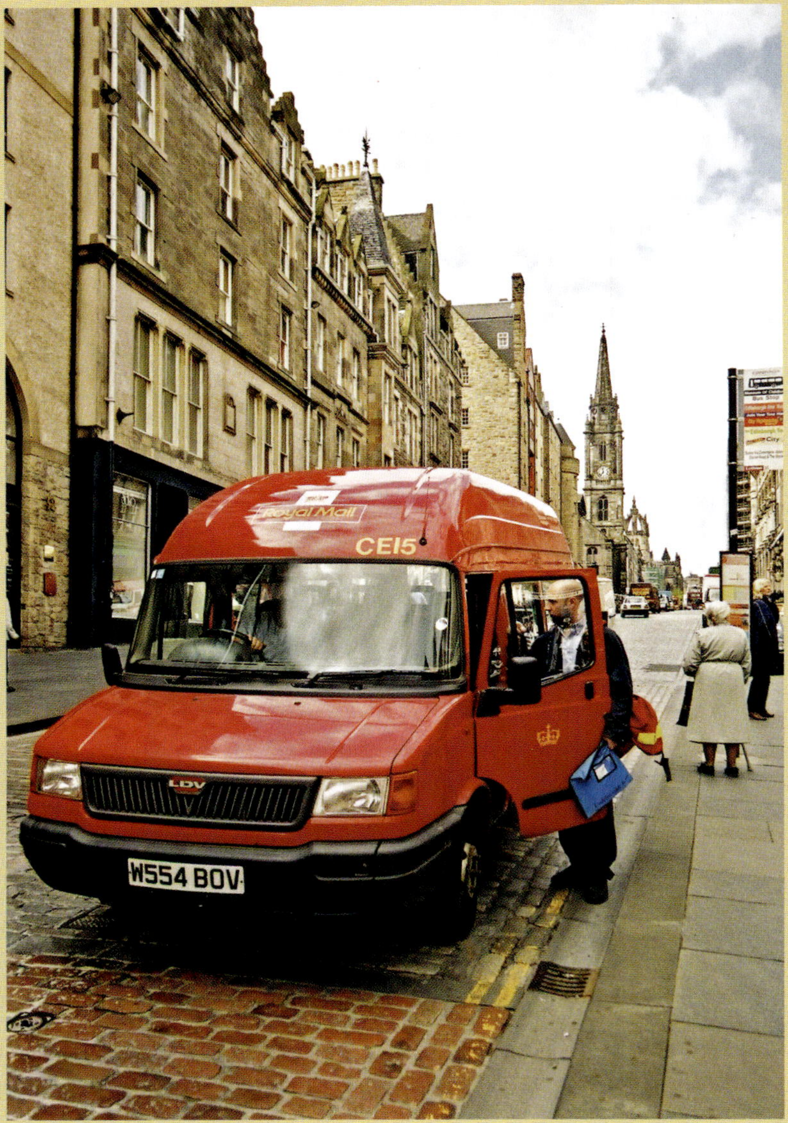

The Old Town of Edinburgh has a strong indigenous population as well as being a magnet for tourists all the year round. Workmen stand by their skip outside the Netherbow Centre in the High Street, while the postman at his van, only a few yards away, retains his concentration. *Photographs by Peter Stubbs.*

PART 2

HIGH STREET

CANONGATE

HOLYROOD PALACE

Part 2 continues the journey down the Royal Mile, beginning with St Giles Cathedral at the top of the High Street and finishing with Holyrood Palace at the foot of the Canongate. The general layout of the main thoroughfare and the closes, wynds and pends has hardly changed in 500 years. It is an area that requires present and future development to be sensitive to its unique setting.

There are 34 illustrations that cover most of the main places of historical importance, but, like Part 1, it would require a much wider selection of pictures to include everything. In this Introduction there are two contrasting photographs showing the interiors of houses in the Old Town. The source of the photographs is unidentified in the sense that there is no accompanying information on the name of the photographer, the date of the photographs, or, most importantly, the reason why the photographs were taken. There is a clear inference that they were taken to record the social conditions prevalent at the time. Several other photographs from the same unidentified album appear throughout Part 2 and convey quite graphic details of the inherent poverty found in parts of the Old Town.

The first group of photographs includes St Giles Cathedral, the Tron Kirk, the City Chambers and John Knox House. St Giles is shown in the 1950s from its west side, along with a contrasting photograph of Parliament Square being used for street entertainment during the Edinburgh Festival. There are two views of the City Chambers, one with the Mercat Cross and the other showing a row of small retail shops built into the arches on the front of the City Chambers. John Knox House is shown in its comparatively modern setting along with a much earlier etching which includes the Netherbow Port, one of the principal defensive entrances to the town.

The next group of photographs relates to the many closes and wynds on either side of the High Street and the Canongate. Three of the most famous are Advocates Close, Old Playhouse Close and Bakehouse Close. The inset picture that accompanies them is of a

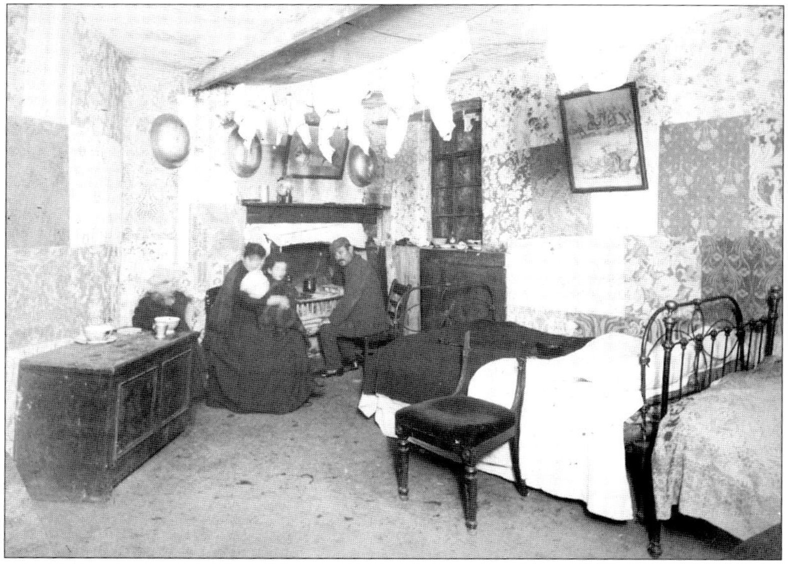

The family is huddled around a very small fire in a room that appears to be used as a dining room, living room and bedroom. It was probably the only room they had. *Courtesy of Robert Murray Stamp Shop.*

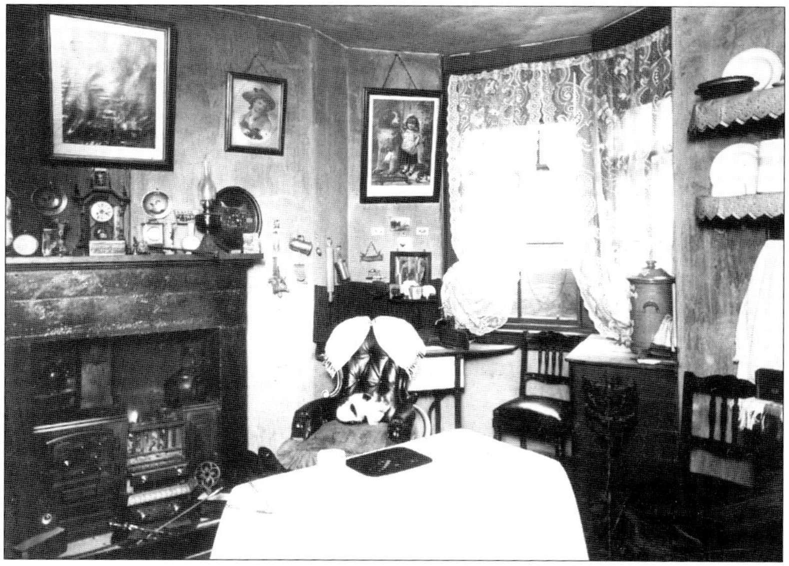

By contrast, this small room has a comfortable look about it with a good fireplace, neat furnishings and several ornaments and pictures. *Courtesy of Robert Murray Stamp Shop.*

lady airing linen at an open fire which was the standard form of heating in all the houses. White Horse Close, used as the royal mews in the sixteenth century, is shown in much poorer condition than at the present day. Lochend Close, recently redeveloped, is shown in the days when it was divided, by an unusual 'island' tenement, into two parts, the smaller section being known as Little Lochend Close.

Two pages are devoted to a selection of the interior and exterior photographs already referred to. These show several mothers and children, as well as a one-man business, a cobbler, probably working from his own single-roomed house. Sitting cheek by jowl with these many closes and wynds is the Canongate Tolbooth, now used as a museum, and Moray House, in the garden of which the 1707 Treaty of Union was signed.

Canongate Kirk, the Canongate Tolbooth and New Street are included in a panoramic view taken from Regent Road. The area between Tolbooth Wynd and New Street is occupied, in the photograph, by the bus garage that was demolished during 2007 for the proposed Caltongate development.

The final group of photographs in Part 2 relates to the foot of the Canongate where the Water Gate stood for many years in the street now known as Abbeyhill. Close by, and still standing, is the oddly shaped, sixteenth-century building known as Queen Mary's Bath. The last two pages have photographs of the Palace of Holyroodhouse by John K. Wilkie and Norward Inglis. The first is of the palace and the ruined abbey, taken from an interesting rock formation on Salisbury Crags, and the second is a very symmetrical picture of the great south gate, now used as the principal processional route to the palace.

Part 2 then leads into the second short colour section by Peter Stubbs. The emphasis is on the people who frequent the streets of the Old Town at the present day, particularly during the Edinburgh International Festival.

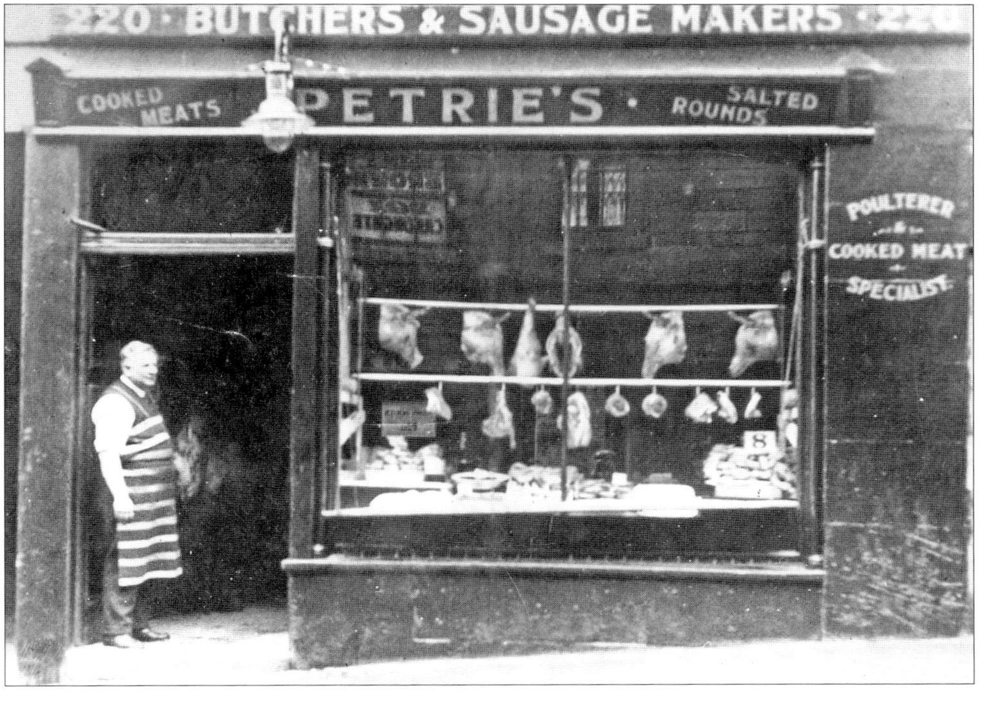

James Petrie was born in Shetland in 1888 and came to Edinburgh as a young boy. He started work as an employee in the butchery trade but later set up his own business at No. 220 Canongate and also at West Port. The photograph shows him outside the Canongate shop in the late 1920s. *Courtesy of Mrs Marissa Bryden, née Petrie.*

Right. The external appearance of St Giles Cathedral has hardly changed in the 50 years since this photograph was taken. There has been a church on the site since at least 1130, its great antiquity alluded to by the Rev. A. Ian Dunlop in *The Kirks of Edinburgh*: 'Its crowned steeple stands over a church, which, albeit changed in outward and inward appearance again and again, has witnessed great national events through the centuries and been used, for worship, by Roman Catholic, Episcopalian, Presbyterian, by General Assembly, Lord High Commissioner, by nobility and Sovereign, and always by ordinary Christian people'. Immediately in front of the cathedral is the statue of the 5th Duke of Buccleuch in the robes of the Order of the Garter. The sculptor was J. Edgar Boehm and the design of the plinth and panels was by Dr Rowand Anderson. One of the old town wells, protected by skew stones to deflect cart wheels, is on the right of the picture. The Tron Church is on the left further down the High Street. It was built between 1636 and 1647 by John Scott, a master wright, and John Mylne Jnr., Master Mason to the Crown. *Photograph by Norward Inglis.*

Below. In 2007, Parliament Square makes a popular venue for impromptu street entertainment during the Festival. *Photograph by Peter Stubbs.*

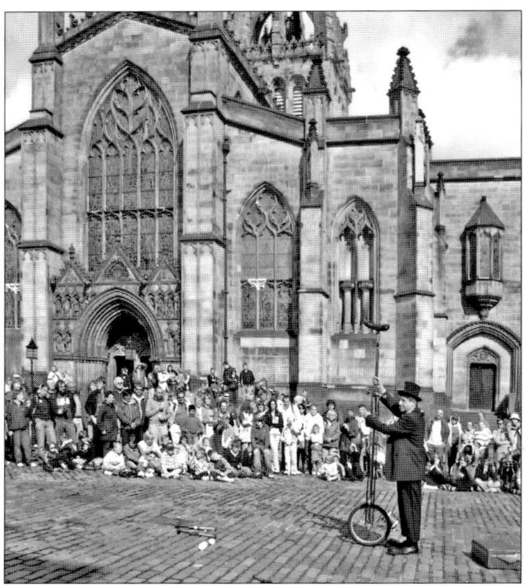

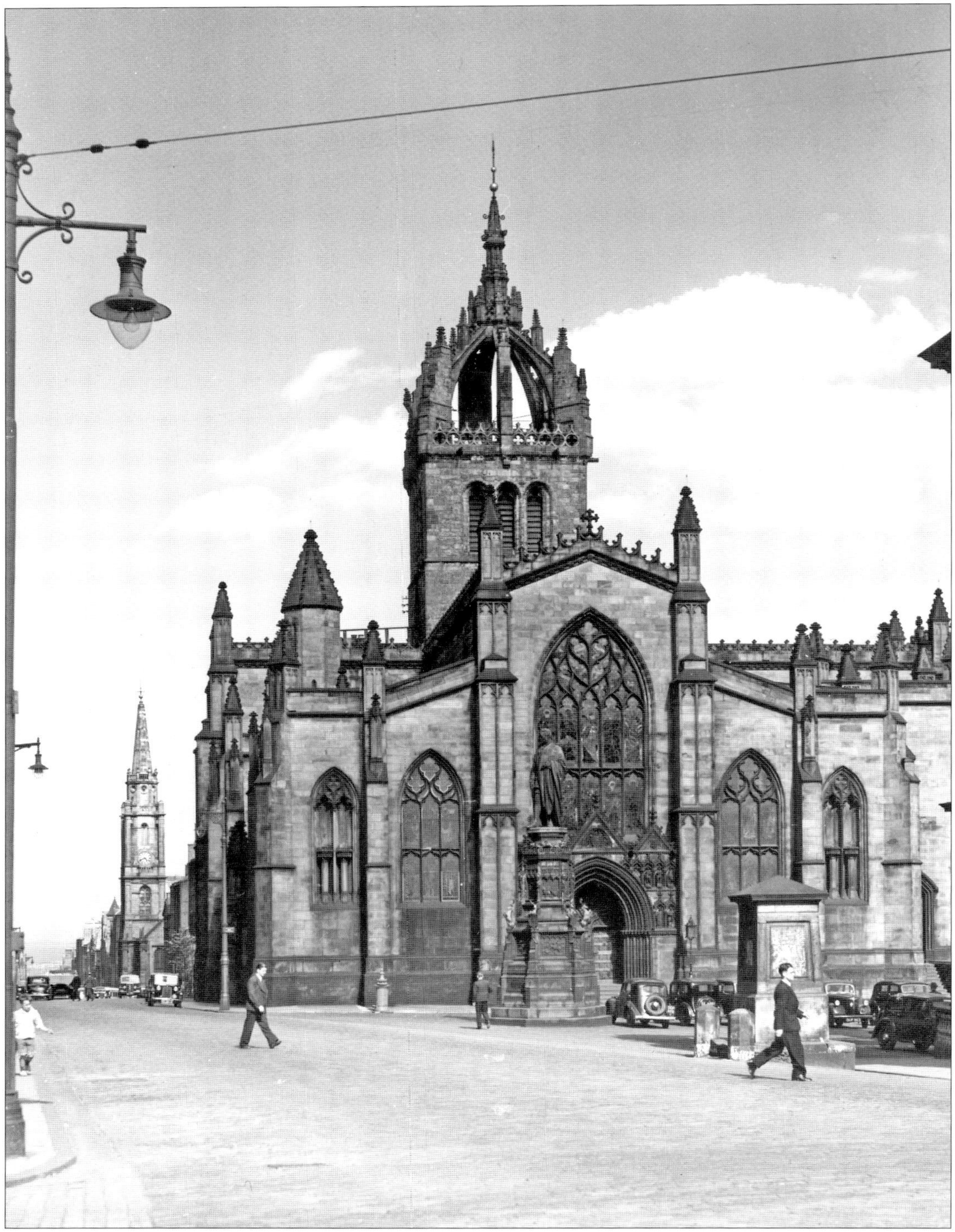

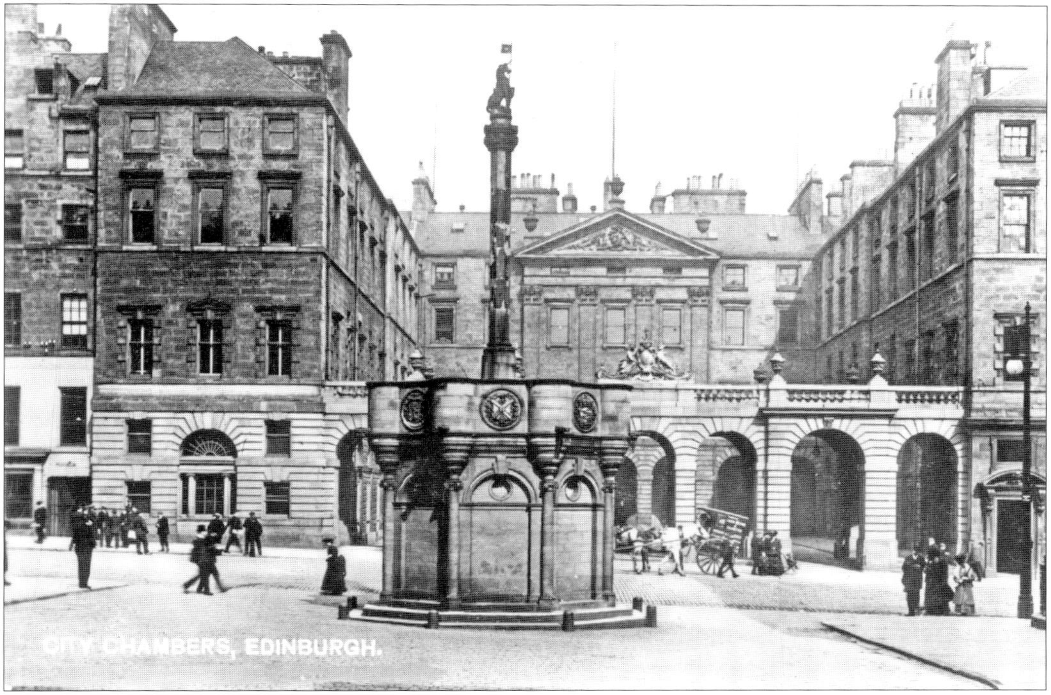

Left. On 13 September 1753 the foundation stone was laid for a Customs House and Exchange, the latter intended as a meeting place for the city's merchants, who had previously preferred to conduct their business in the open, usually in Parliament Square. When the building was completed in 1761, only one public office was located there, the remainder being used as the Exchange. The Town Council gradually increased its presence until 1811 when the building became known as the City Chambers. *Malcolm Cant Collection.*

Below left. In this picture, the elegant arches in front of the City Chambers are occupied, somewhat inappropriately, by several small retail businesses, including George Hardie 'the practical hatter'. On the left, the Exchange Hotel maintains a link with the building's first use.
Courtesy of Mrs Hamish Mearns.

Below. The 1st Battalion of the Argyll and Sutherland Highlanders marching down the High Street in 1892. After being stationed in Hong Kong, the battalion returned to Scotland and was in Edinburgh from 1892 to 1894.
Malcolm Cant Collection.

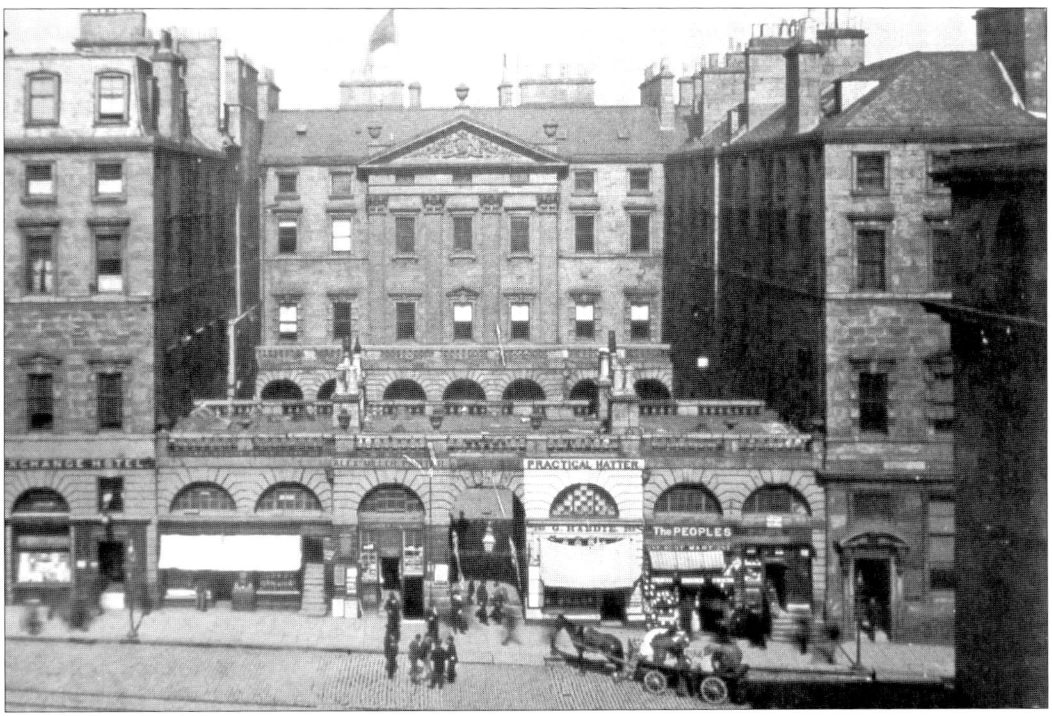

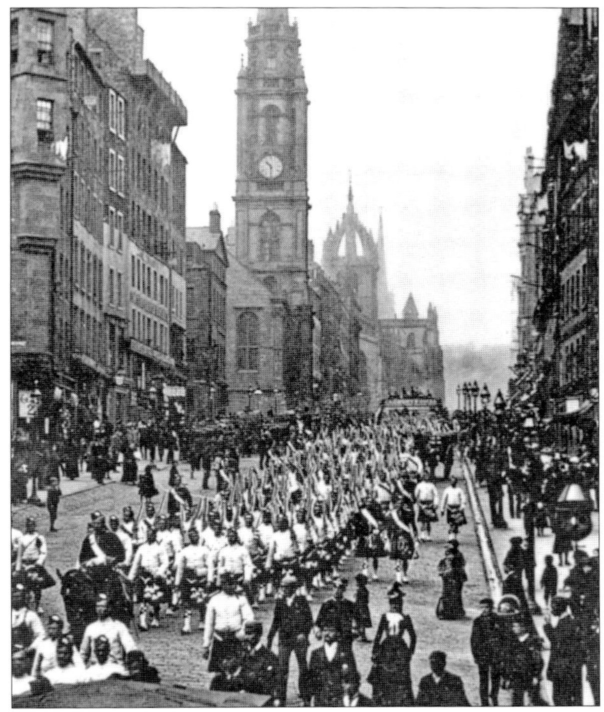

Right. John Knox House is among the most picturesque buildings in the Old Town, projecting southwards partially to close the vista down the High Street. There is doubt about its exact age: the Edinburgh volume of *The Buildings of Scotland* describes it as 'largely genuine C 16', but other authorities maintain that it is much older. Ironically, the man most closely associated with the house, James Mosman, Goldsmith to Mary Queen of Scots, was no admirer of Knox's reforming zeal. John Knox died in the house on 24 November 1572 shortly after delivering one of his fiery sermons at St Giles Cathedral. He was buried in the graveyard on the south side of St Giles, the spot now being marked by a brass plate I K 1572, near one of the parking bays for the Court of Session. Although Knox's tenure of the High Street house was brief in 1572, there is strong evidence that he also lived there at an earlier period. *Photograph by Norward Inglis.*

Below. The etching, *c.* 1760, shows John Knox House with the Netherbow Port blocking the roadway at the boundary between Edinburgh and the Canongate. *From* Old Houses in Edinburgh.

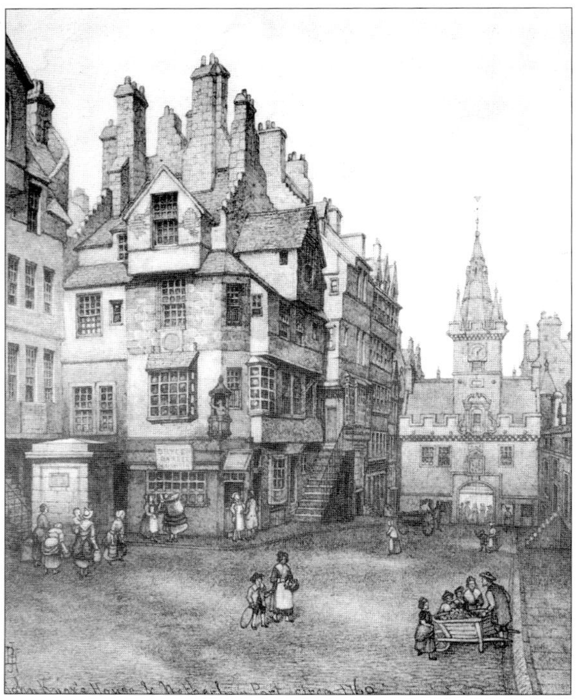

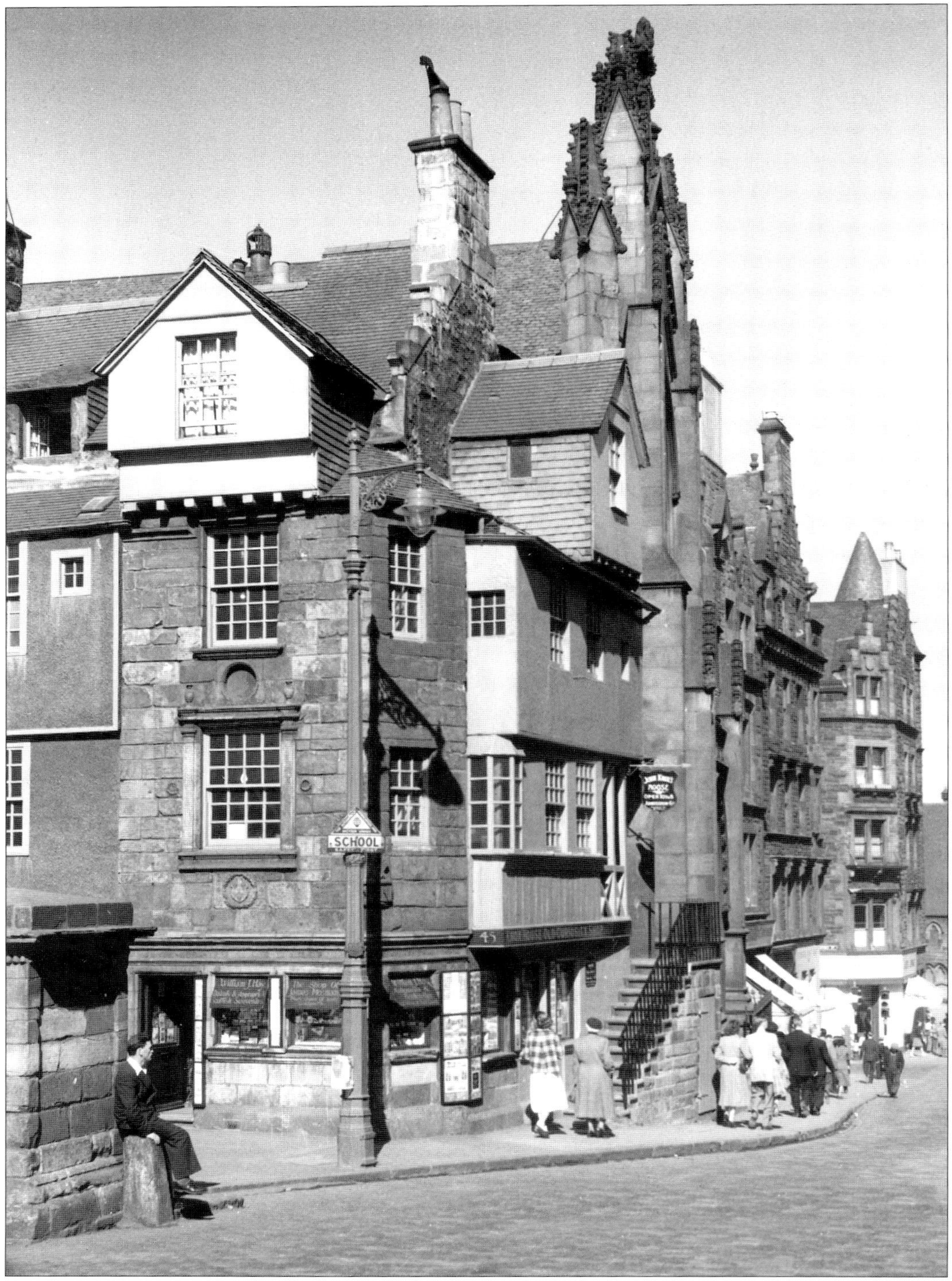

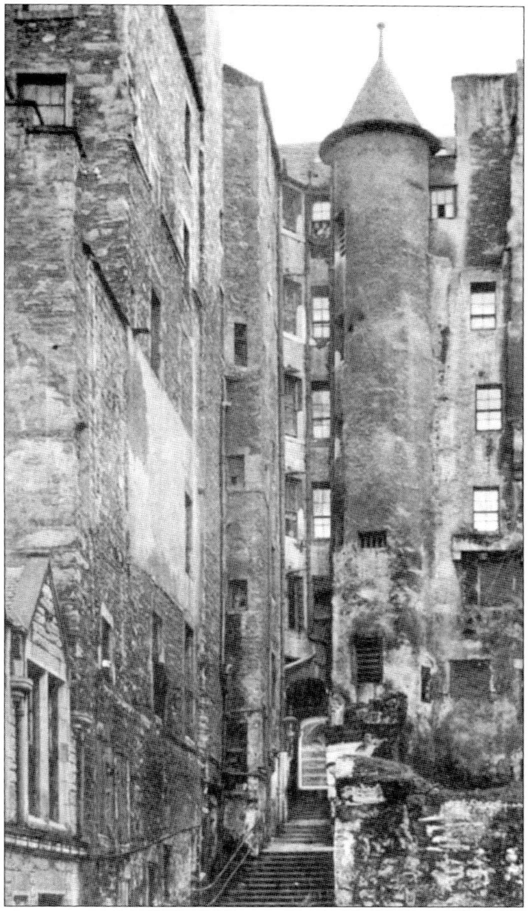

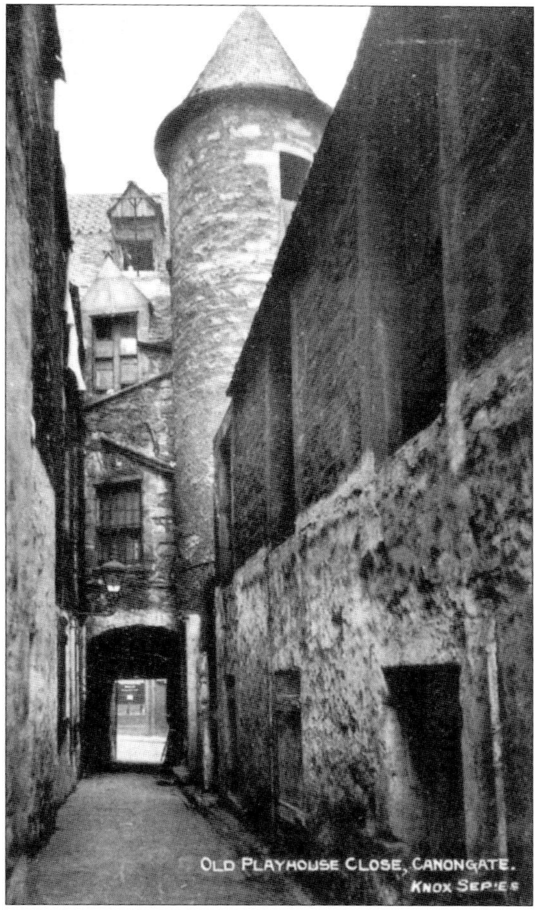

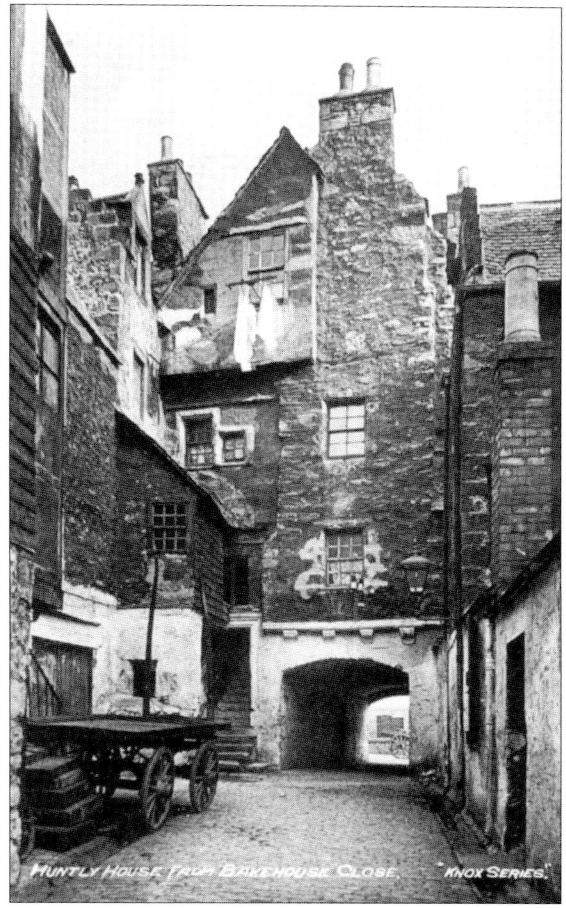

Right. The presence of the camera appears to have startled this housewife as she goes about the task of airing linen in front of the open fire. It is a Dow's range, 'By Her Majesty's Royal Letters Patent'. *Courtesy of Robert Murray Stamp Shop*

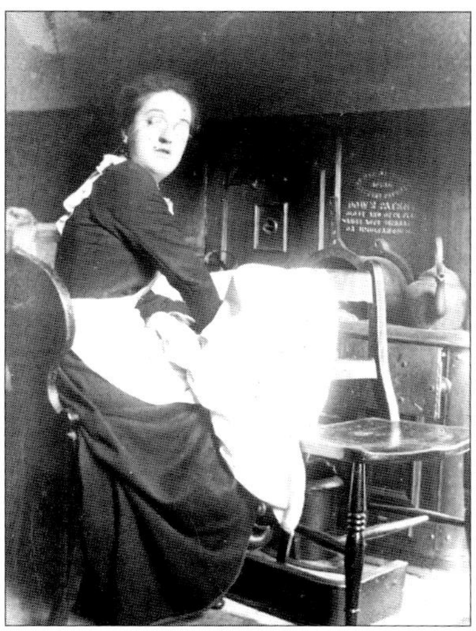

Above left. The entrance to Advocates Close is on the High Street, opposite St Giles' Cathedral. It is very narrow as it runs under the tenements but widens considerably nearer to Cockburn Street. Much of the lower part of the close was rebuilt after extensive demolition in 1880. The close is named after its most famous resident, Sir James Stewart, Lord Advocate from 1692 to 1713.

Above centre. Old Playhouse Close is on the south side of the Canongate, a few yards uphill from the pend that leads to St John's Street. There were two closes of that name: the one nearer to Holyrood Palace was Old Playhouse Close and the one nearer to Edinburgh Castle was (Upper) Playhouse Close. They both gave access to Edinburgh's first purpose-built public theatre, opened in 1747, but replaced when the Theatre Royal was opened in 1769 in Shakespeare Square.

Above right. Bakehouse Close lies on the south side of the Canongate, on the east, or lower, side of Huntly House. The close takes its name from the Incorporation of Bakers of Canongate who built a bakehouse there in the late eighteenth century. An important building lies on either side: Huntly House, occupied in the mid-eighteenth century by the Dowager Duchess of Gordon; and Acheson House, built for Sir Archibald Acheson, Secretary of State to Charles I. *All Malcolm Cant Collection.*

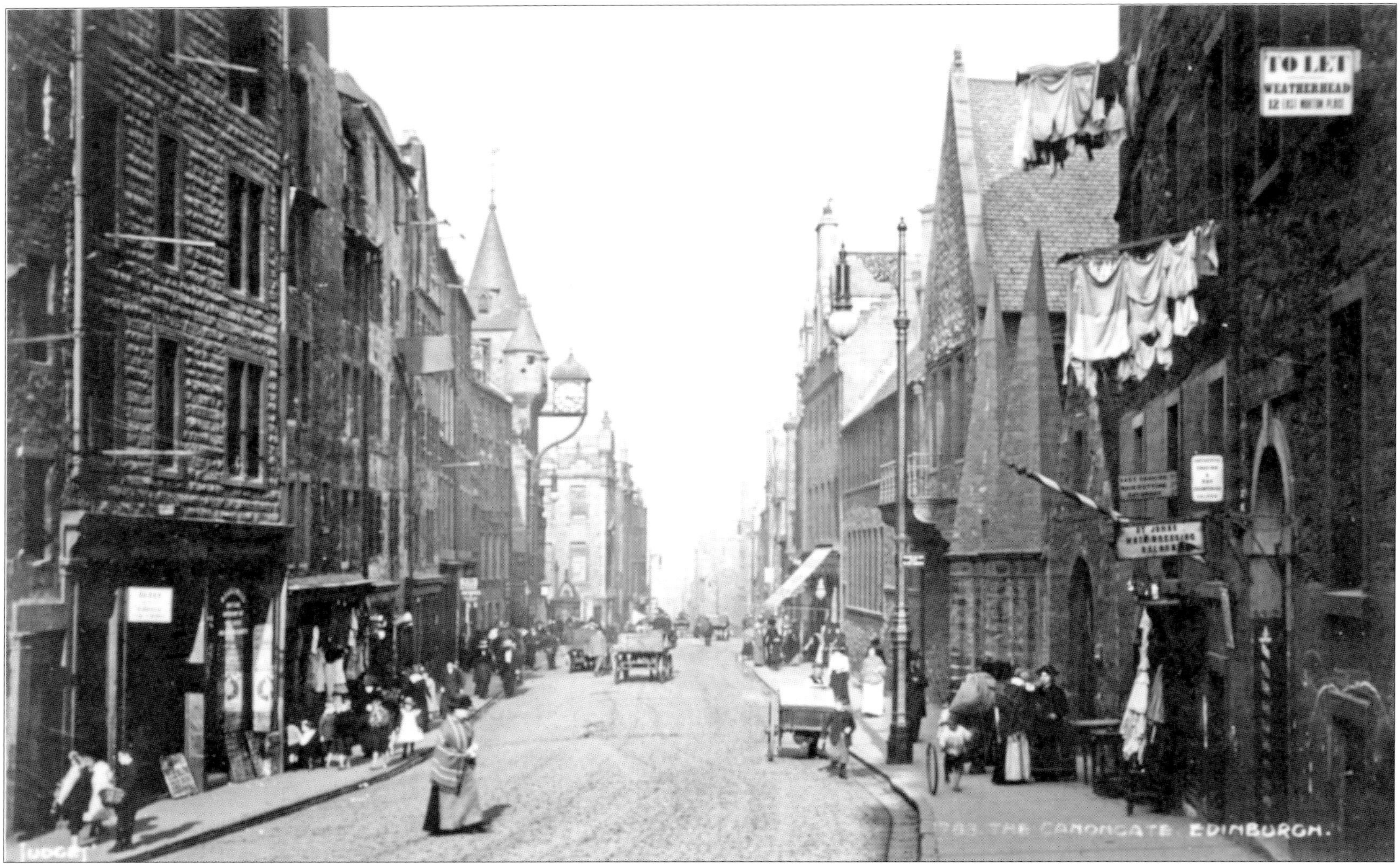

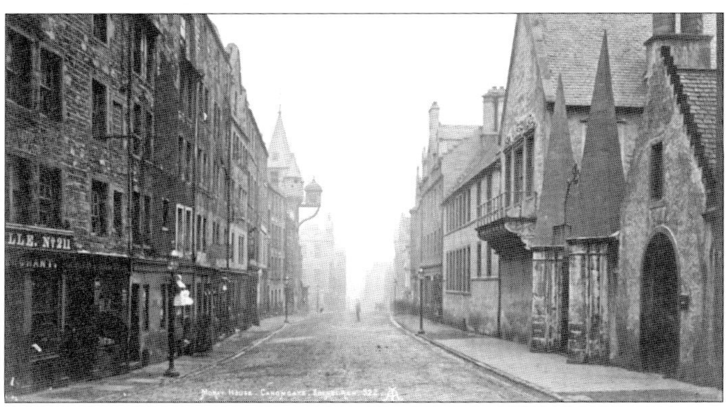

The two photographs, taken from about the same position, show very different views of the Canongate: the upper picture depicts a busy street scene whereas the lower, much older picture, is almost devoid of people and traffic. On the left of both pictures, the bracket clock, dated 1884, projects from the Canongate Tolbooth, built in 1591 to replace an earlier one on the same site. Originally, it was used for the collection of public dues but was later used as a prison, a courthouse, and, at the present day, a museum, the People's Story. On the right of the pictures, the massive conical stone obelisks mark the entrance to Moray House, built *c.* 1625 by Dowager Countess of Home. On her death, the property passed to her daughter, Margaret, Countess of Moray. It remained in the Moray family for almost two centuries. The summerhouse in which the Treaty of Union was signed in 1707 lay to the south of the entrance.

At a more mundane level, there is a sign for St John's Hairdressing Salon which offers 'Antiseptic Shaving and Dry Shampooing'.
Malcolm Cant Collection.

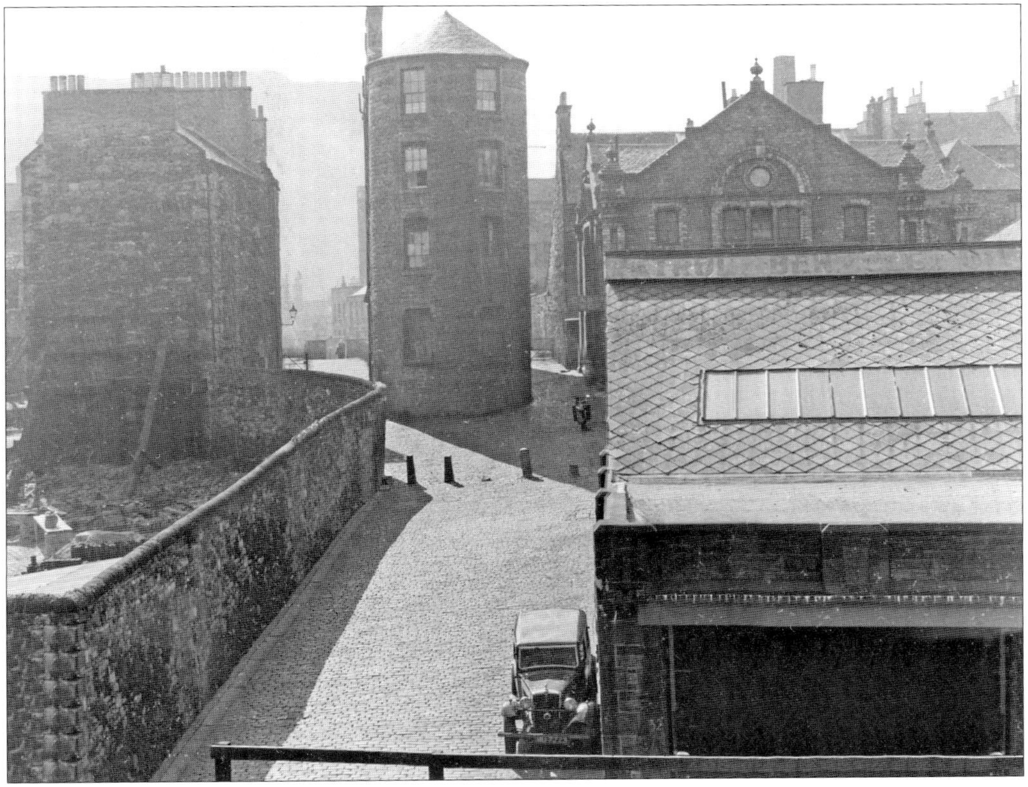

Left. This early 1950s photograph shows Lochend Close which ran from Calton Road southwards to the Canongate. The curious 'island' tenement divided Lochend Close from the narrower one on the right, Little Lochend Close. The Highland Society School was located in Lochend Close in the 1880s. *Photograph by Duncan McMillan.*

Below left. White Horse Close, on the north side of the Canongate, looks very run down in this illustration: at the present day it is in excellent repair but much altered from the original. The site was used as the royal mews in the sixteenth century but was rebuilt a century later by Laurence Ord. *Malcolm Cant Collection.*

Below. The rear of White Horse Close faces onto Calton Road, previously named North Back of Canongate. Clearly it is in domestic use with several of the old stable doorways still evident. *Malcolm Cant Collection.*

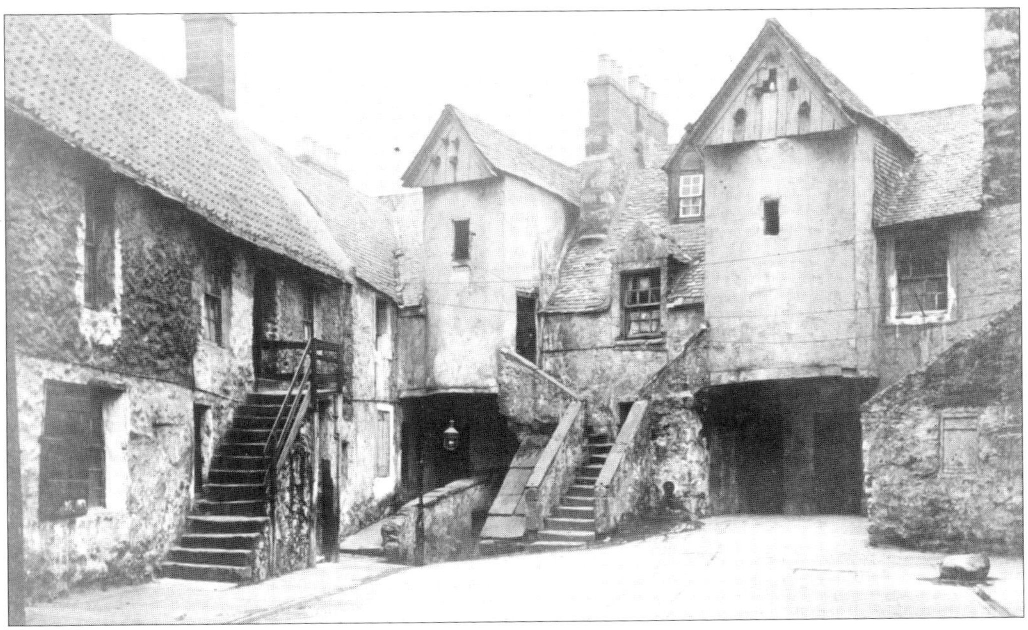

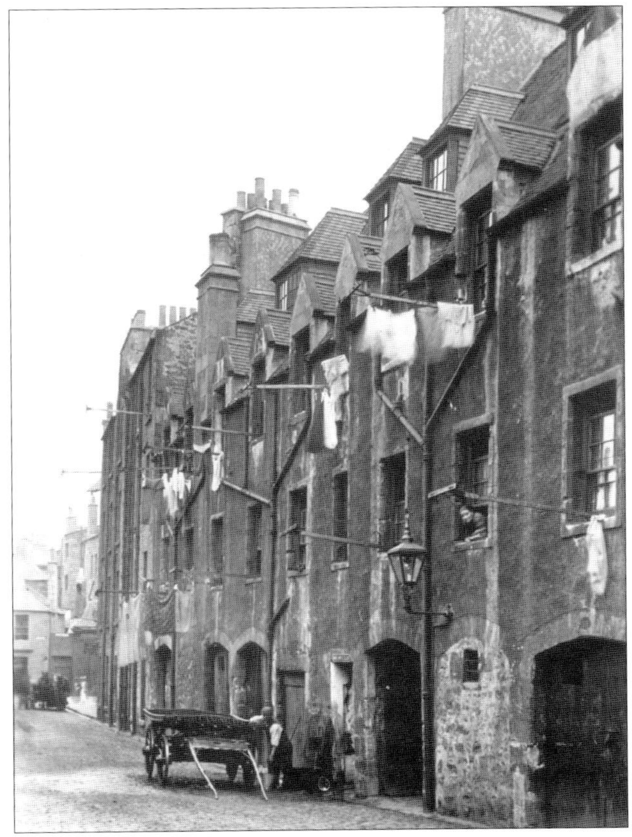

The photographs on this, and the opposite page come from a series of undated and unidentified images of the Old Town of Edinburgh. Presumably they were taken to record the appalling state of some of the tenements and the hardship endured by the occupants. The two interior photographs on this page are believed to relate to the close shown below. Perhaps the cobbler lived and worked in a single room, hoping to attract sufficient business for his modest requirements. The upper picture gives the impression of being slightly more 'affluent' than the lower one. *All courtesy of Robert Murray Stamp Shop.*

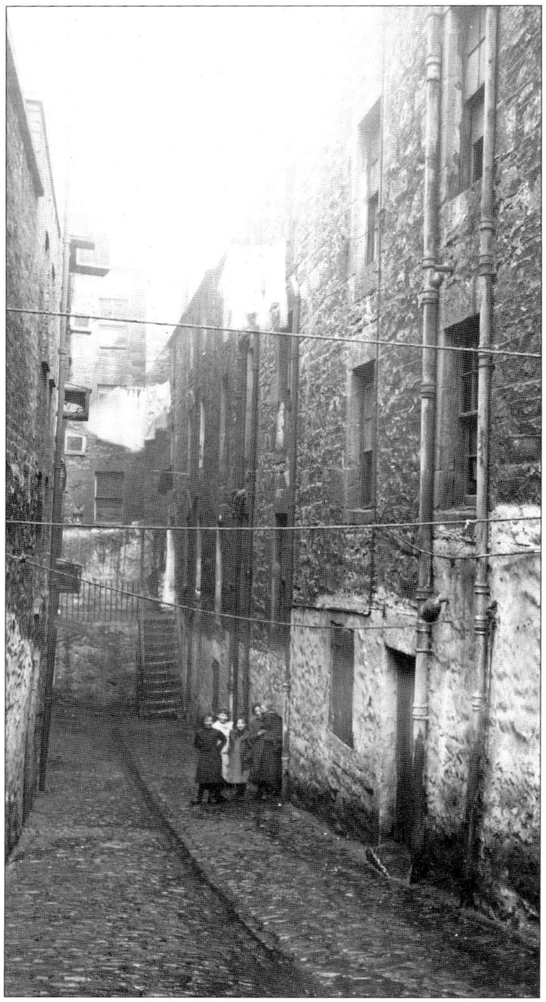

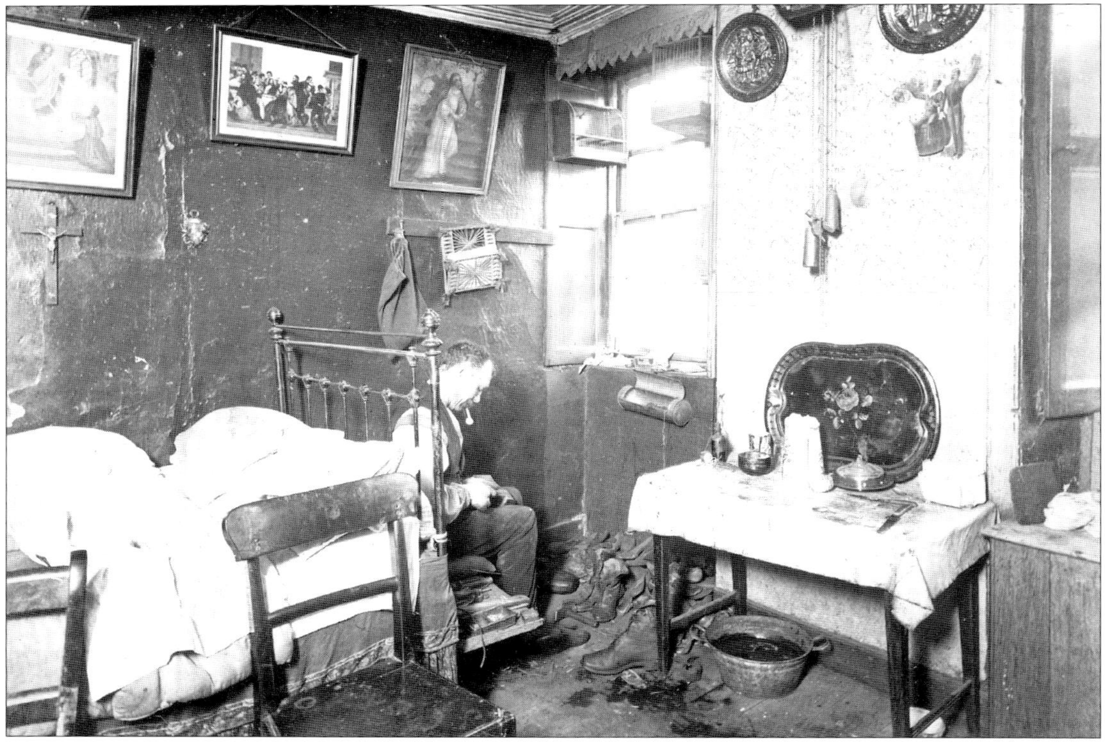

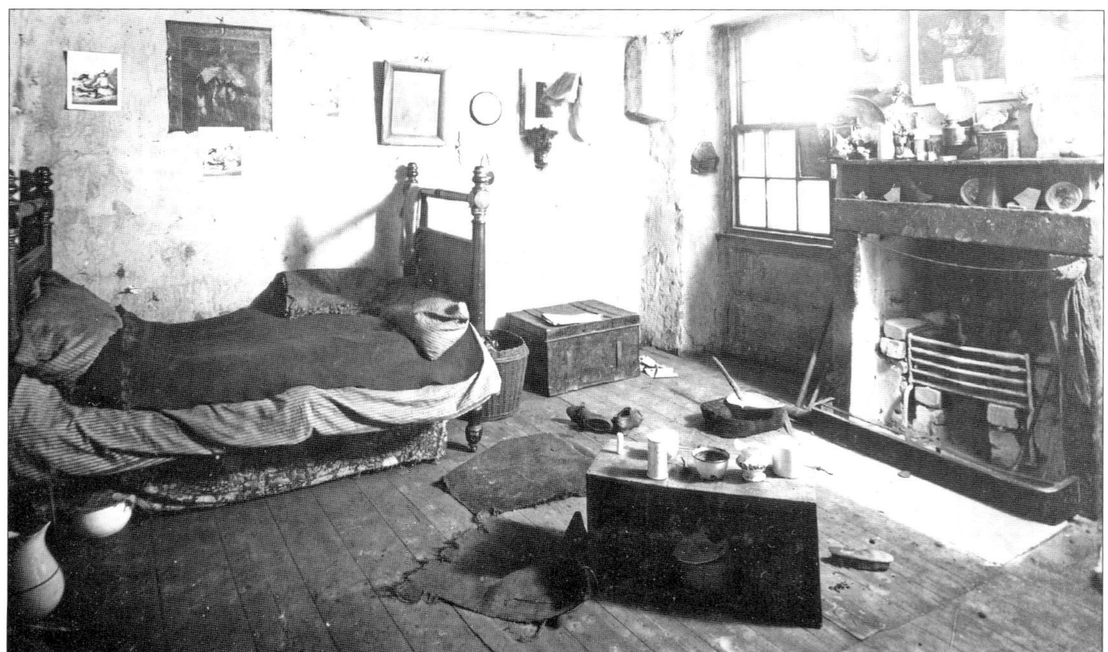

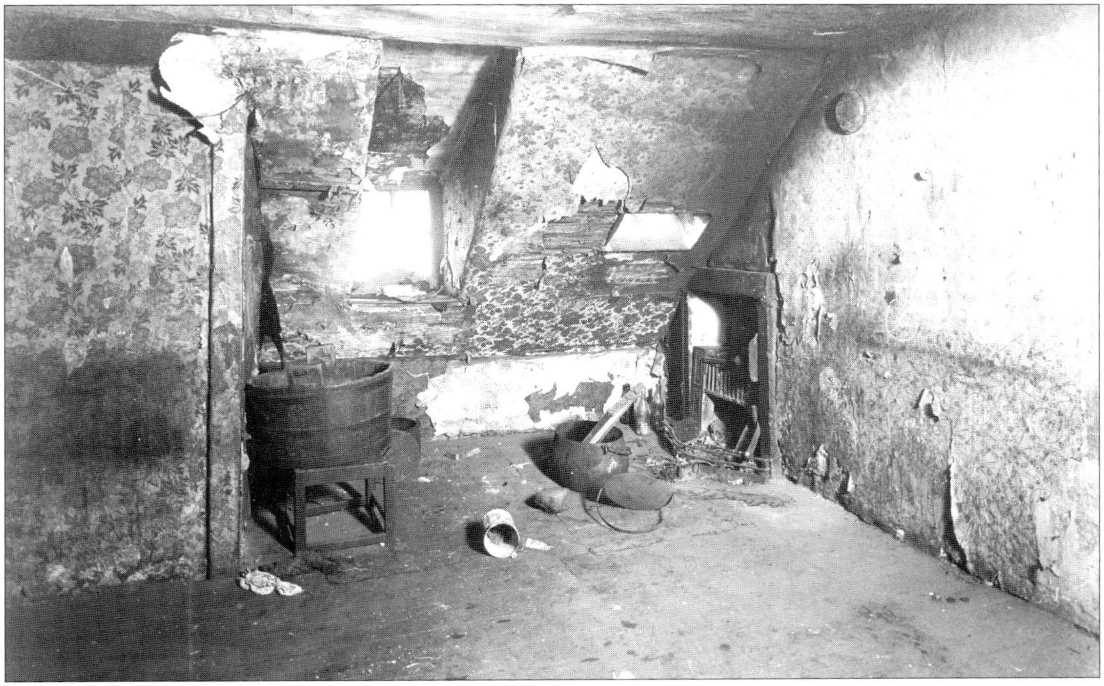

The people in the close look reasonably well turned out but their living quarters would be very modest. Some parts of the tenement were without running water and bathrooms were completely unheard of. Flush toilets, where fitted, would be communal and situated either in the backgreen area or on the landing off the common staircase. Washing facilities were usually a communal, single cold-water tap often on the ground floor. The two interior photographs are obviously of the attic accommodation with very small dormer windows and a fireplace built dangerously close to the roof timbers. As the tenement gradually became unfit for human habitation, the attic and upper floors would succumb more quickly than the rooms at a lower level. The rooms illustrated show extensive deterioration of the lath and plaster walls and ceiling, with some wallpaper remaining.
All courtesy of Robert Murray Stamp Shop

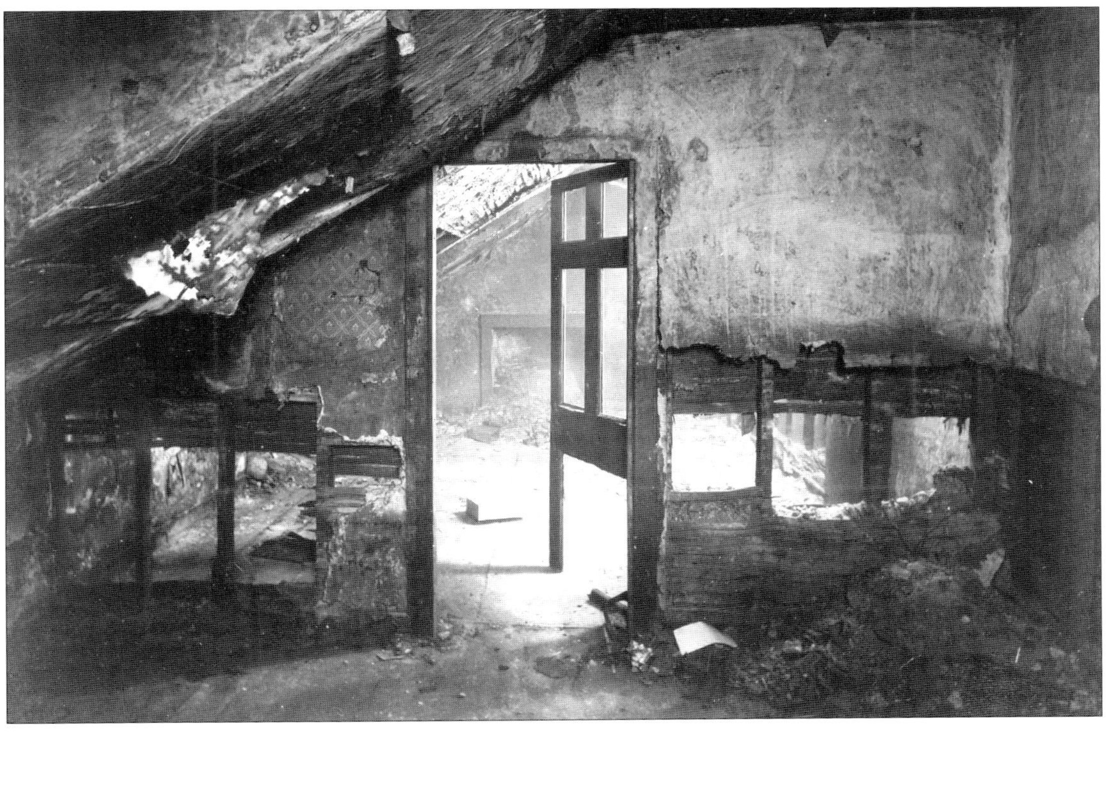

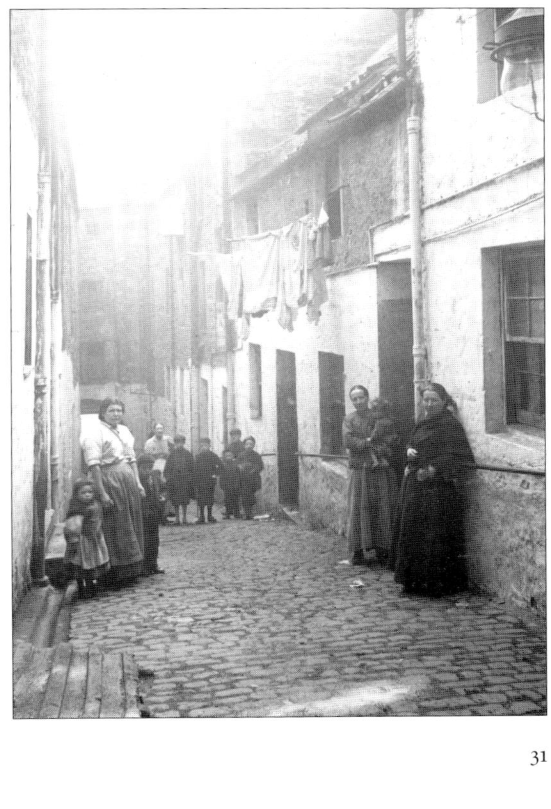

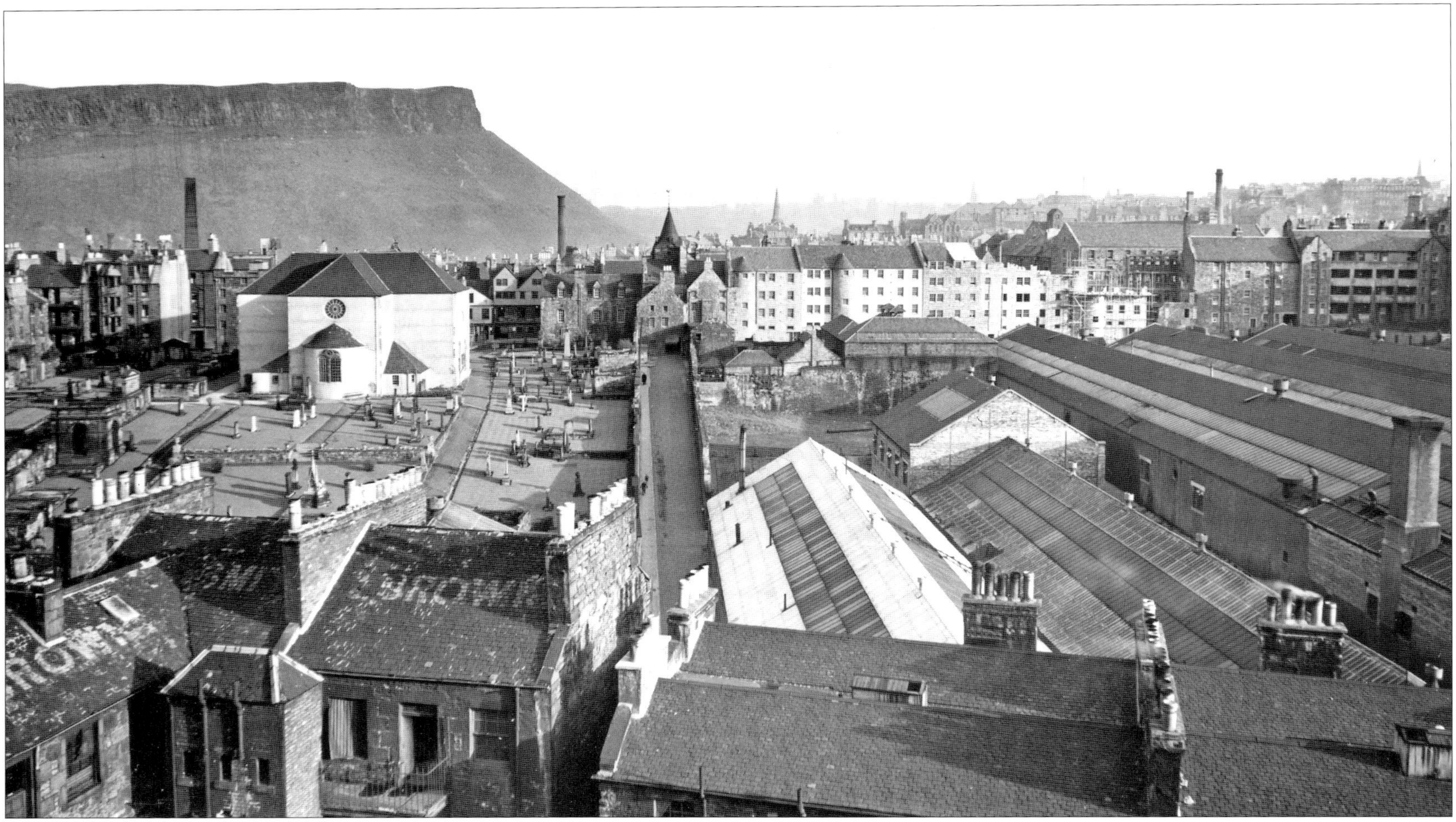

The photograph was taken from the sloping ground between Regent Road and Calton Road in the mid-1950s. The very narrow lane in the centre of the picture is Tolbooth Wynd, which takes its name from the Canongate Tolbooth, the spire of which can be seen against the sky-line. Near the foot of the Wynd, on its east side (close to the building in the photograph which has BROWN written on the roof), the Charity Workhouse was opened in 1761. According to Grant's *Old and New Edinburgh*: 'It was established by subscription and opened for the reception of the poor, the expense being defrayed by collections at the church doors and voluntary contributions'.

To the left of Tolbooth Wynd is the rear view of Canongate Kirk which dates from 1691. Its ancient graveyard contains many interesting tombs but there are just as many unmarked graves. Among the many distinguished citizens buried there are: Lord Provost George Drummond (1687–1766); the economist Adam Smith (1723–90); the hospital founder, George Chalmers (1773–1836) and the poet, Robert Fergusson (1750–74) whose life-size statue stands on the pavement outside the kirk gate in the Canongate.

The pitched roofs to the right of Tolbooth Wynd belong to the former Eastern Scottish bus garage, built in 1927. The Edinburgh volume of *The Buildings of Scotland* dismisses it with one short phrase: 'red brick with no attempt at architecture'. The site was cleared in 2007 to make way for the hugely controversial development, Caltongate, which, hopefully, will not fall into the same category. Before the bus station was built, the site was occupied by the remaining buildings of the Edinburgh Gas Light Company which began distribution of gas in 1818. A few years later, in 1823, the company was faced with stiff competition, firstly from the Edinburgh & Leith Gas Light Company which had its works in Baltic Street in Leith, and then by the Edinburgh Oil Gas Company at Tanfield, Canonmills. The Edinburgh Oil Gas Company was later absorbed by the Edinburgh Gas Light Company but the remaining two fought it out for customers, even to the extent of laying their own separate gas mains. With an eye to economy, the two companies agreed, in 1866, to limit their costs by carving up the total area between them. Granton Gasworks did not open until 1902.
Photograph by Norward Inglis.

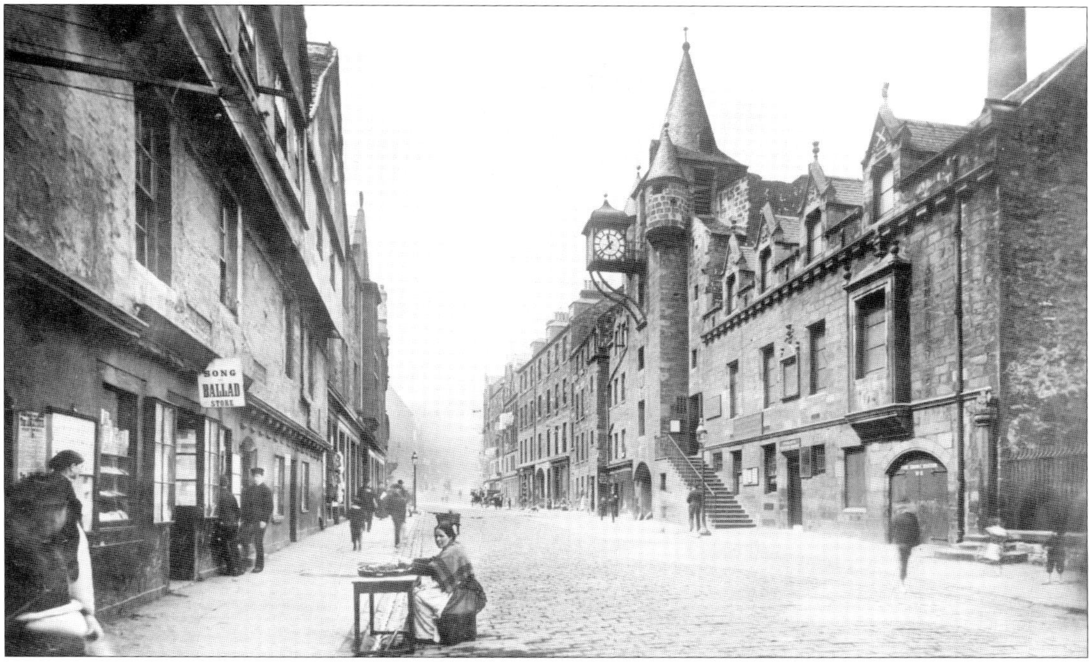

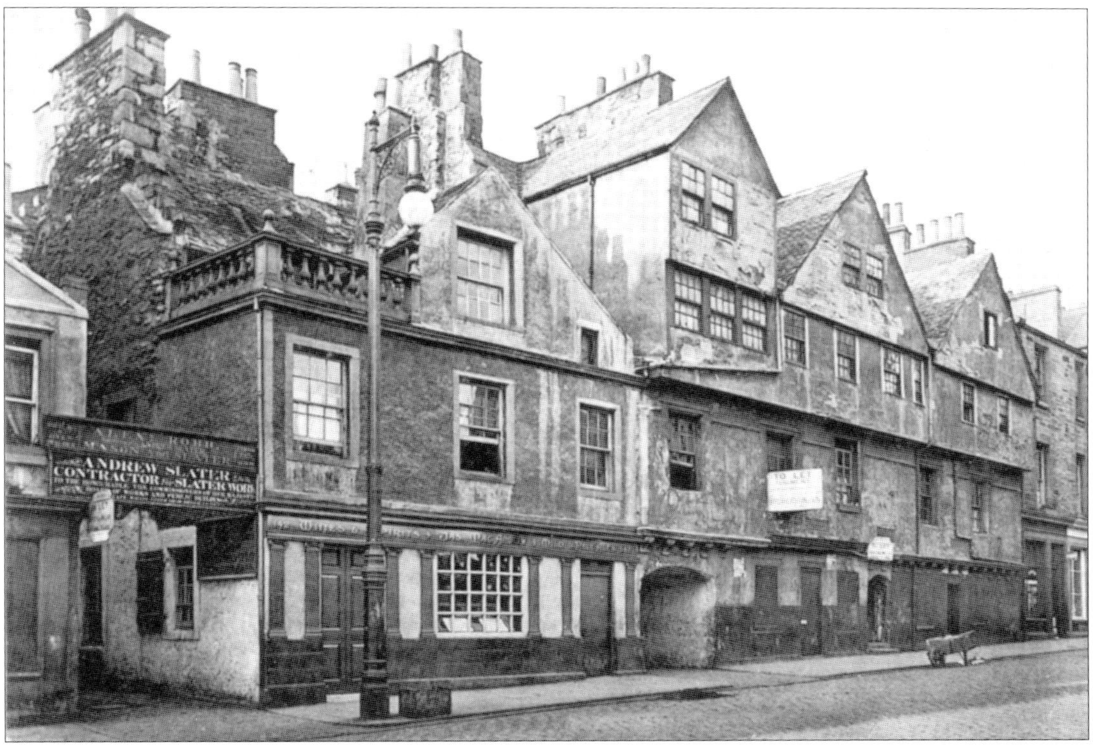

Left. In the Canongate, the female vendor is sitting at her small table outside a shop which has the sign, 'Song and Ballad Store', but there is no indication of what she is selling. The shop forms part of the sixteenth-century building, Huntly House. The building on the right, with the projecting bracket clock, is the Canongate Tolbooth. The door in the rounded arch says, 'Fire Engine Station' and the smaller door, nearer to the flight of stairs, says, 'Police Station Entrance'.

Below left. The building on the right, with the three pitched gables, is Huntly House, now the home of the Museum of Edinburgh. Its tenuous connection with the Gordons of Huntly appears to be that the Duchess of Gordon had an apartment there long after it was built. On the extreme left there is a name board for Andrew Slater, Contractor for Slater Work, whose trade connections must have been the envy of his competitors: 'SLATERS TO THE HONOURABLE THE COMMISSIONERS OF HER MAJESTY'S BOARD OF WORKS AND PUBLIC BUILDINGS'.

Below. Canongate Kirk, dating from 1691, has a Doric porch, above which are the arms of Thomas Moodie, its benefactor. Above the circular window are the royal arms for William III. Outside the church, on the left, is the Canongate Cross, now resited behind the railings on the right. The well has long since disappeared but the approximate site of it is currently occupied by a statue of the poet, Robert Fergusson.
All Malcolm Cant Collection.

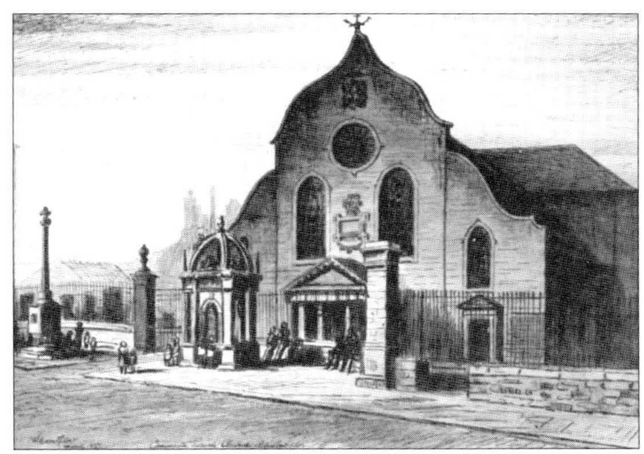

Below. The Water Gate (Yett) stood at the junction of the Canongate and what is now Abbeyhill. According to Stuart Harris in *The Place Names of Edinburgh*, it was called the Water Yett because it was near the small Tummel burn. As can be seen from this 1820 drawing, the gate was never constructed for defence, but was frequently blocked up in times of trouble. Its importance as a principal entrance to the city had obviously declined by the sixteenth century when it was known as the Dung Port, on account of the inhabitants using the Tummel as an open sewer. *From* Storer's Views of Edinburgh.

Below right. This very odd-shaped, lumpy building, recently dated to 1565, which still stands in Abbeyhill, has always been known as Queen Mary's Bath. It was probably built for Mary as a pavilion or summerhouse in the corner of her Privy Garden. *Malcolm Cant Collection.*

Right. The substantial, four-storey block on the left dates from the early sixteenth century but has been altered on several occasions since. The smaller building, nearer to Holyrood Palace, dates from a century later. The bus is about to enter Horse Wynd where the side view of Holyrood Free Church (now the Queen's Gallery) can just be seen. *Photograph by John K. Wilkie.*

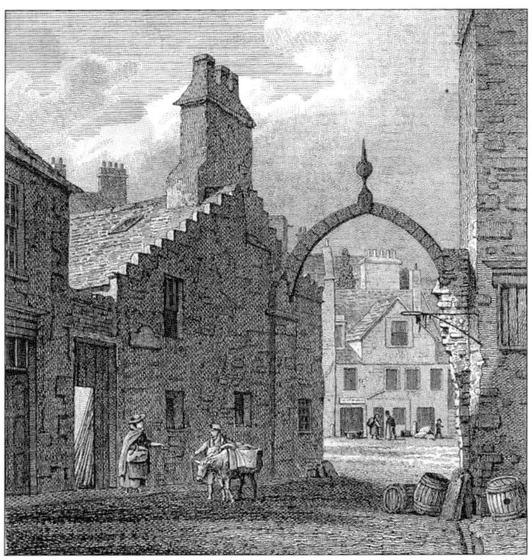

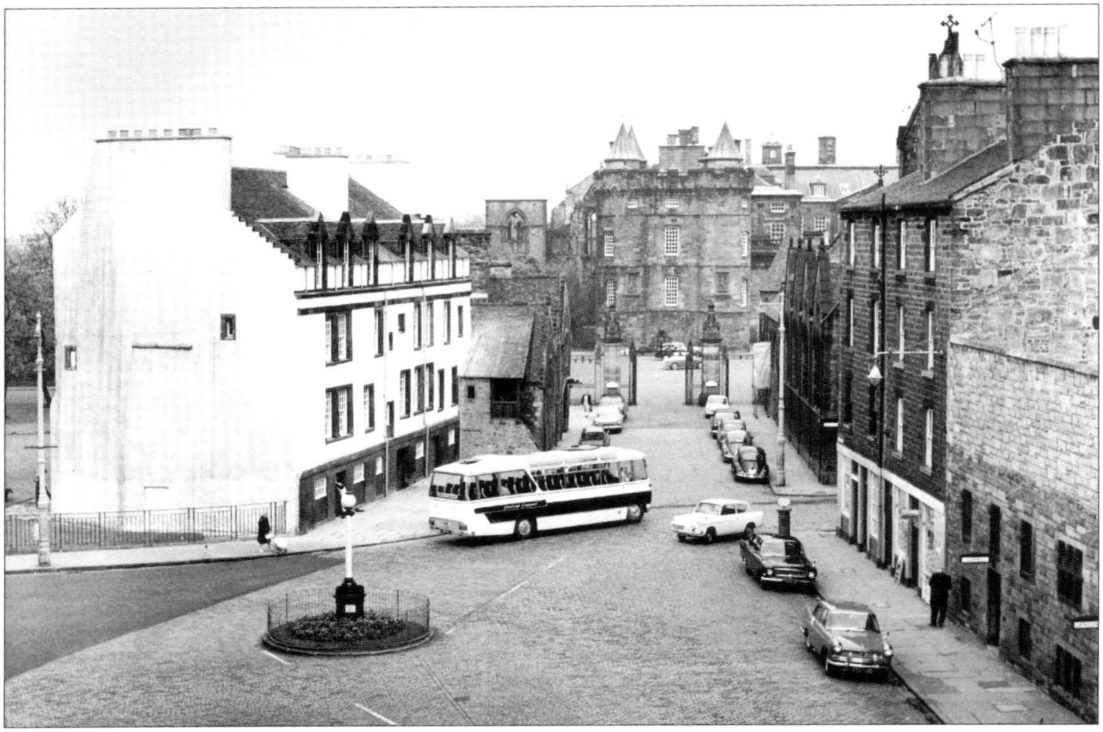

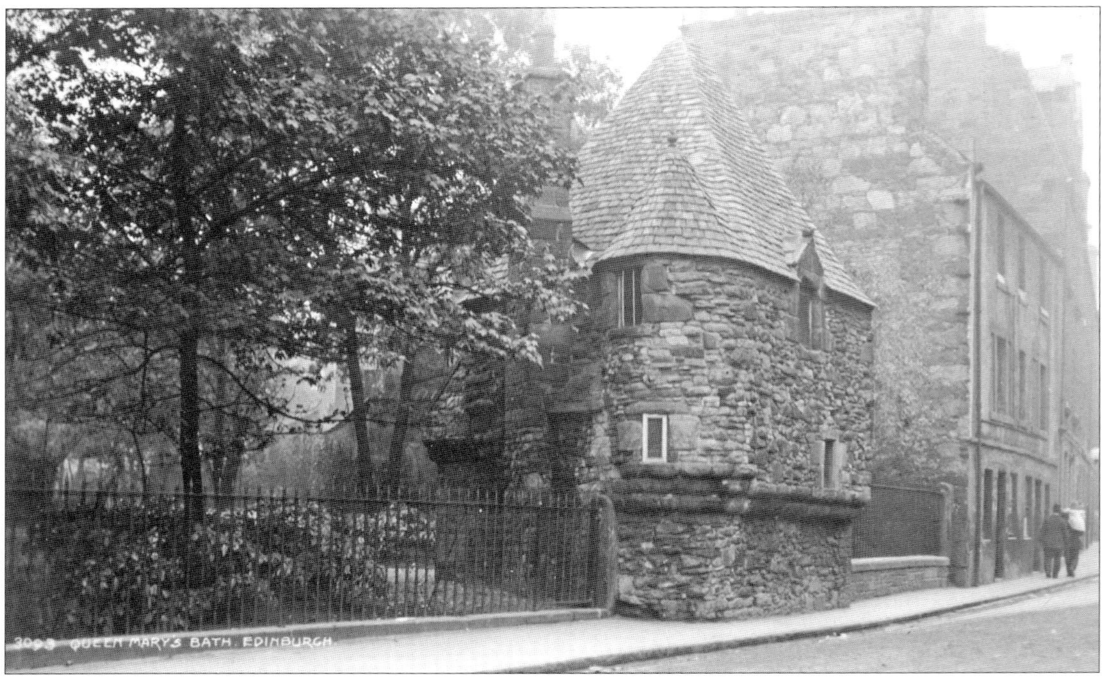

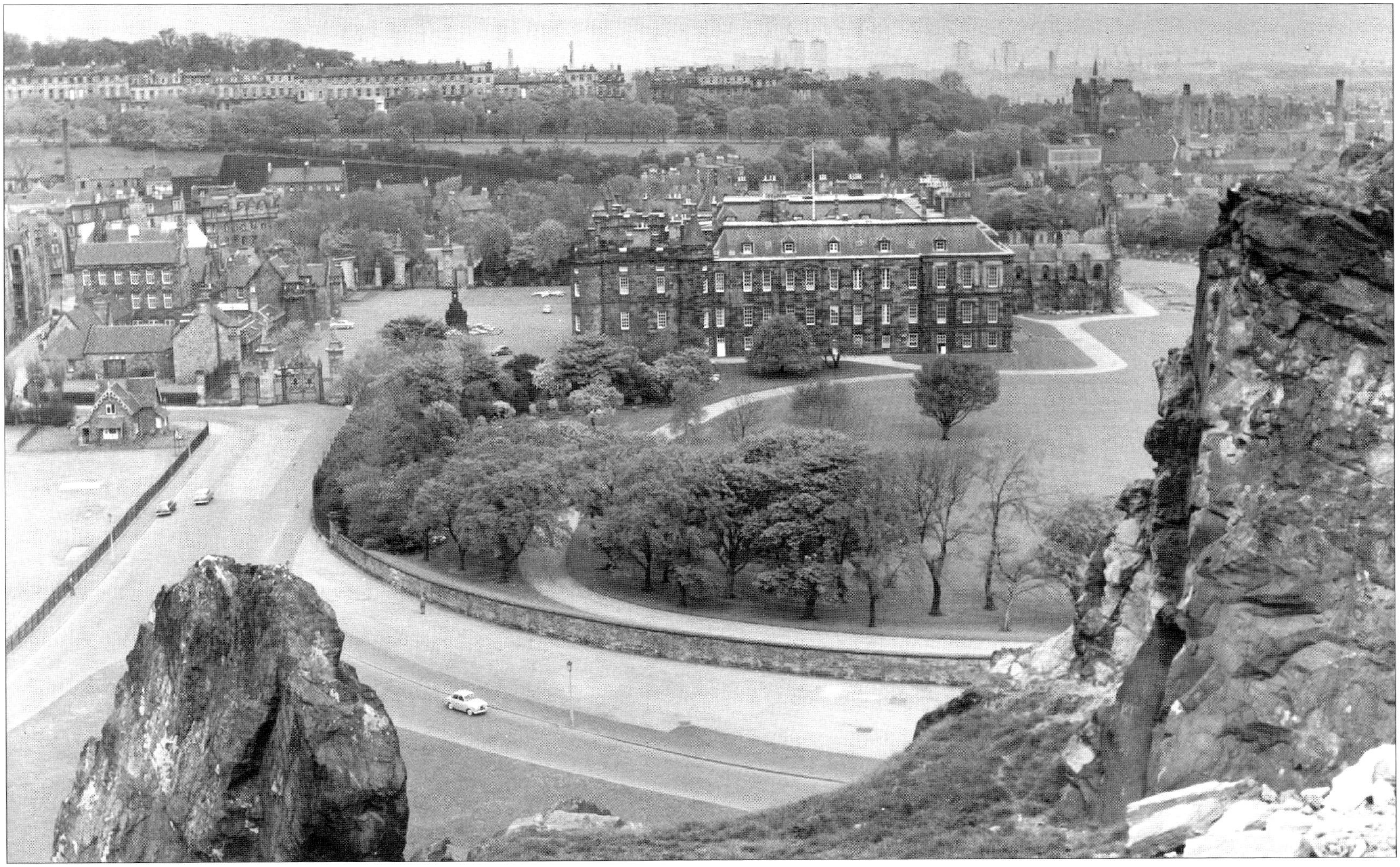

Over a period of almost 1,000 years, the Palace of Holyroodhouse has changed its use on numerous occasions to include monastery, royal residence, parliament, parish church, debtors' sanctuary and leading tourist attraction. The abbey was founded in 1128 by David I as a comparatively modest structure and rebuilt between 1195 and 1230 on a much grander scale. The new building was erected around the old abbey, allowing it to continue in use until the new abbey was completed, after which the old building was demolished. It was extensively damaged during the Hertford invasion of 1544. After a serious roof fall in 1768, the abbey entered a long period of neglect, resulting in its present-day appearance as a romantic ruin. Restoration schemes proposed in 1906 and again in 1945 came to nothing. Holyrood was probably a royal residence from the start: James II was born there in 1430. Between 1501 and 1505 James IV built a new palace (probably incorporating some of the monastic buildings) and the work was continued by his son, James V, between 1528 and 1532. The oldest surviving part of the palace is James V's great north-west tower, dating from *c.* 1530. The remainder of the building that we see today is largely the work of Charles II's architect, Sir William Bruce, and master mason, Robert Mylne, who began reconstruction in 1672. Holyrood was greatly reinforced as a royal residence in 1822 during George IV's visit to Scotland, even though he opted for the overnight comforts of Dalkeith Palace. Queen Victoria began the process of restoring the palace to its former glory. At the present day, the Queen and several members of the Royal Family make frequent use of the palace, particularly during the Queen's annual official visit in June or July and also for the General Assembly of the Church of Scotland, held annually in May. The photograph shows the palace in the 1950s with the nave of the abbey visible on the right. *Photograph by John K. Wilkie.*

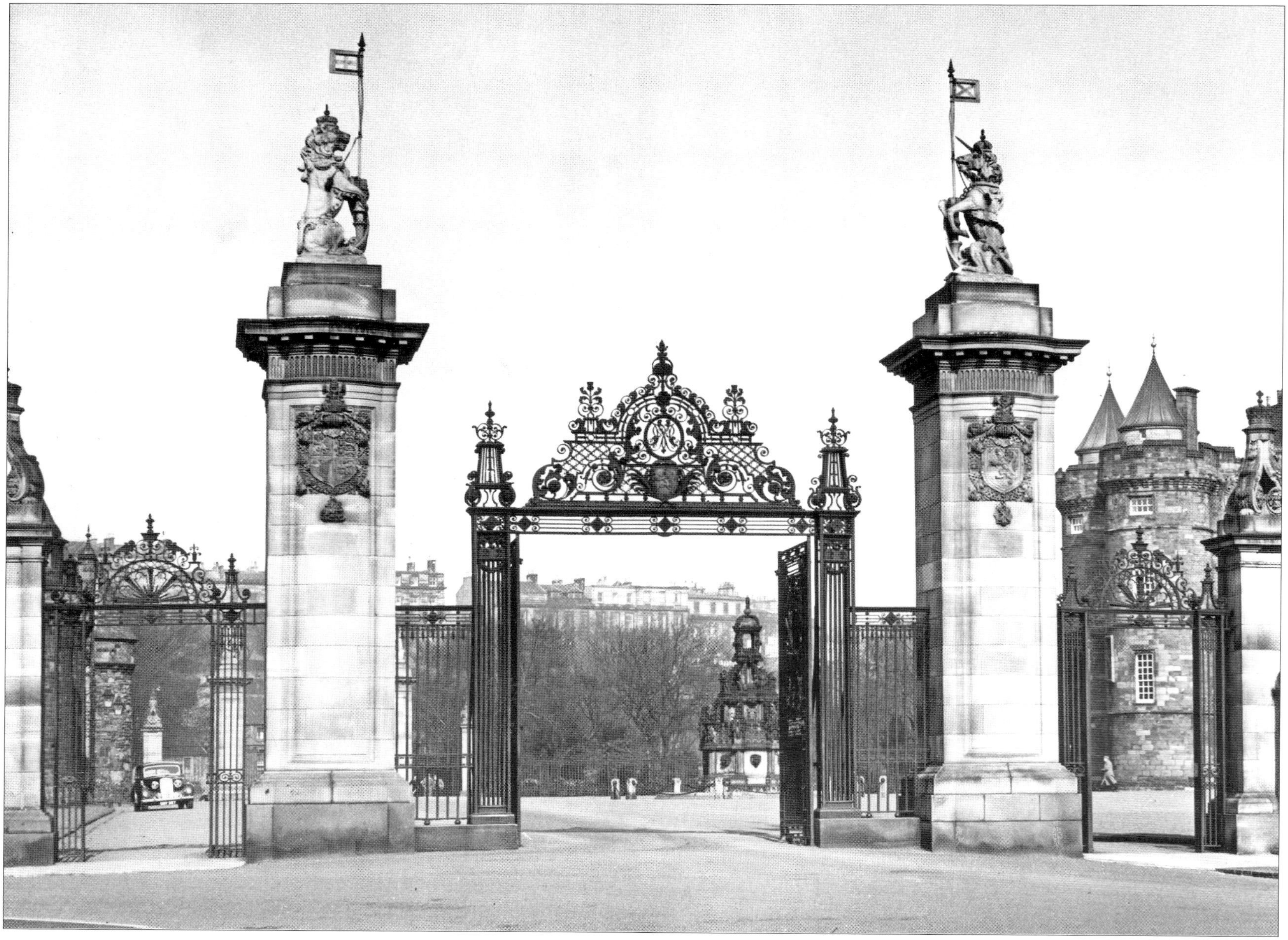

The south gate, facing Holyrood Park, is used as the principal processional route to the palace. The gates were erected between 1920 and 1922 as part of the Scottish National Memorial to Edward VII. The architect was George Washington Browne and the ironwork was by J. Starkie Gardner. The pillars carry the lion, on the left, and the unicorn, on the right, along with the respective national and royal emblems.

An octagonal fountain can be seen beyond the main gate. It was erected in 1859 at the same time as the new garden and carriage approach was built from Abbeyhill. The design, by Robert Matheson, principal architect of the Office of Works in Scotland, was modelled on the 1628 Cross Well at Linlithgow. The crown spire and historical figures were designed by Charles Doyle and carved by John Thomas. The great tower of James V, built *c.* 1530, can be seen beyond the right-hand gate.

Photograph by Norward Inglis.

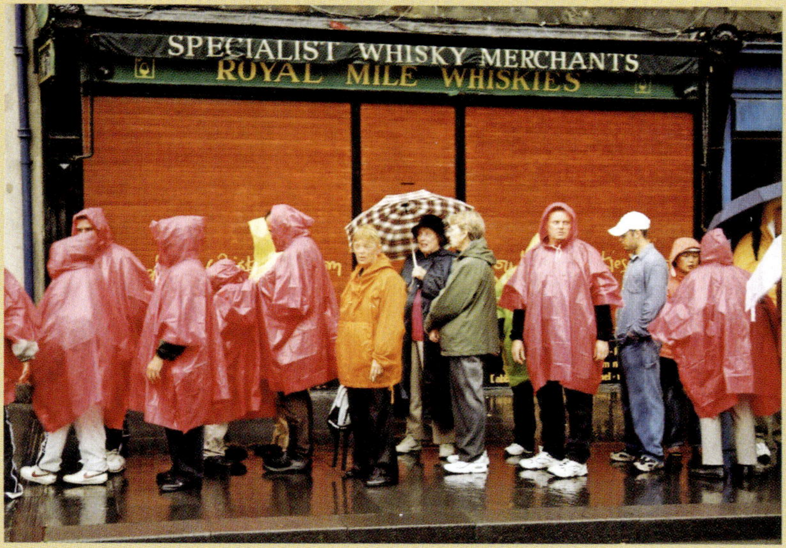

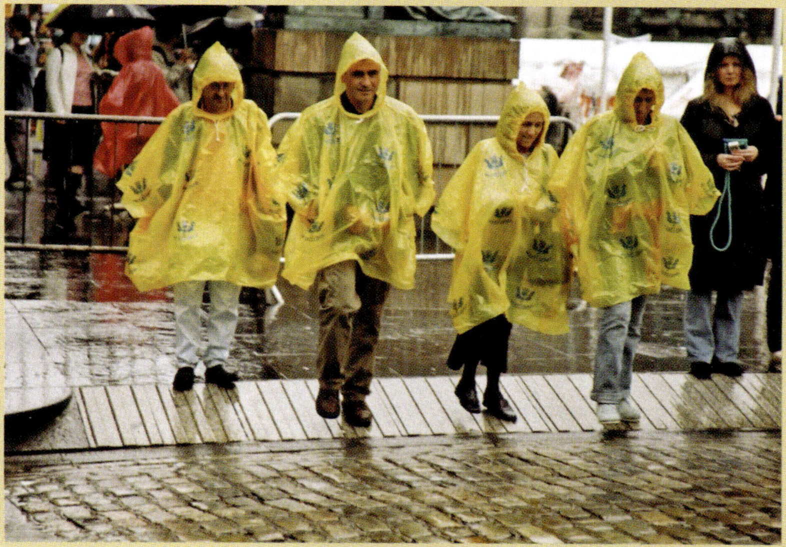

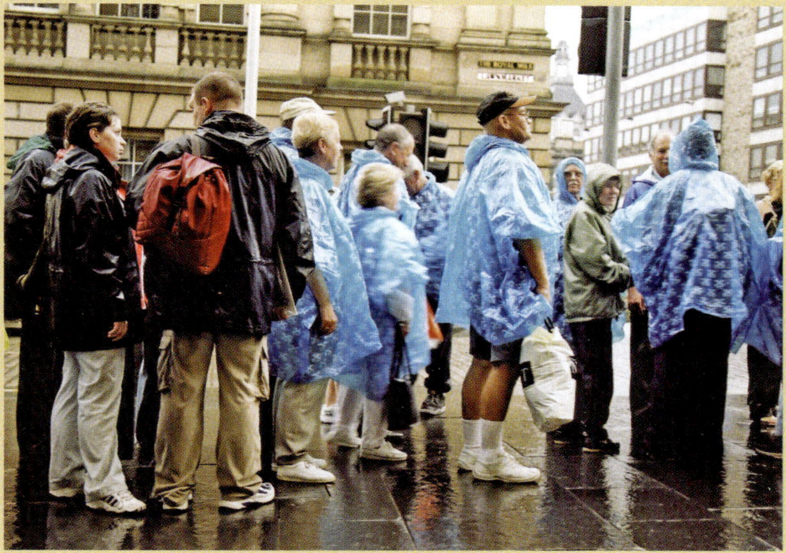

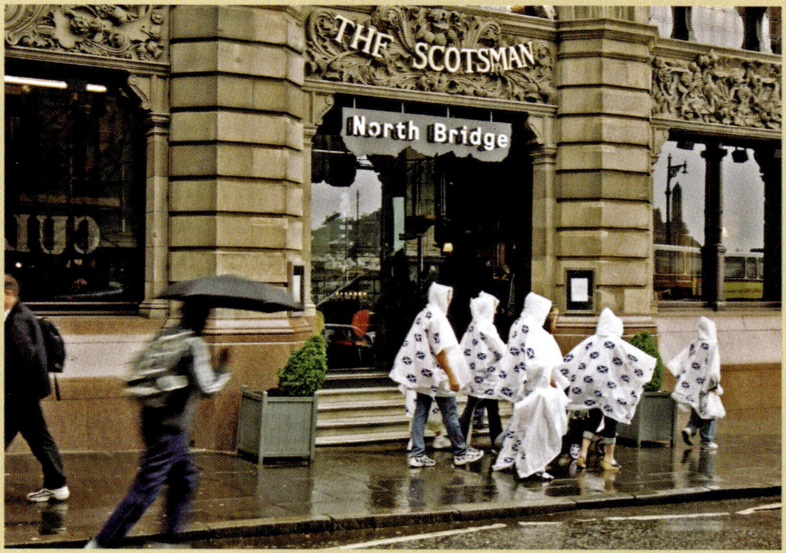

Edinburgh's annual rainfall is actually lower than the average for Scotland but in 2002 it all seemed to fall during the International Festival in August. Visitors retain their group identity with their colour-coded capes at various locations: the High Street; the top of Bank Street; the Lawnmarket; and outside the Scotsman Hotel on North Bridge.
Photographs by Peter Stubbs.

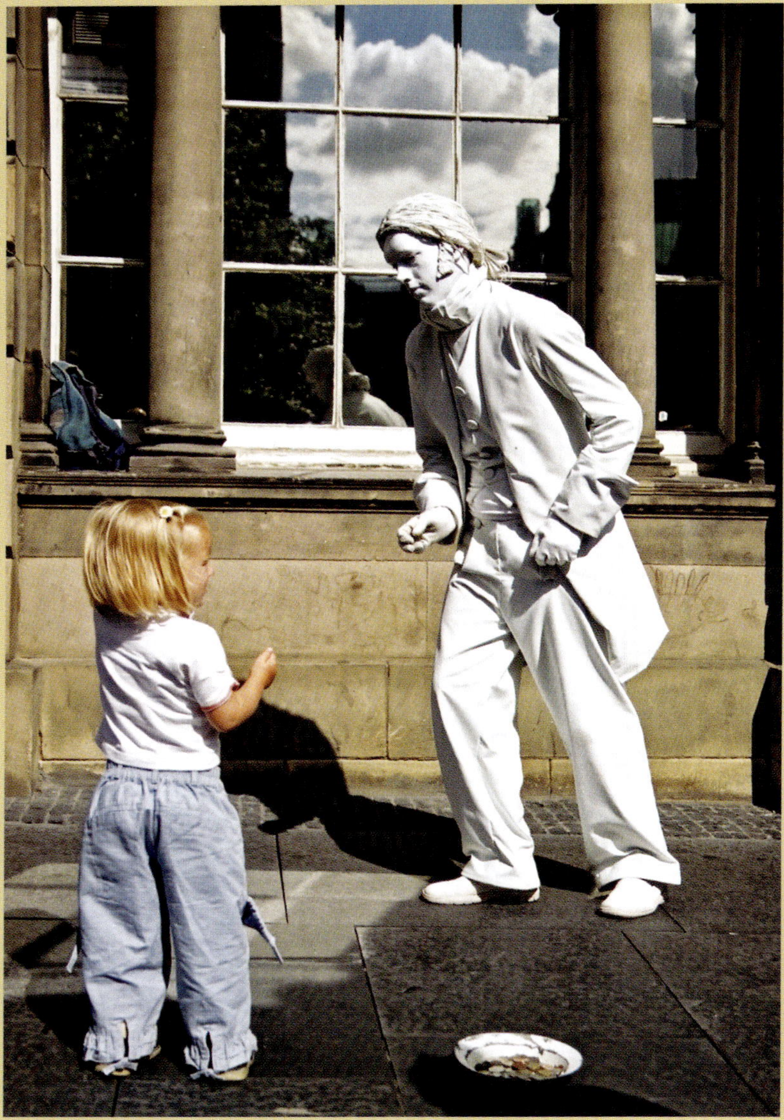

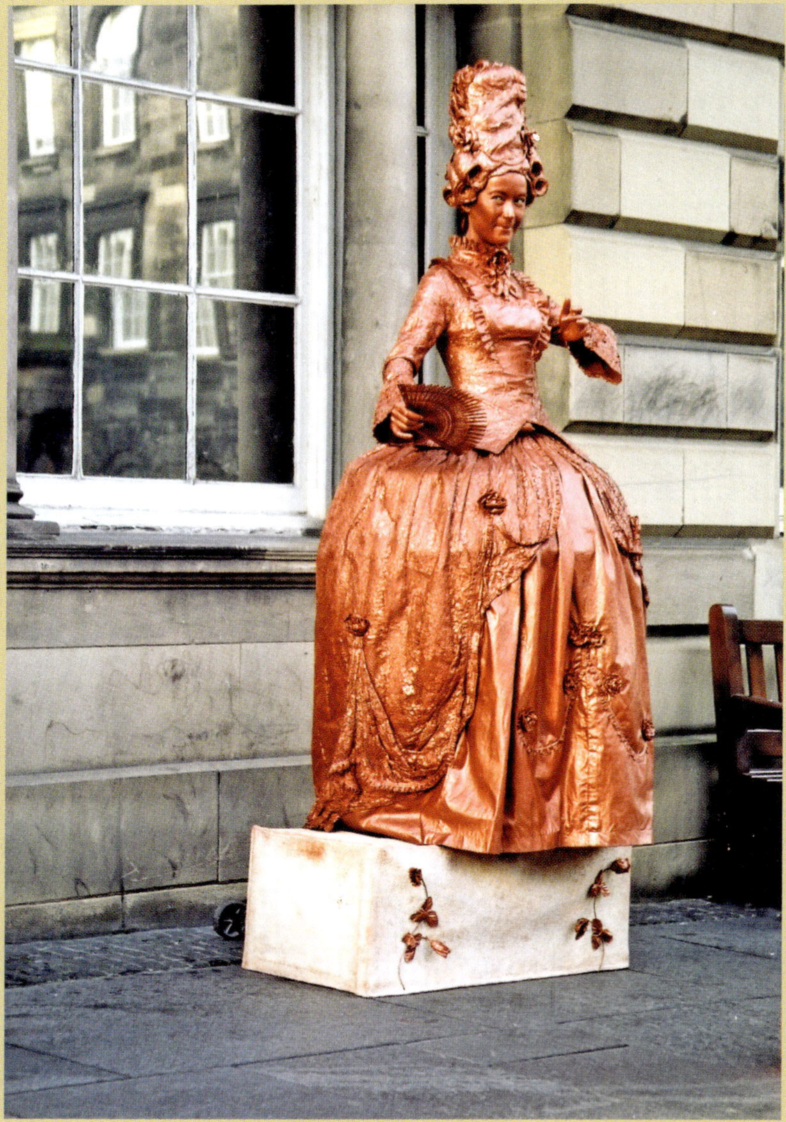

The young girl cannot quite make up her mind if what she is seeing is a real man or a statue. The same child might have had a similar problem watching the crinoline lady outside the City Chambers. *Photographs by Peter Stubbs.*

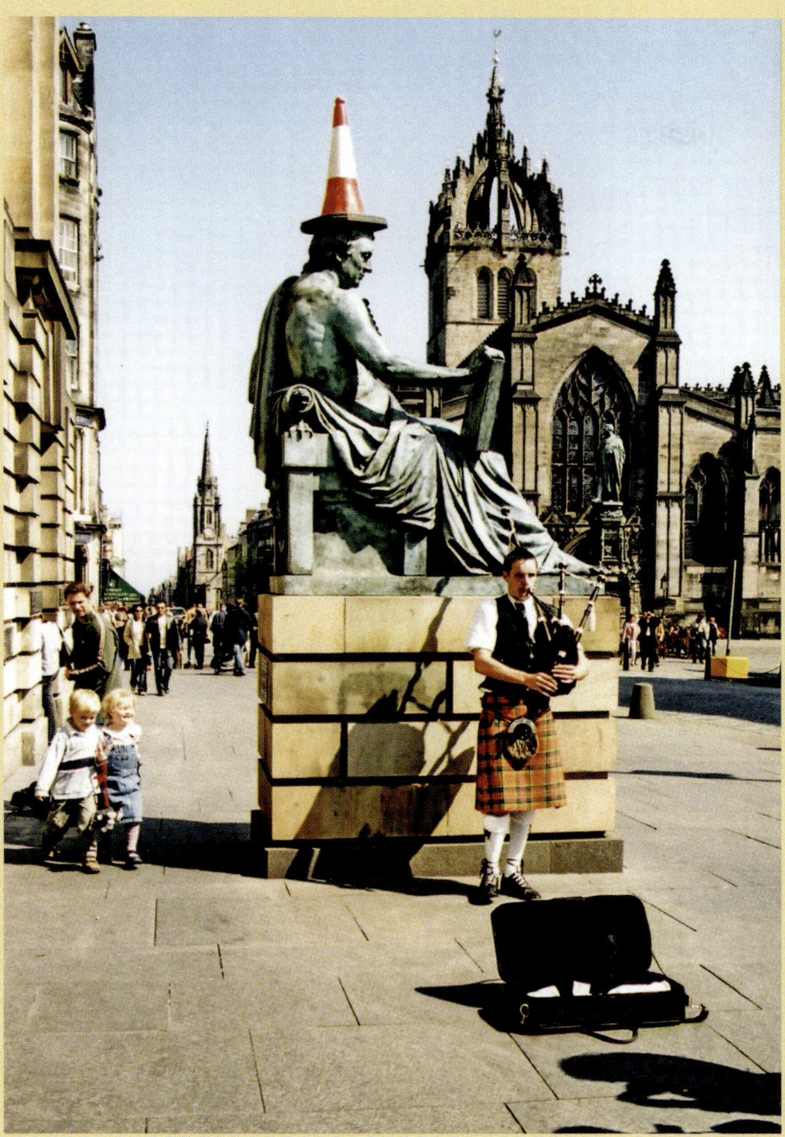

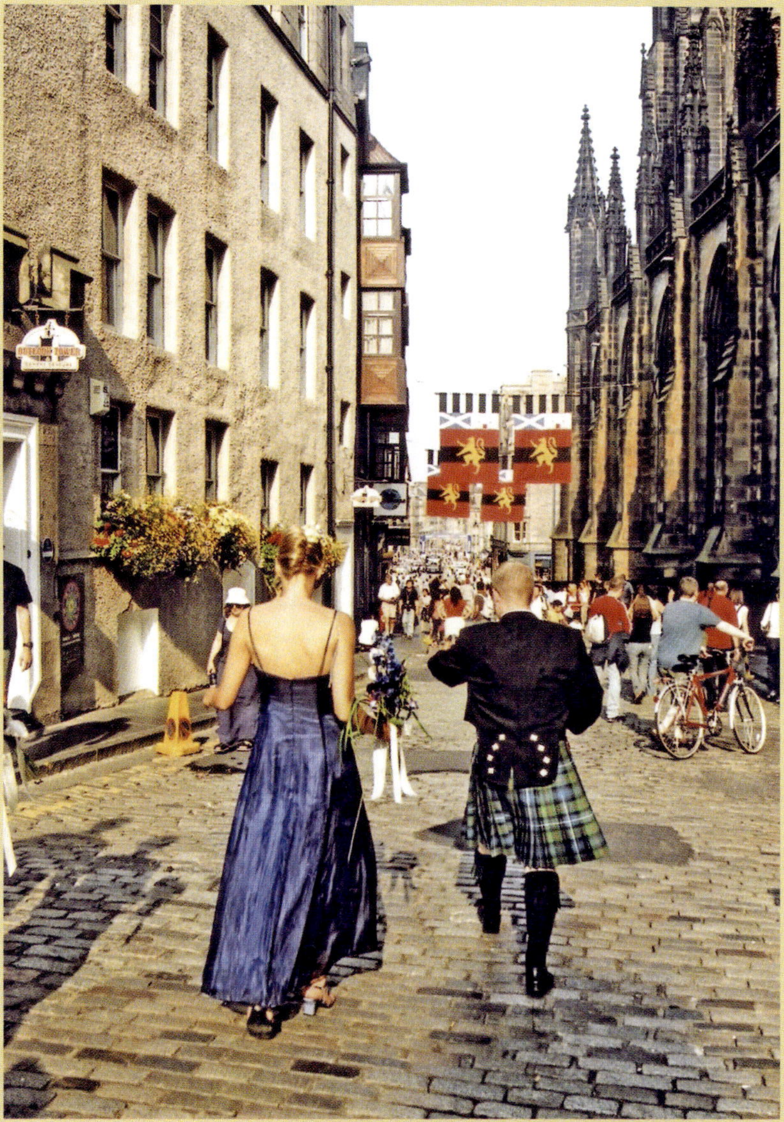

Two young children are attracted to the skirl of the pipes beside the statue of David Hume, who is still wearing his customary 'Friday night' headgear.

A young couple, dressed for a wedding reception or other formal function, make their way down Castlehill past the Outlook Tower. *Photographs by Peter Stubbs.*

Below. A single musician provides additional entertainment as people visit the Mercat Cross during Doors Open day.

Right. The 'rubbish busters', sponsored by the Royal Bank of Scotland, take a few moments' rest from their never-ending task of keeping the streets clear of litter.

Below right. The adults question the city's policy on public toilets while the children look on in amazement. *Photographs by Peter Stubbs.*

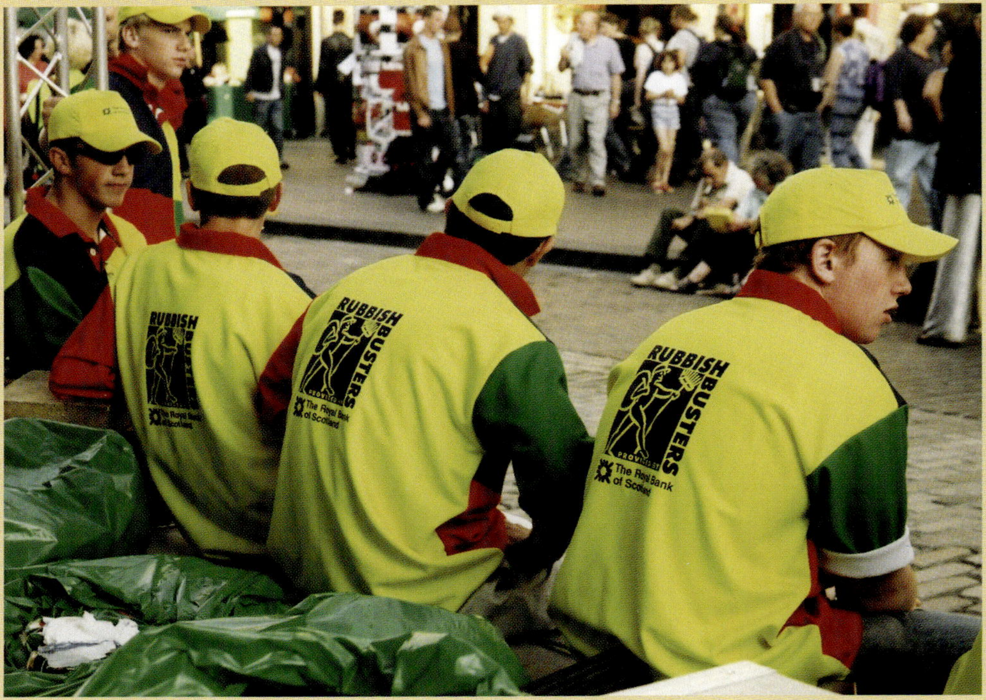

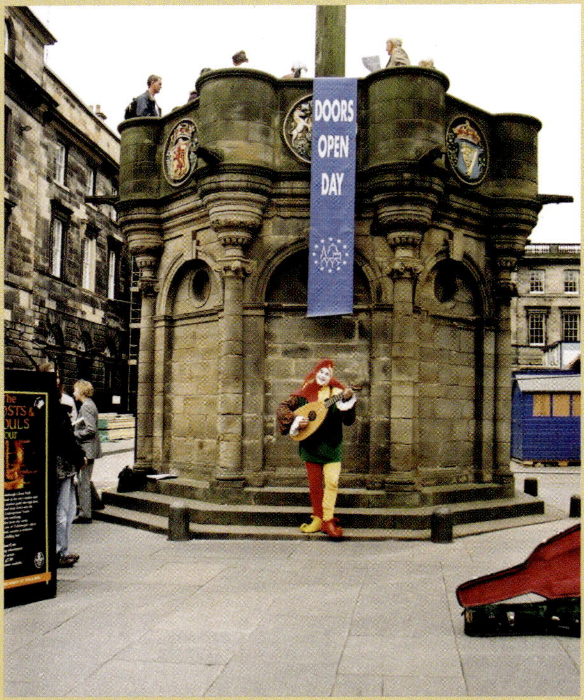

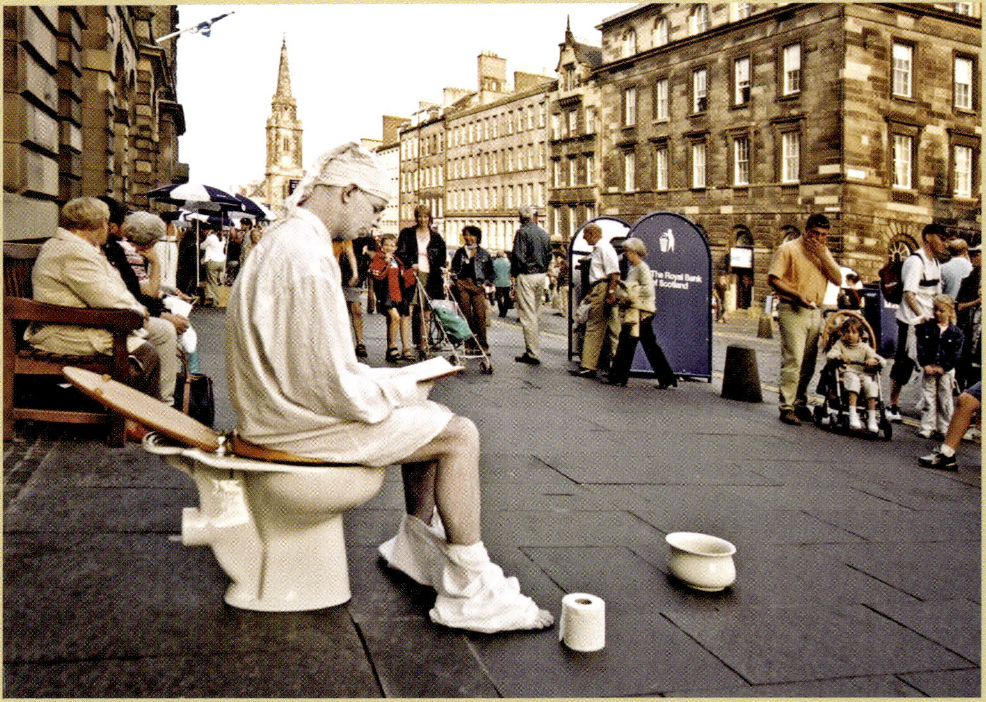

PART 3

SCOTTISH PARLIAMENT

HOLYROOD ROAD

COWGATE

GRASSMARKET

WEST PORT

VICTORIA STREET

GEORGE IV BRIDGE

NORTH BRIDGE

SOUTH BRIDGE

Part 3 deals with a slightly wider geographical area to that covered by Parts 1 and 2 of the book. There are 55 images, covering Holyrood Road, Cowgate, Grassmarket, West Port, West Bow, George IV Bridge, North Bridge and South Bridge. It is an area of many contrasts as is evident from the illustrations in this Introduction. The slum dwellings of Guthrie Street are woefully inadequate when compared to the grandeur of the public buildings in Chambers Street.

The journey begins at the foot of Holyrood Road where the headquarters of Scottish & Newcastle Breweries were swept away for the construction of the Scottish Parliament. In addition to the many brewers' premises in Holyrood Road, there were other associated industries, notably the Holyrood Flint Glass Company, run by several generations of the Ford family. Although the factory has long since been demolished, a curious link with the past has been preserved in the form of the sculptured panels now on the façade of the Macdonald Hotel.

There are several photographs associated with the area around what was known as Cowgate Port at the junction of what is now Cowgate and St Mary's Street. They include: the interior of hostels for homeless people; the sharp, clean lines of St Patrick's Church; and the exterior of Tailors' Hall and A. Campbell & Co., brewers. Further west there is the Grassmarket and the various roads radiating from it. The Grassmarket picture includes several hostelries, two of which, the Black Bull and the Beehive Inn, still operate from the same premises. Nearby is West Port, King's Stables Road and West Bow, all of which have preserved many, but not all, of the older buildings.

Probably the most interesting photograph in the book is of George IV Bridge, taken sometime between 1895 and 1899. Its principal interest is as a transport picture, showing two horse-drawn trams which Edinburgh purchased from the Glasgow Tramway & Omnibus Company. The picture also includes the Sheriff Court (on the site of the present National Library of Scotland) and the rear elevation of County Hall which backed onto Libberton Wynd, before George IV Bridge was even built. At the south end of George IV Bridge there are photographs at Greyfriars and Bristo Port.

The photograph shows a very dilapidated tenement on the corner of Guthrie Street and the Cowgate, probably in the early 1900s, when the corner premises were occupied by Richard Jordan who ran a woollen, rag and paper store from No. 179 Cowgate. The small print on the face of the building says: 'Highest prices given for rags, bones & tailors'clippings'. The other photograph is of an interior similar to those in the Guthrie Street building. *Courtesy of Robert Murray Stamp Shop.*

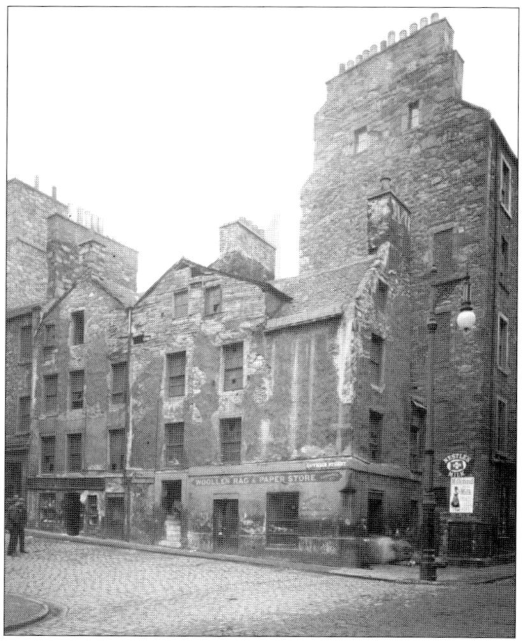

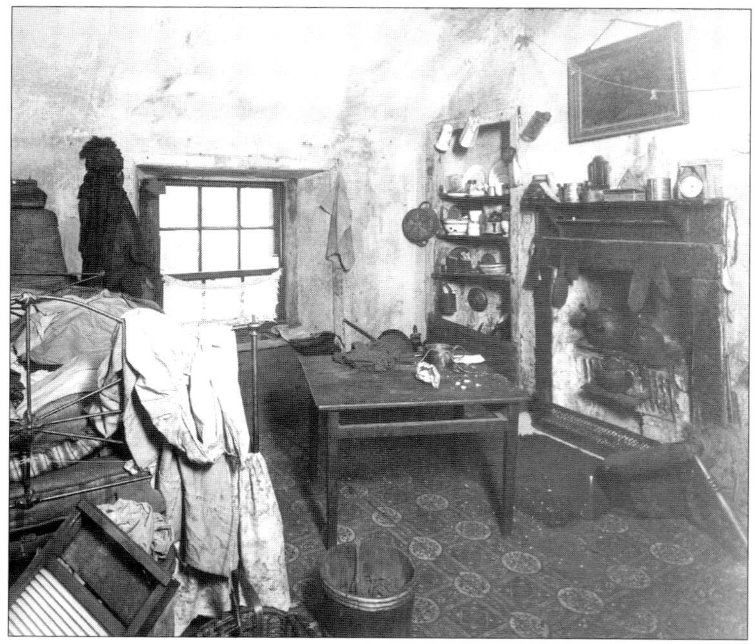

In the middle of the eighteenth century, Edinburgh was still largely confined to the area of the Old Town but there were proposals to extend both to the north and the south. The foundation stone for the first North Bridge was laid on 21 October 1763 which gave access to the feued ground that was laid out as the New Town. A photograph of the first North Bridge is included which was later replaced by the second North Bridge, begun in 1896. South Bridge, with 19 arches, all of which are closed except the one which crosses the Cowgate, was designed by Robert Kay and built between 1785 and 1788. Several photographs are included of general street scenes and also of two major public buildings. The first is of the Old Quad of Edinburgh University, designed by Robert Adam and William H. Playfair, and the second is the Royal College of Surgeons of Edinburgh, also by Playfair. The general street scenes of South Bridge and Nicolson Street date from the days of Edinburgh's tram systems. The first picture is of a cable car in the 1920s but most of the others are from the 1950s when Edinburgh's tramway system was being run down in favour of buses. The pictures are sufficiently detailed to see route numbers, destination boards, street furniture and a host of shop premises, which, at one time, were household names, for example, Peter Allan, the Draper, Macraes Furniture and Baird, the Bootmaker.

The last page of Part 3 is devoted to the story of the Great Lafayette who perished, with others, in the Empire Theatre on 9 May 1911 when an act by the great illusionist went wrong and set fire to the stage. Apparently, a stage lamp fell and ignited drapes which had been arranged for the grand finale, 'The Lion's Bride'. The story was greatly dramatised by the cruel irony of two incidents. Lafayette's pet dog, Beauty, had died of natural causes a few days earlier and had been buried in Piershill Cemetery on the strict understanding that Lafayette would be buried in the same lair when the time came. That time came much sooner than Lafayette had expected – with complications that had not been anticipated. Apparently, his body was found in the debris of the Empire and was moved to Glasgow for cremation before being returned to Edinburgh for the ashes to be buried at Piershill. Shortly before the interment, when the real body of Lafayette was discovered under the stage at the Empire, it was realised that the first body was that of Charles Richards, Lafayette's stage double, who assisted with the illusions.

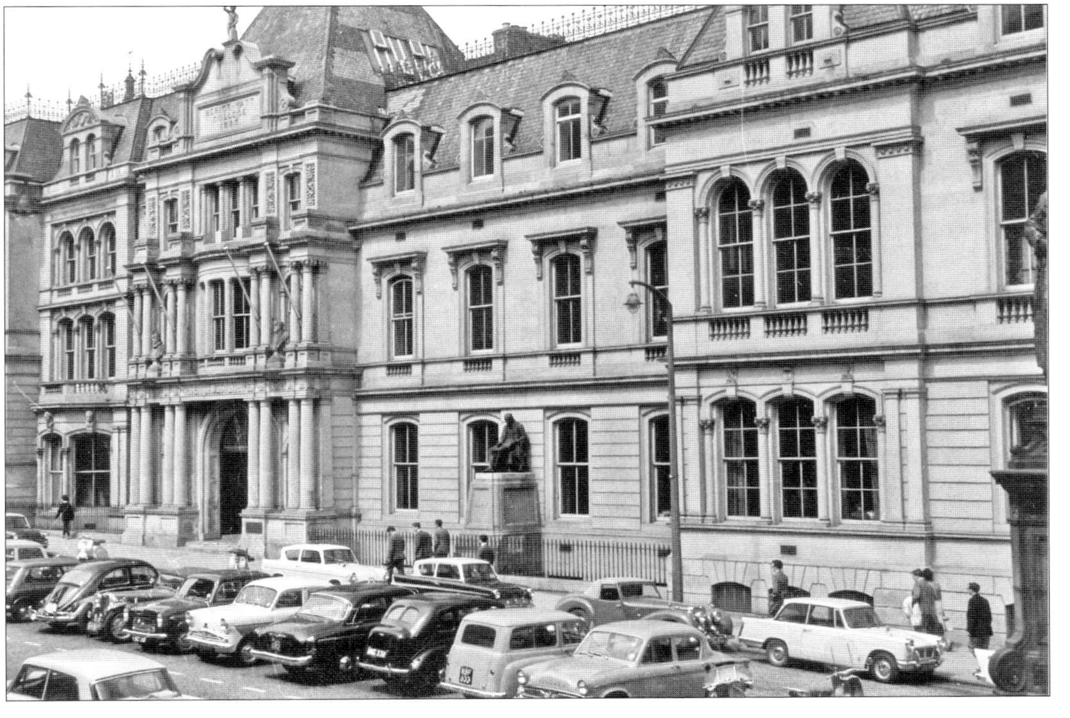

In 1962, when this photograph was taken, the north side of Chambers Street was dominated by the imposing façade of Heriot-Watt College (now University). The date, 1887, on the front of the building, refers to the alterations done between 1886 and 1888 by the architect, John Chesser. The statue of James Watt, to the right of the entrance, now stands at the university's campus at Riccarton. The Chambers Street building has been occupied by the Crown Office since 1996. *Courtesy of Colin Dale.*

Right. The head office of Scottish & Newcastle Breweries was at the junction of Holyrood Road and Horse Wynd. This 1998 photograph shows, on the front of the building, the separate names of William Younger & Co. Ltd., and William McEwan & Co. Ltd. Younger's opened their first brewery in Leith in 1749 and McEwan's opened the Fountain Brewery in 1856. In 1931, Younger's and McEwan's merged to form Scottish Brewers, which became Scottish & Newcastle in 1960. The section of the building nearer to the camera dates from 1903, and the plainer section, on the corner, from 1961. *Malcolm Cant Collection.*

Below. The entrance to the headquarters of Scottish & Newcastle Breweries at No. 111 Holyrood Road was recessed between the 1903 and 1961 sections of the building. *Malcolm Cant Collection.*

Below right. The brewery buildings were demolished for the construction of the Scottish Parliament. In July 1998, the Barcelona architects, EMBT, and their partners, RMJM Scotland, won an international competition to design the new parliament building. The resultant design and cost were hugely controversial. The photograph was taken from the south and includes the renovated Queensberry House on the extreme left. *Photograph by Peter Stubbs.*

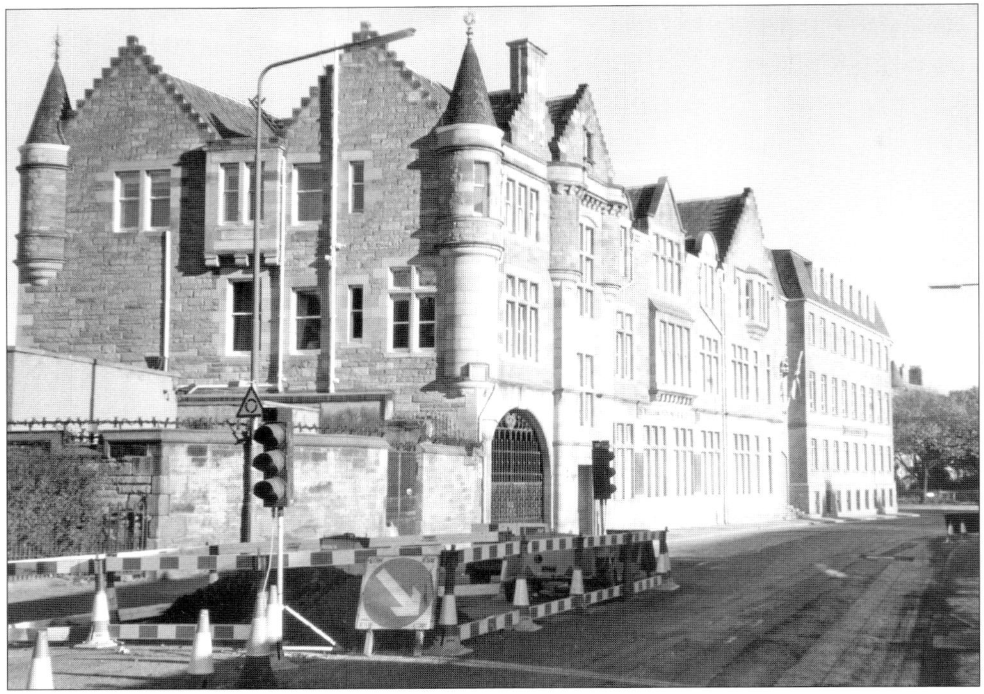

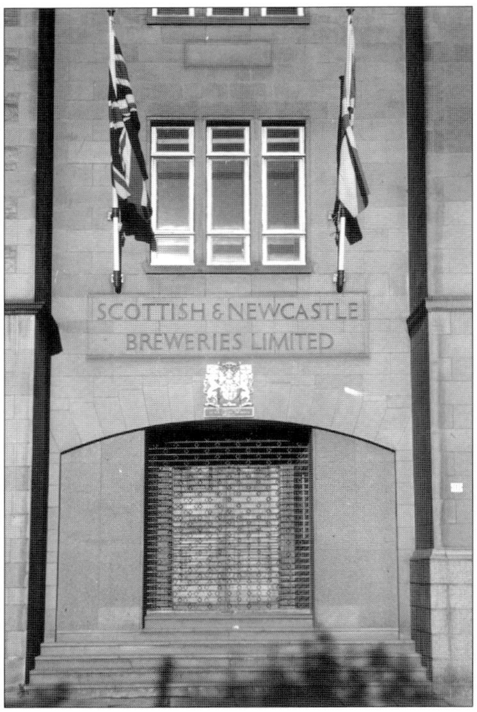

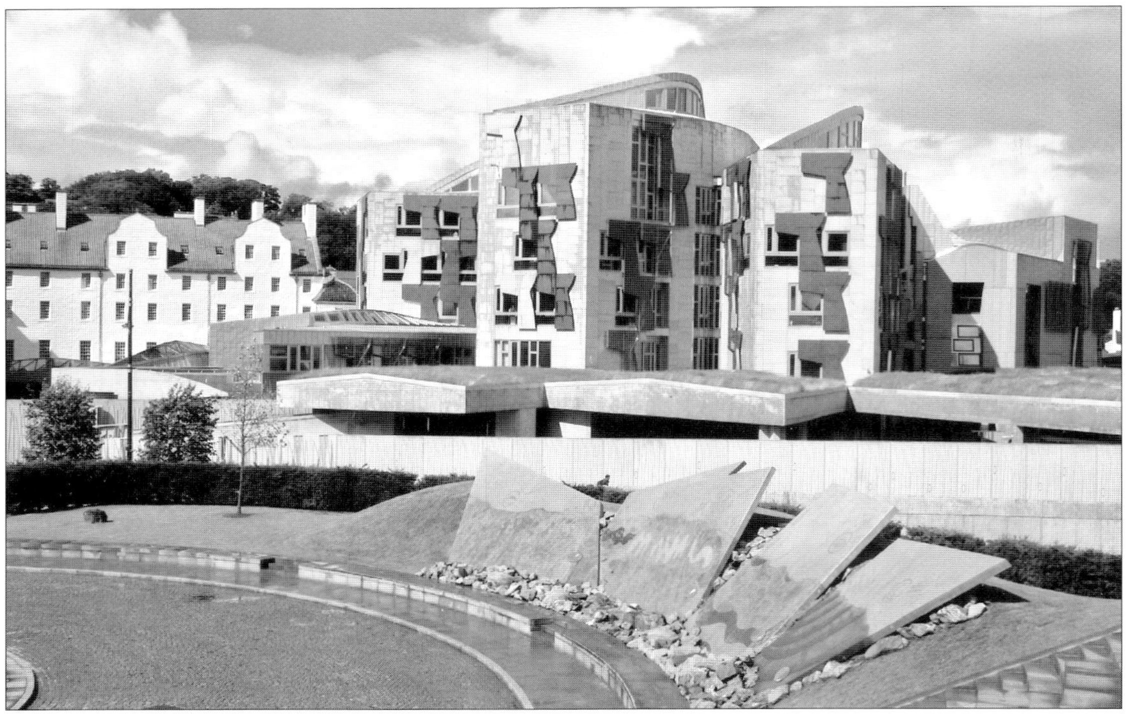

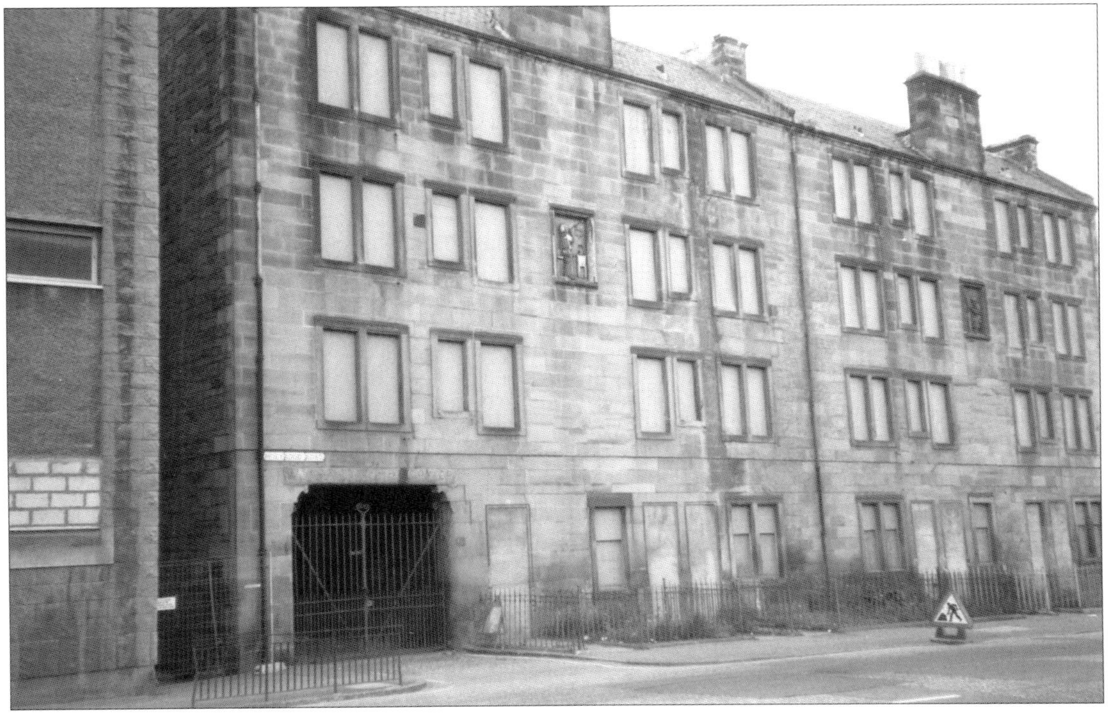

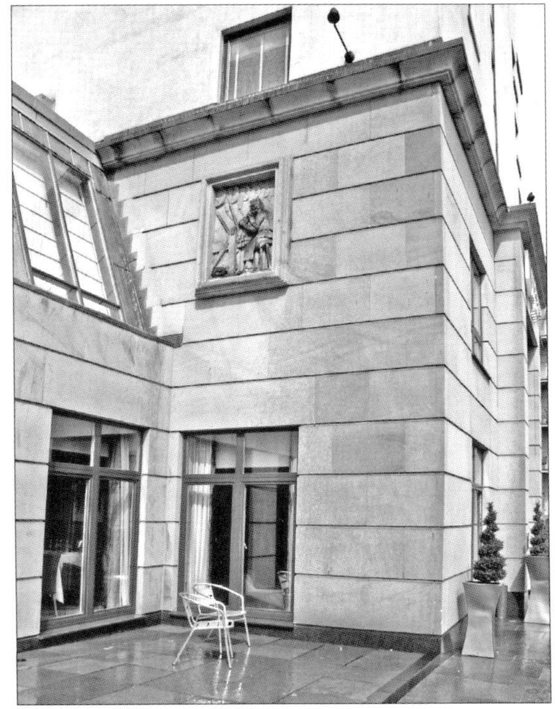

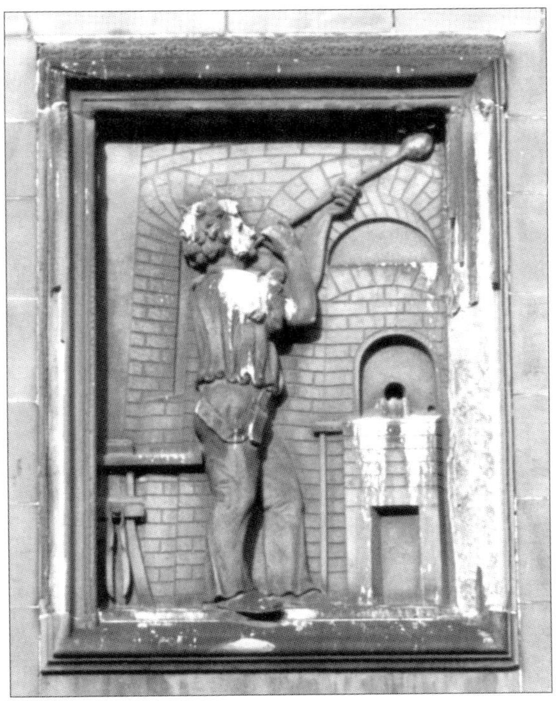

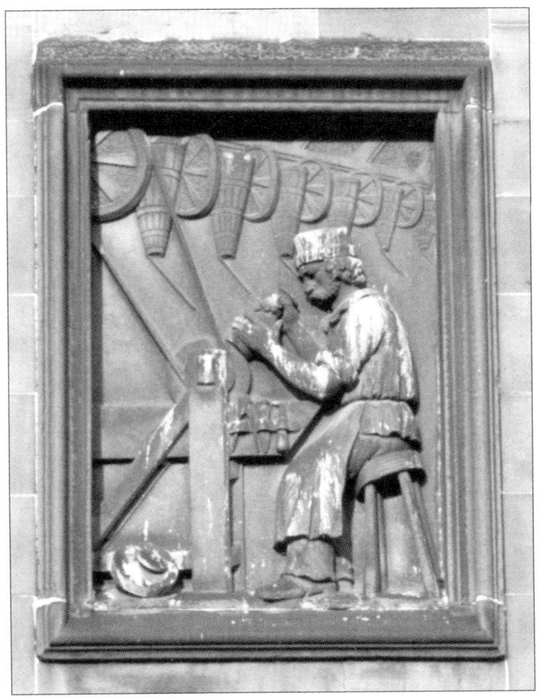

Above left. The tenement buildings on the north side of Holyrood Road, with the pend on the left giving access to industrial premises, were erected in 1907. Two sculpted stone panels can be seen on the face of the building at third-storey level. *Malcolm Cant Collection.*

Left. The stone panels have caught the imagination of architects and developers over the years, and have been photographed many times. The one on the far left is clearly a glass blower working in the traditional manner of blowing through a hollow rod to expand the molten glass. The other stone depicts a glass worker forming patterns on a goblet. *Crown Copyright: RCAHMS.*

Above. In 2000, when the Macdonald Hotel was built on the site of the old tenement, the opportunity was taken to save the stone panels and incorporate them in the new building. *Photograph by Peter Stubbs.*

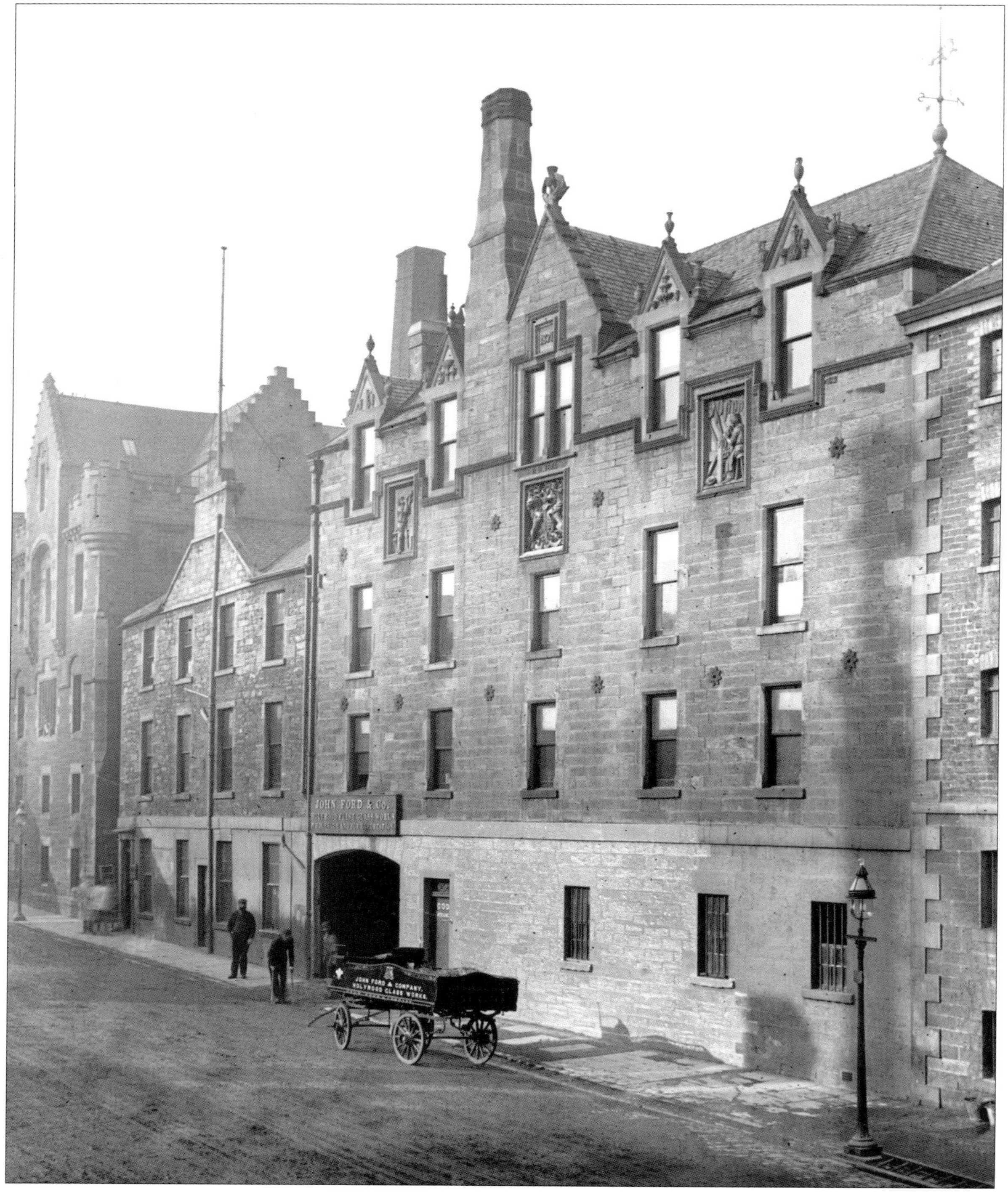

This undated photograph is of the Holyrood Flint Glass Works on the north side of Holyrood Road, founded in 1815 by William Ford. At that time, Holyrood Road was called South Back of the Canongate. Although Ford's had been in existence since the early nineteenth century, it was not until 1871 that the new headquarters were built. In *Scotland Today and Edinburgh its Capital*, published in 1890, Ford's frontage is described as 'enriched with figures and designs emblematic of the trade'. The present photograph shows several ornamentations along the roof line, and there are three stone panels on the face of the building. The centre one is the Royal Coat of Arms and the other two are clearly the stone panels referred to and illustrated on page 45. The board above the pend reads: 'JOHN FORD & CO. HOLYROOD FLINT GLASS WORKS. WHOLESALE AND FOR EXPORTATION'. The small door behind the cart is marked 'GOODS ENTRANCE'.

The four-storey building was, originally, a much older tenement of three storeys only, owned by Ford & Co., which used it to house their employees. On 14 April 1871, William Ford applied to the Dean of Guild Court to remove the roof of the old tenement and add a fourth storey, including the embellishments already referred to. Presumably the sculpted panels of the Royal Coat of Arms and the two glass workers date from that time. The architect for the new building was R. Thornton Shields at No. 62 George Street, Edinburgh, but, sadly, no record has been found to identify the sculptor. Ford & Co. remained at Holyrood Road until about 1907 by which time the buildings had been sold to John Brodie Smith who petitioned the Dean of Guild Court to demolish them and construct the two tenements shown on page 45. The architect inserted the comment, 'Old Panel Refixed' on the front elevation drawing of the new tenement.
Courtesy of the Museum of Edinburgh.

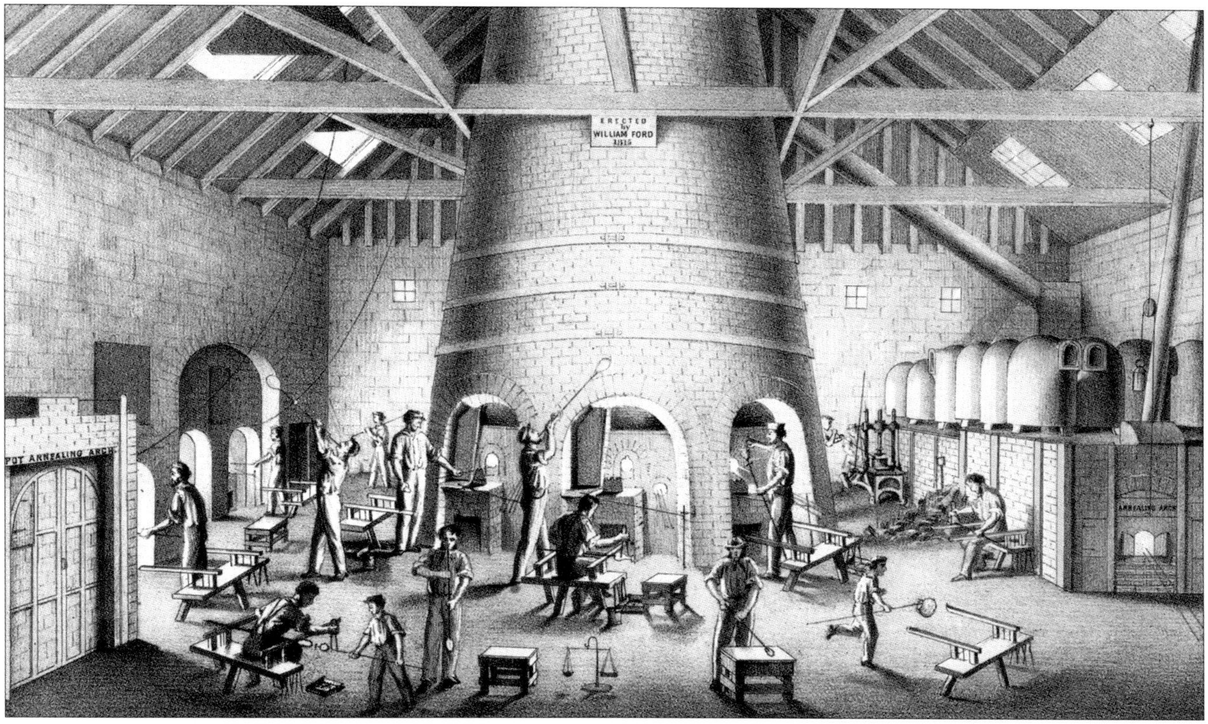

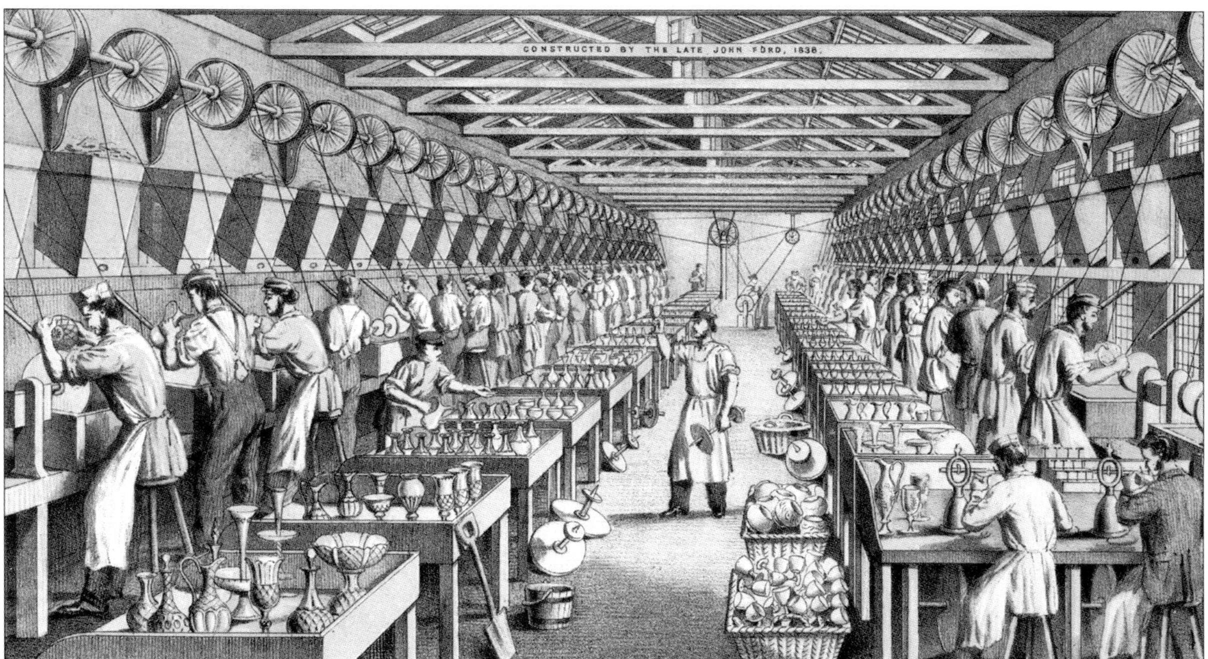

These two illustrations of the interior of the Holyrood Flint Glass Works give an excellent idea of some of the processes undertaken.

The upper picture shows the central, brick-built cone, erected by William Ford in 1875, with three chambers to the front where the glass was heated. There are several benches fitted with extended 'arms' on which the operative rolled the molten glass (on the end of a rod) into the requisite shape. On the left, the doorway leads to the 'pot-annealing arch', and, on the right, there are several large, rounded pots used in the kilns. The central cone would have extended much further up and out through the timber roof.

The lower picture shows at least twenty operatives on each side, cutting and engraving a wide variety of products which can be seen in the trays. Different wheels would be used for different tasks: the spares are lying on the floor near the trays. All the overhead revolving wheels would be powered from a system of shafts and pulleys, driven by a single static steam engine located outside the work area. At the far end a man is adjusting the tension on the belts to ensure that the system works at a uniform speed. The large square boxes above the heads of the operatives were filled with glass polishing powder which could be fed, through a tube, onto the work, as required. The process is very similar to that depicted in the stone panel, except that in the panel, the supply of powder appears to be held in a container made of near-vertical slats of wood held together with hasps. At the bottom right-hand corner of the picture, two highly skilled operatives are using copper wheel machines for more delicate patterns.

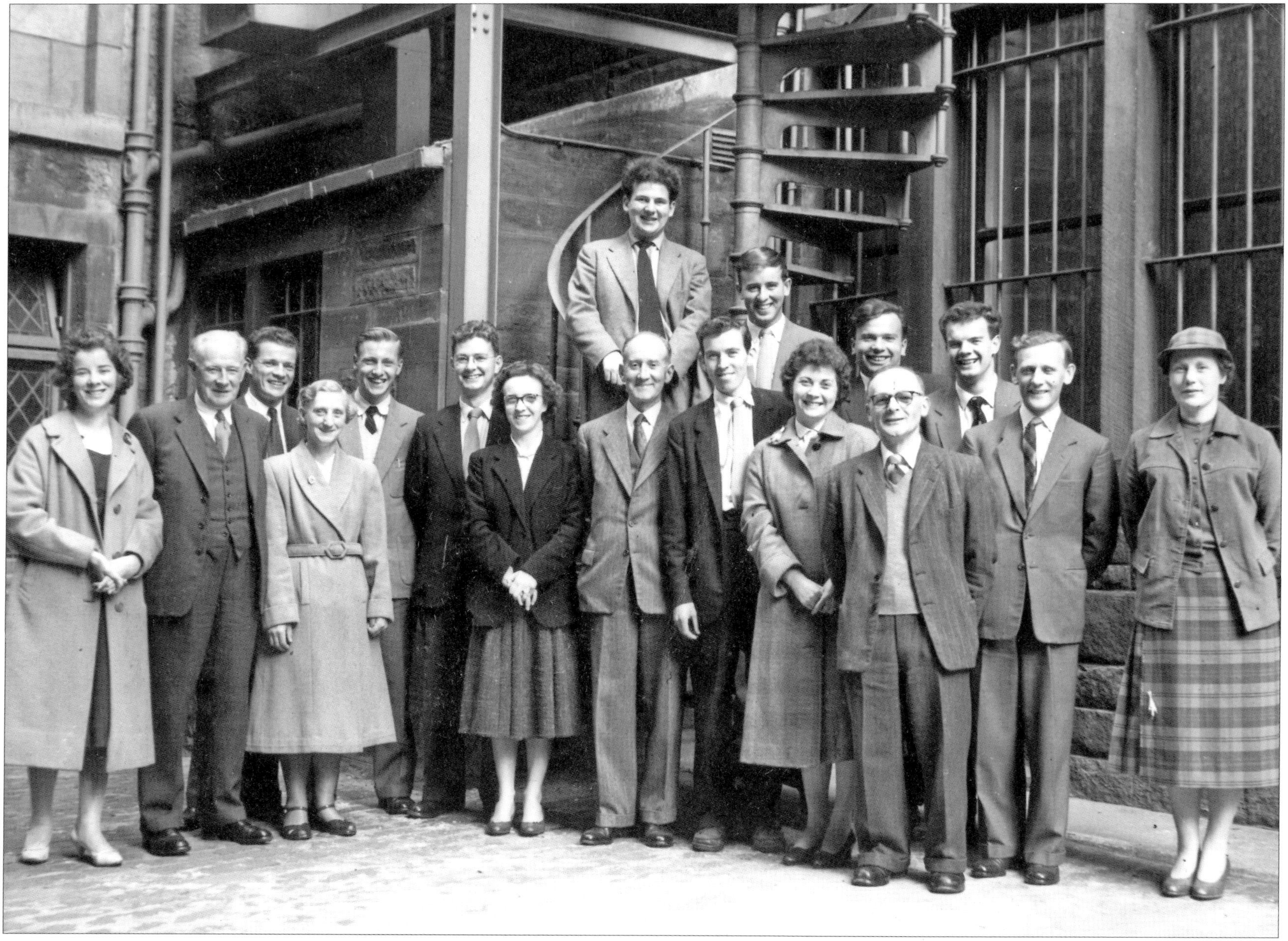

The staff of William Younger's Brewery photographed at Holyrood Brewery, *c.* 1959. From left to right: Betty Richardson, secretary; Louis Fletcher, chief chemist; Bob Denholm, chemist; Jean?, cleaner; Willie Sinclair, stores assistant; Hugh Aird, chemist; Jean Wallace, microbiologist; John Westwood, deputy chief chemist; Alastair Brown, stores assistant; Alan Arthur, senior apprentice; Edith ?, secretary; Lachlan McKenzie, microbiologist; David Kennedy, storeman; Colin Dale, apprentice; Ralph Aitken, malting chemist; lady with checked skirt, cleaner; Bill Robertson, apprentice, is standing on the stairs at the back. *Courtesy of Colin Dale.*

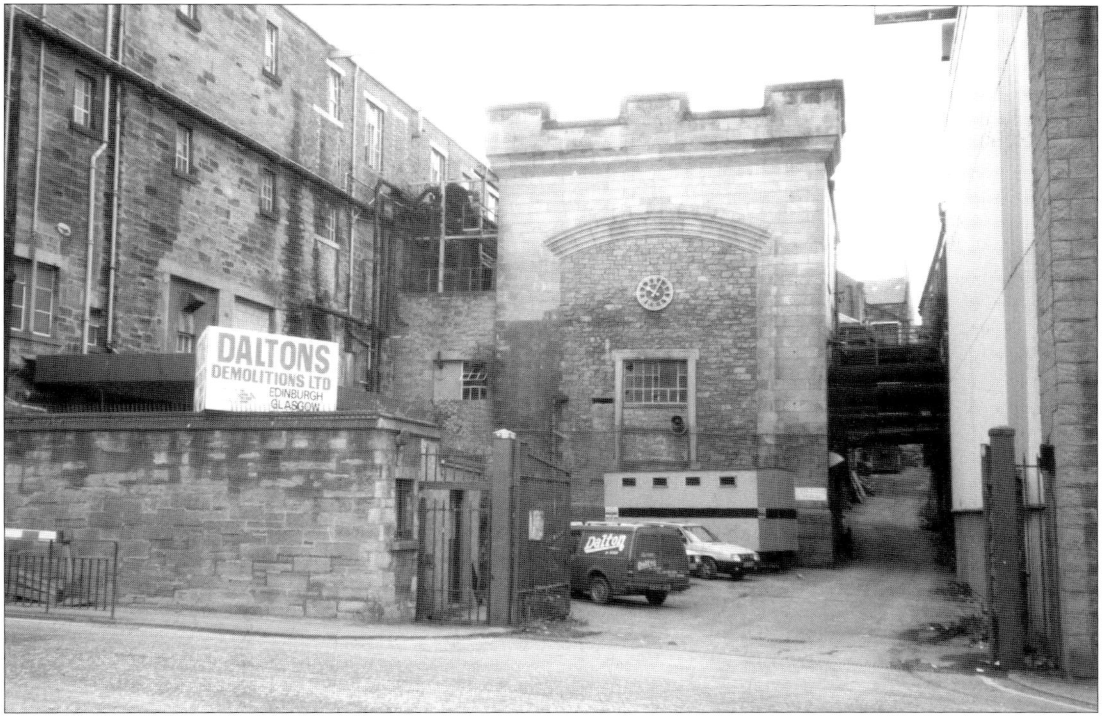

Left. In this 1995 photograph, Daltons have moved into the site but the castellated building, at one time used for yeast storage, was not demolished. Immediately behind this building was the experimental brewhouse where trials were conducted prior to main production. The malt lorries entered from the Canongate. The building on the left is the Coronation Tun Room and the one on the right is the East Tun Room. *Photograph by Phyllis Cant.*

Below left. The castellated building, still known as The Tun, was restored with indoor and outdoor accommodation as Pizza Express.
Photograph by Peter Stubbs.

Below. When this photograph was taken in 1995, Younger's Brewery, at No.71, was clearly not in use. However, the stone panel on the face of the building could still be read: 'Established 1749'. The other date, 1872, below the shield, is the year in which the building was constructed. *Photograph by Phyllis Cant.*

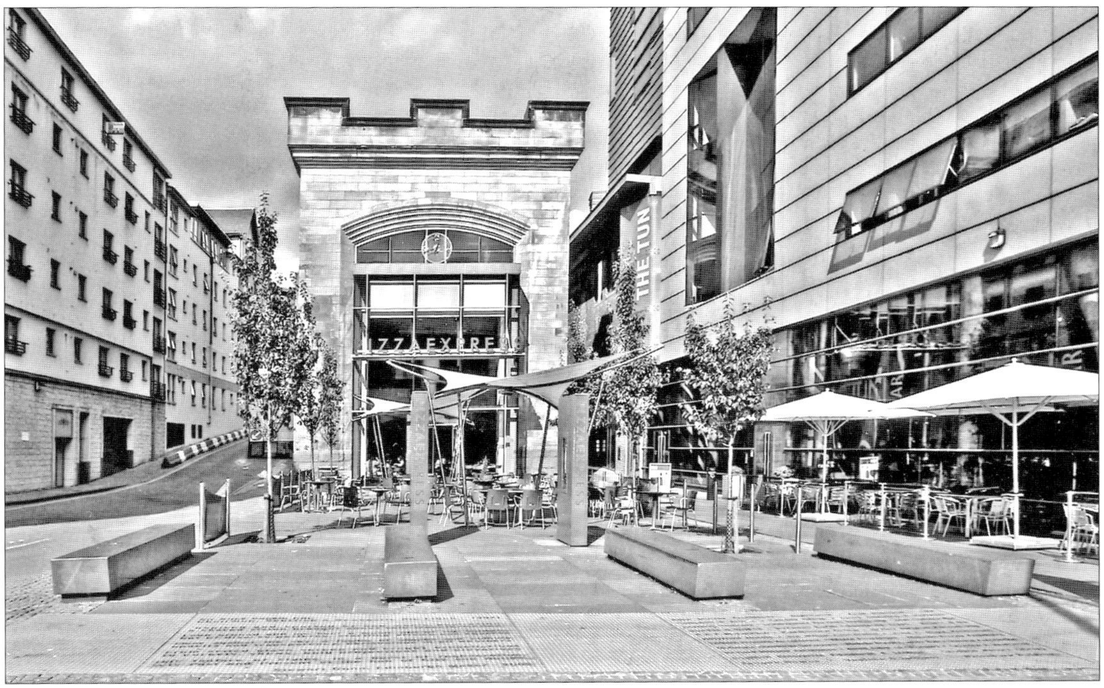

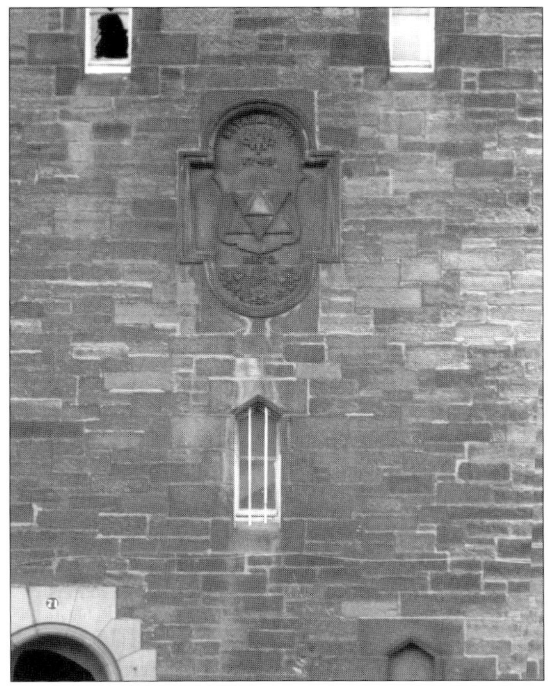

Right and below right. In the early part of the twentieth century, communal living in one of the many hostels for homeless people provided some of life's essentials, but little or no privacy. The layout was very basic, the slightly raised communal berths having no individual division. Each allotted space is marked only by the upper end of the timber supports. The communal berths on either side are separated by a narrow walkway with a very small coal-burning stove at one end. The upper picture shows the dormitory for women and children and the lower one for the men. The facilities, or lack of them, appear identical in each dormitory. *Courtesy of Robert Murray Stamp Shop.*

Below. The practical problems of communal living dictate that even in 1970 the basic layout is not dissimilar at the hostel run by the Salvation Army in the Pleasance. Although there was little or no privacy, the room was warm and dry, the beds had mattresses and the linen was clean and tidy. There was also a great deal of support given by Salvation Army staff to get inmates back into society. *Courtesy of the Salvation Army. Photograph by Murdo Macleod.*

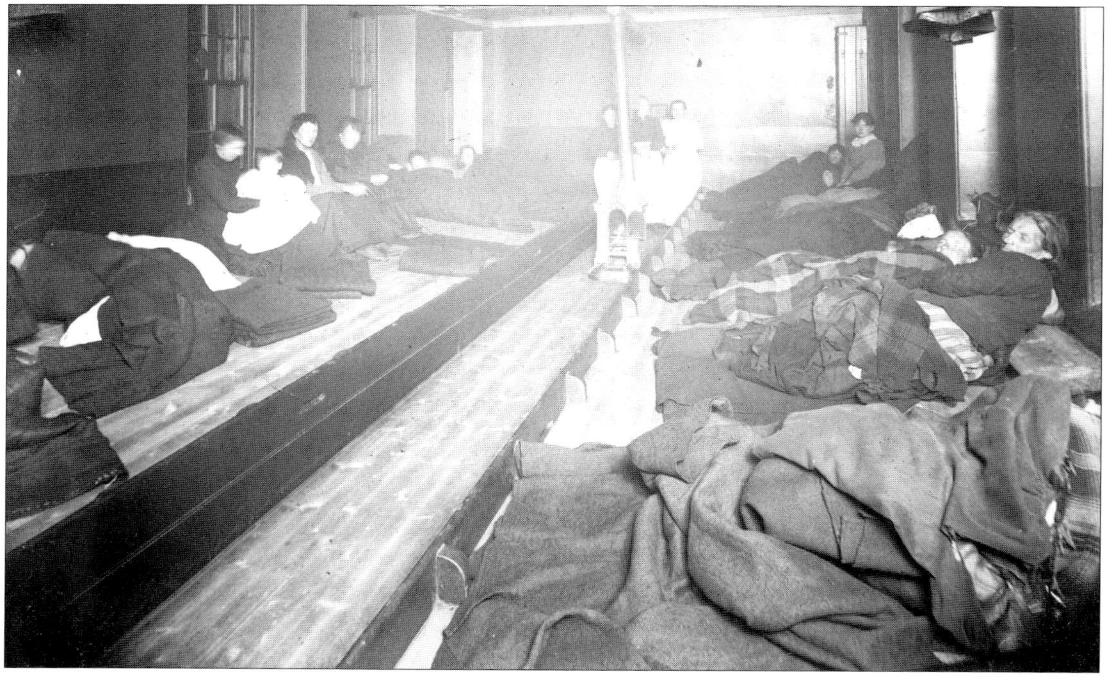

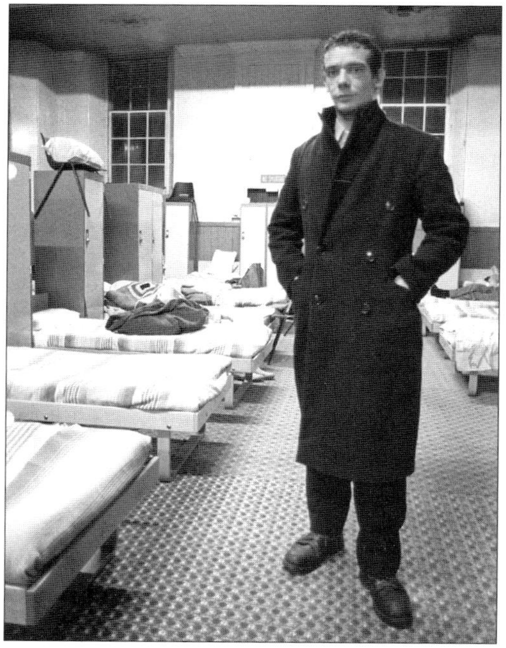

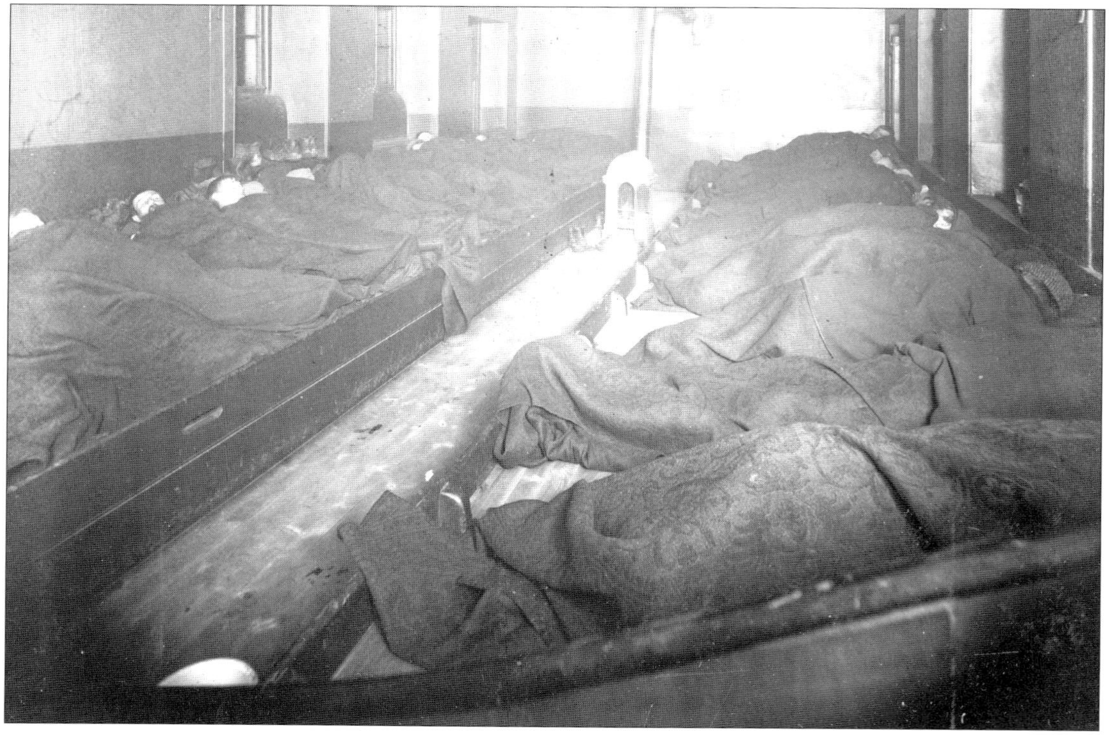

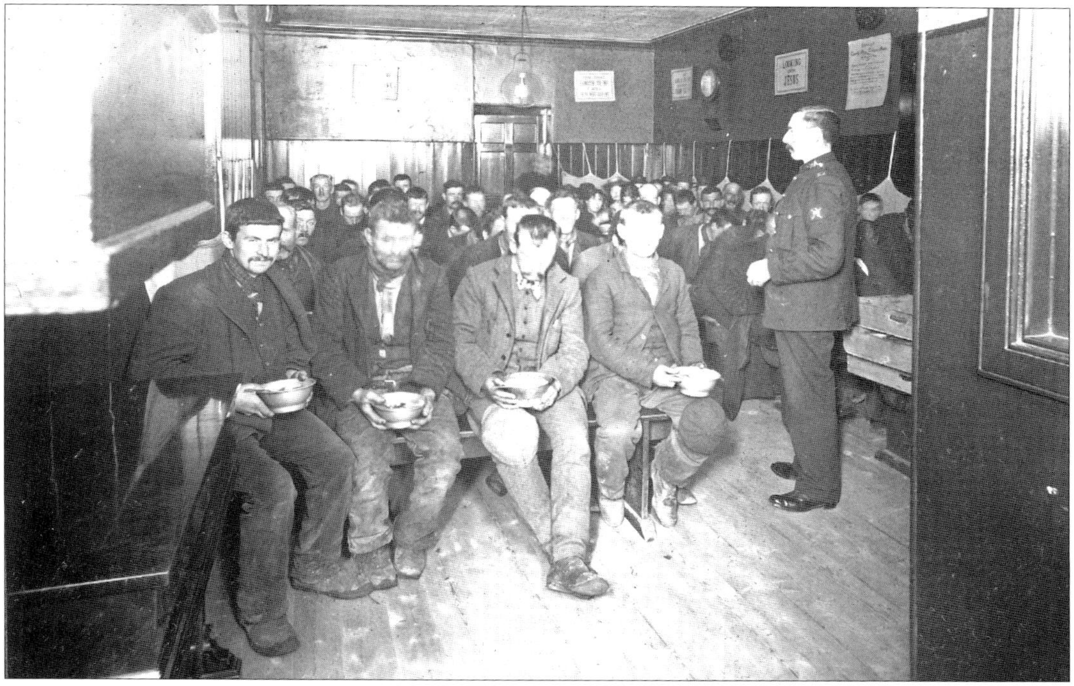

Left. In addition to the many hostels for homeless people, there were several soup kitchens, usually run in conjunction with the hostels. This one obviously catered for quite a large group of men. The notices on the upper part of the walls carry various exhortations based on the scriptures: 'Him that cometh to me I will in no way cast out'; 'Looking unto Jesus'; and, on the extreme right, 'Edinburgh Church Army Labour House'.

Below left. The neat and tidy dormitory, with individual beds, was probably part of the same organisation. *Both photographs courtesy of Robert Murray Stamp Shop.*

Below. This ancient pend gave access 'To Counting Room by East Gate', part of the brewing premises of A. Campbell & Co., which later became Campbell, Hope & King. The pedimented panel above, with the open scissors, marks the location of the original Tailors' Hall founded in 1621. *Courtesy of Pat Scoular.*

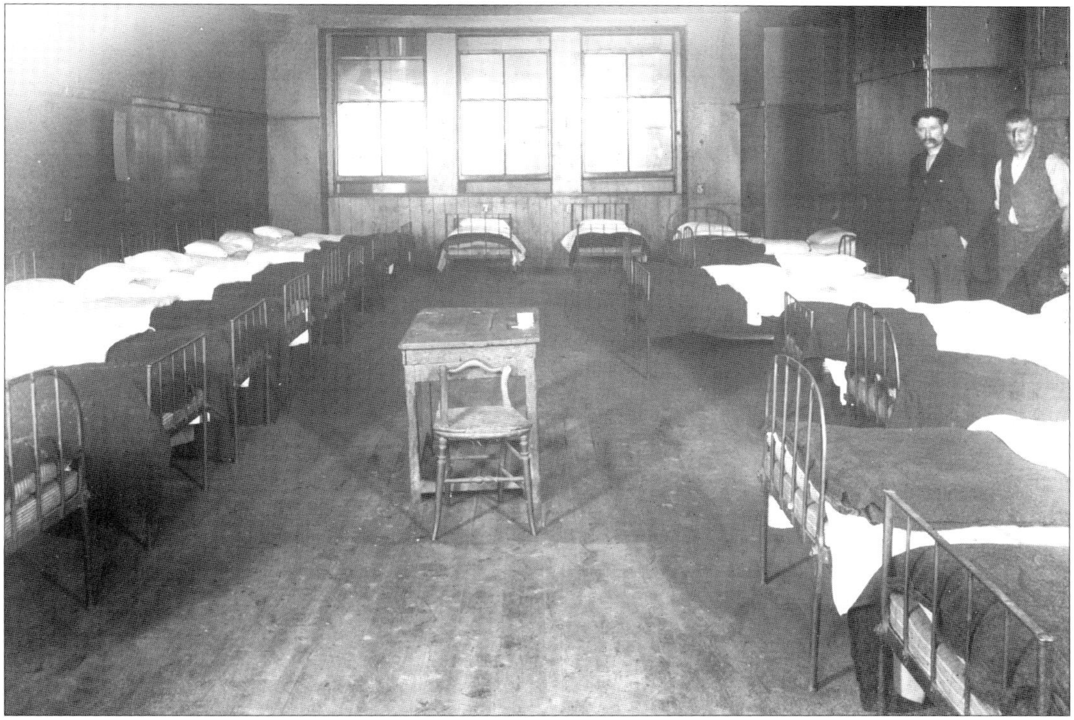

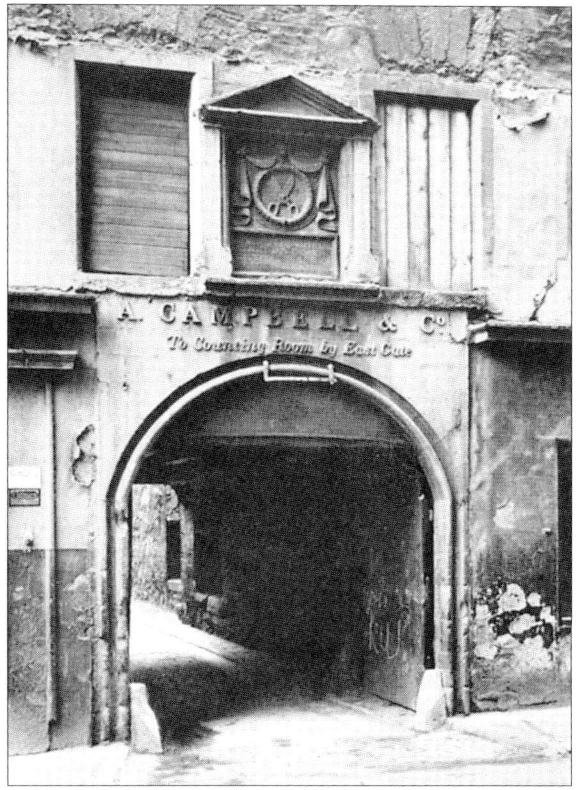

Right. The building now occupied as St Patrick's Roman Catholic Church was built in 1772 by the Episcopalians. The tower and octagonal belfry date from the original building but much of the remainder was encased by later additions after it was bought by the Roman Catholics in 1856. The façade and imposing arch were the work of Reginald Fairlie, the architect, in 1929. *Malcolm Cant Collection.*

Below right. This dilapidated pile stood on the west corner of the Cowgate and St Mary's Wynd (Street), the site now being occupied by the Travelodge hotel. The photograph by Archibald Burns was taken in, or before, 1866. The premises on the left is occupied by William Stirling, Cabinetmaker & Undertaker, and the shop in St Mary's Wynd is James White, China Merchant. *Malcolm Cant Collection.*

Below. Dating from *c.* 1900, this unidentified close is typical of many others in the Old Town. *Courtesy of Robert Murray Stamp Shop.*

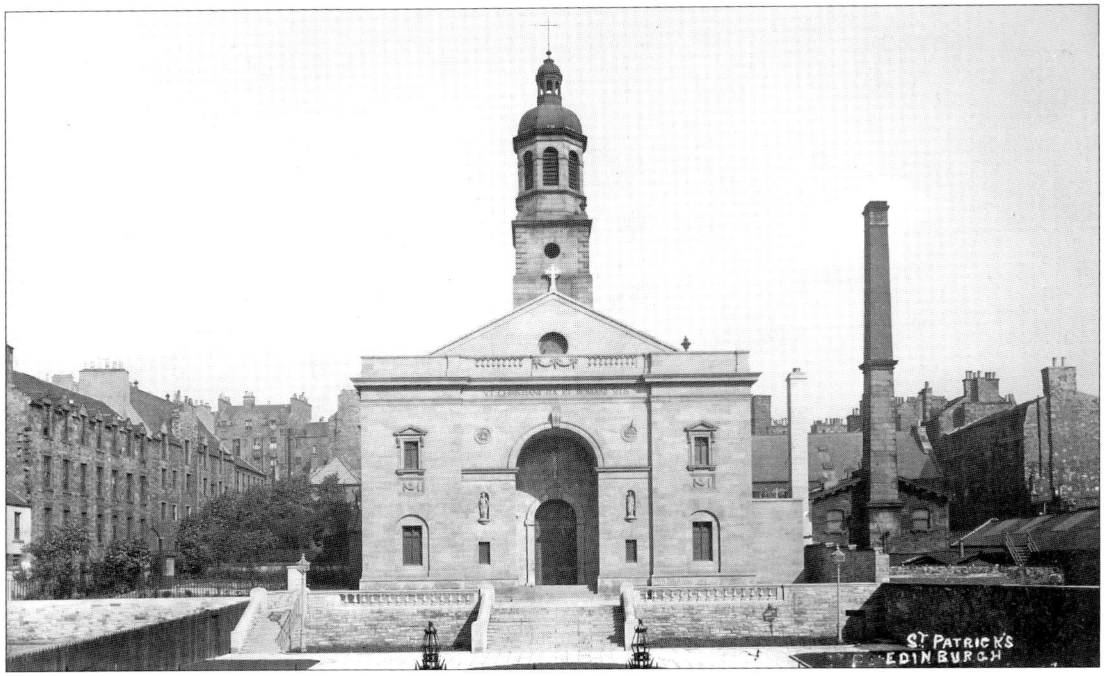

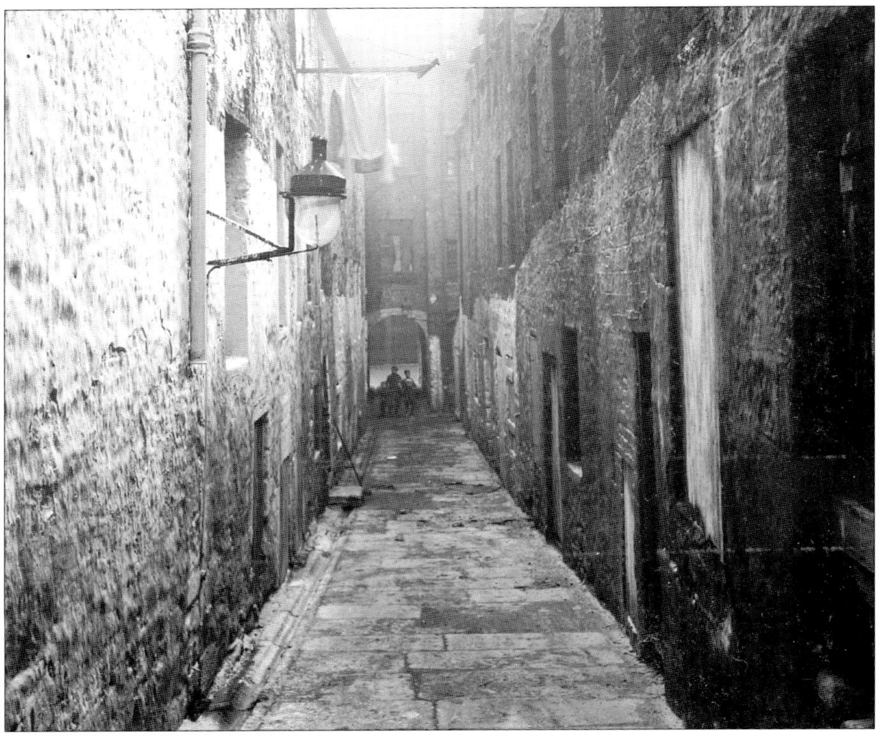

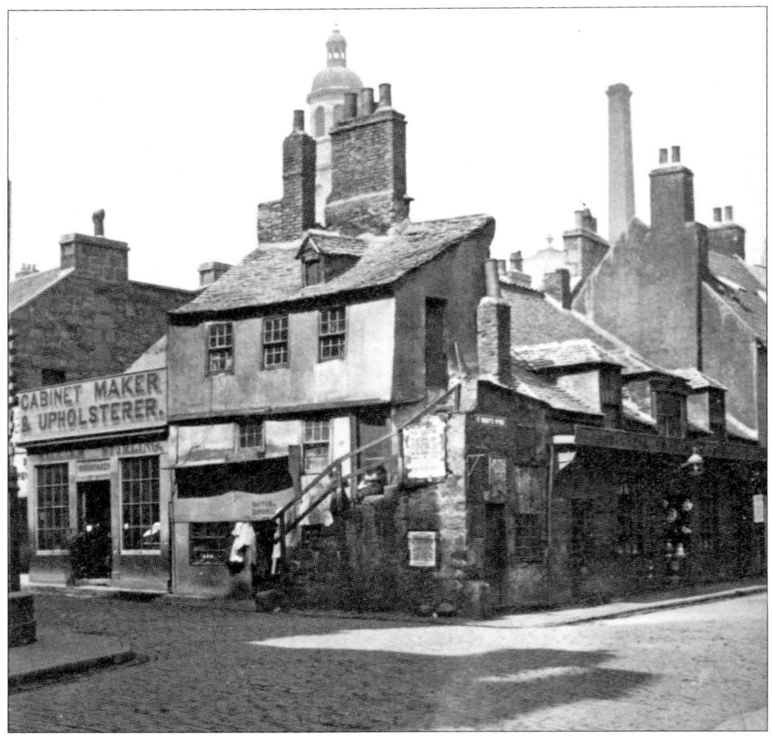

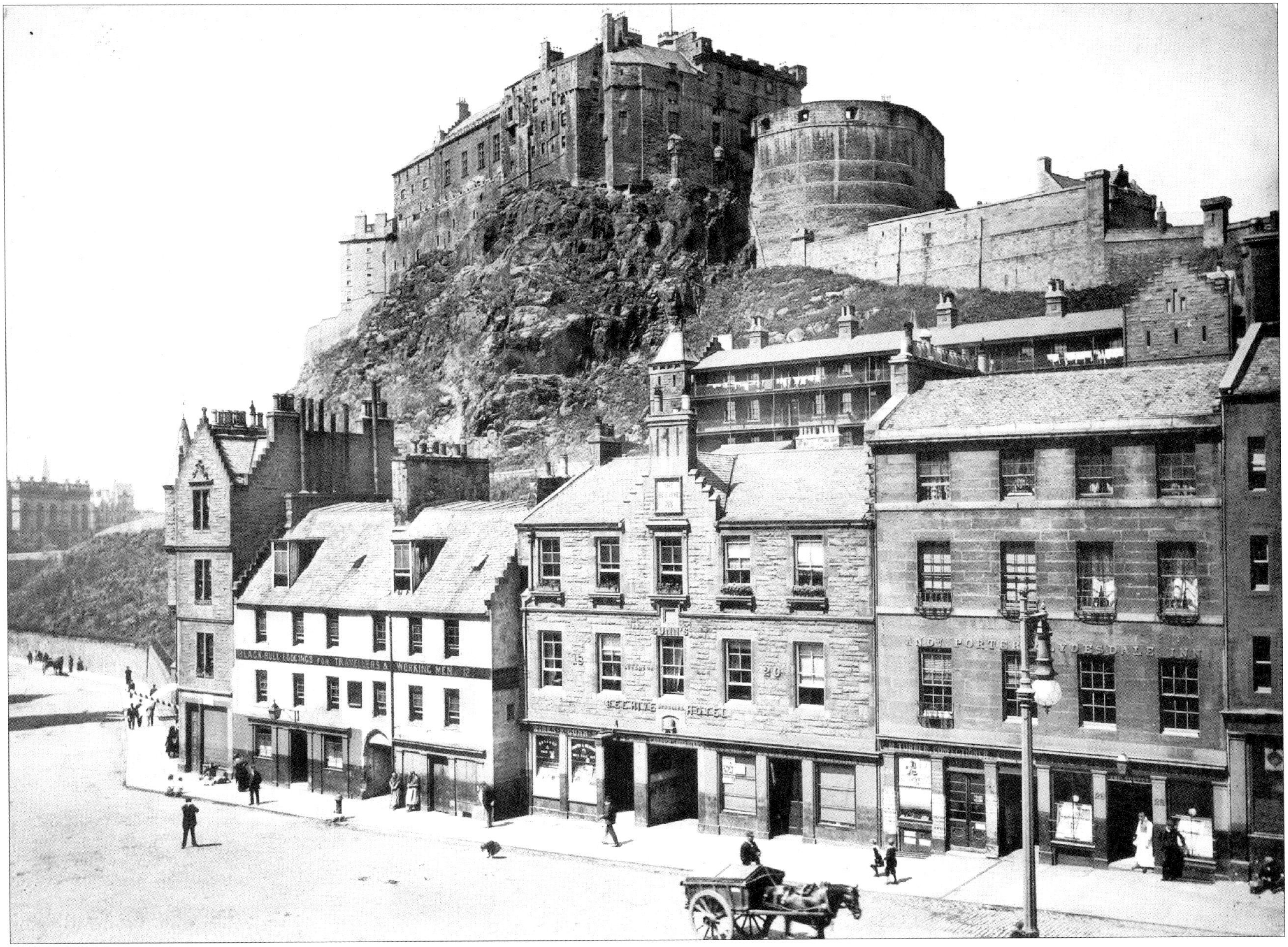

Photographs of the Grassmarket, probably taken from the former Corn Exchange building, are always greatly enhanced by the backcloth of Edinburgh Castle's Great Hall, the Royal Palace and the Half Moon Battery. In the Grassmarket there are three important hostelries: on the left, the Black Bull Lodgings for Travellers and Working Men, at No.12; in the centre, Gunn's Beehive Hotel, offering luncheons, bars and stabling; and, on the right, Andrew Porter's Clydesdale Inn. On the corner, near the junction with King's Stables Road, the barber advertises 'shavings', and the pend in the middle of the Beehive building leads to the Carriers' Quarters. Mr Turner, the confectioner, has his small shop in the Clydesdale Inn building. On the extreme left of the photograph is the Poole's Synod Hall in Castle Terrace that was demolished in anticipation of an opera house which was never built. The site is now occupied by Saltire Court. *Malcolm Cant Collection.*

Below. The Cowgate, looking west to the Grassmarket in 1860, is flanked by rundown properties and 'brokers' who dealt in second-hand furniture and general goods. The huge arches of George IV Bridge cross the Cowgate at what was Excise Office Close. On the extreme left of the picture, the sign protruding from the first-floor window says 'Lodgings' and the shop front with the semi-circular doorway was last used as a provision and spirit merchant. At the present day, the south-east bridge pier has a plaque commemorating James Connolly (1870-1916) who was born in the Cowgate, educated at St Patrick's School and later joined the Royal Scots. After a period of political and trade union involvement he went to Ireland where he organised, with James Larkin, the transport strike in Dublin. He took part in the Easter Rising of 1916 and was later arrested and executed on 12 May the same year. *From* Yerbury: A Photographic Collection 1850–1993.

Right. The photograph shows the lower section of West Bow with the tenements of Victoria Terrace at the back. The shop on the left is a confectioner's and the one on the right is the Grassmarket Post Office. The premises with the men standing outside appear to be the Bethamy Mission Hall. On the extreme right of the picture, the property with the railings of Victoria Terrace on its wallhead is No.46 Victoria Street. Below this point is the original West Bow which was truncated in the 1827 improvement schemes for the Old Town. *Malcolm Cant Collection.*

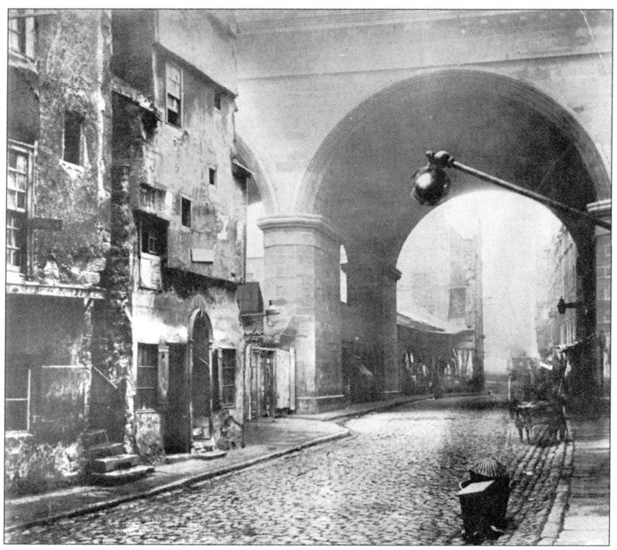

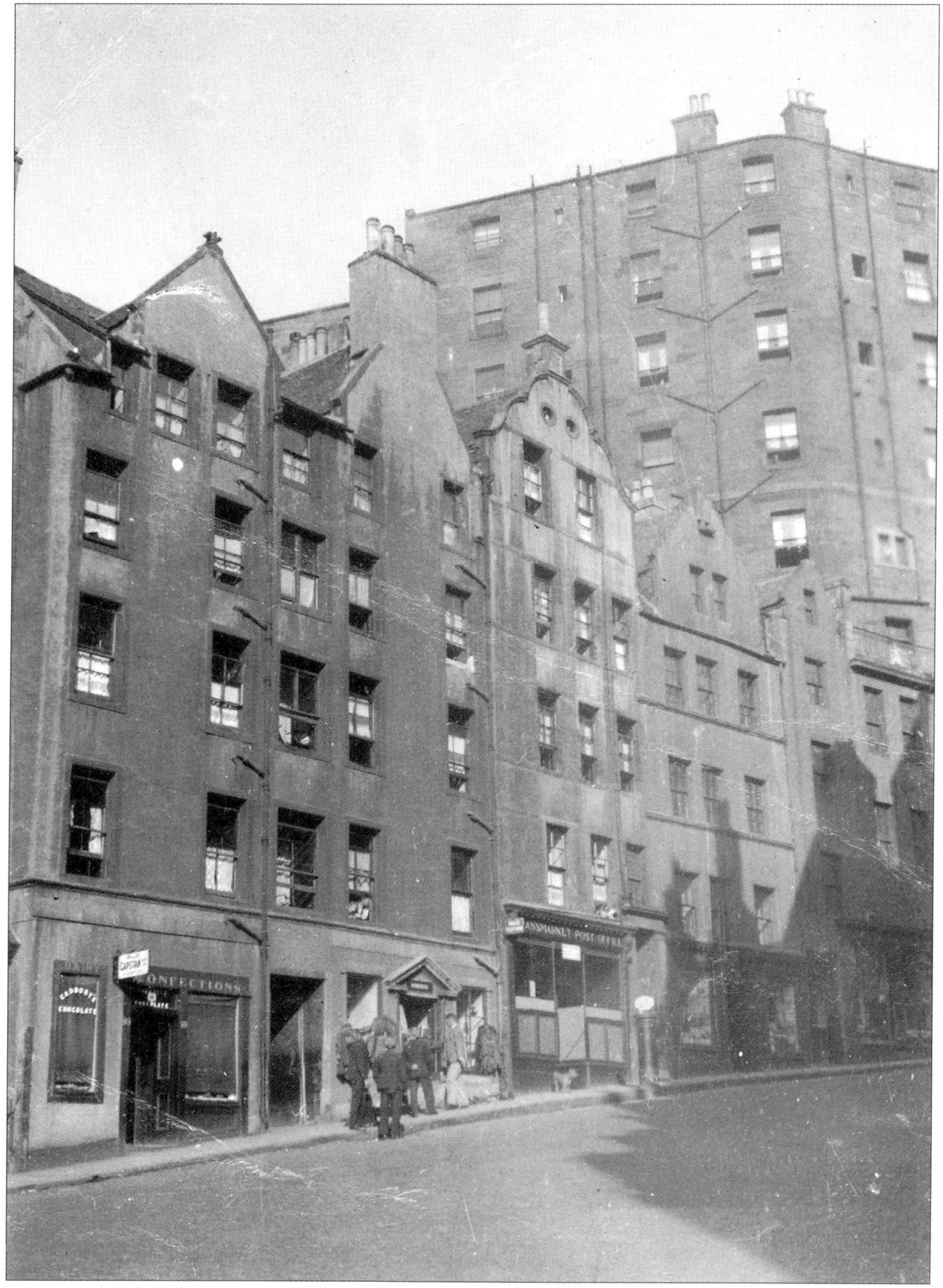

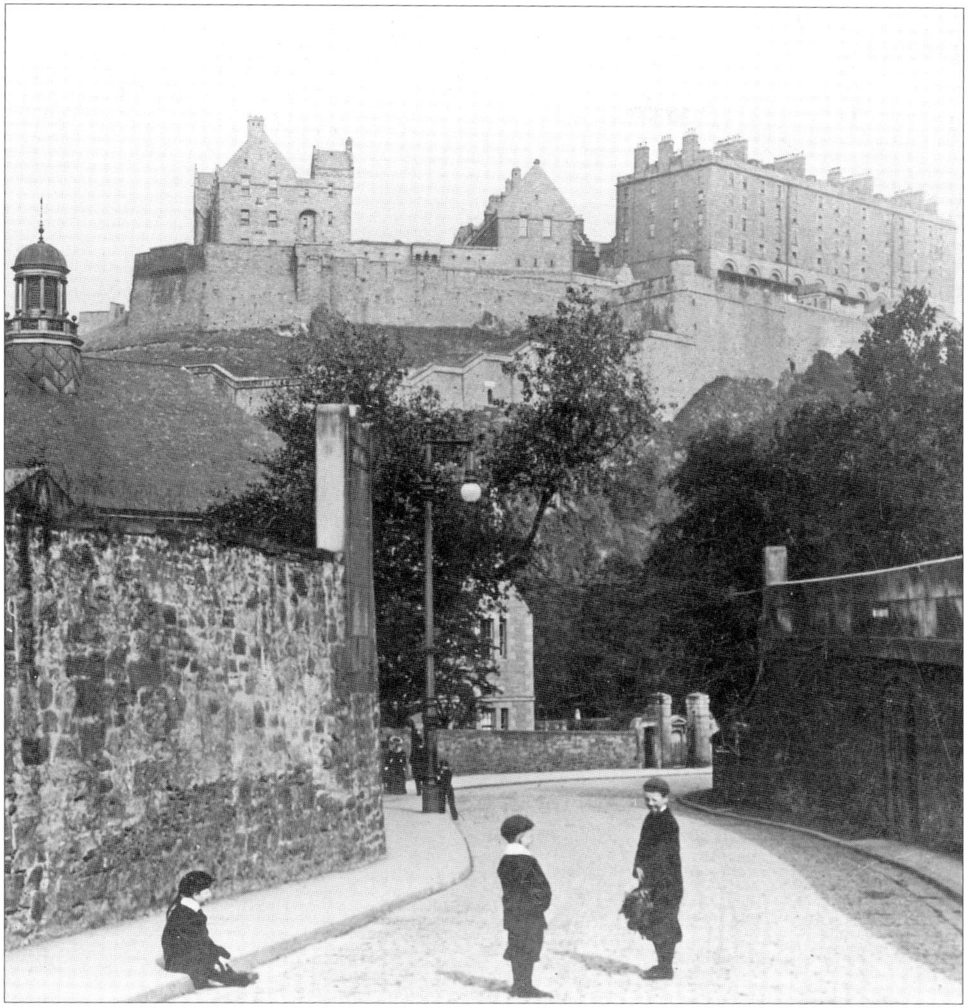

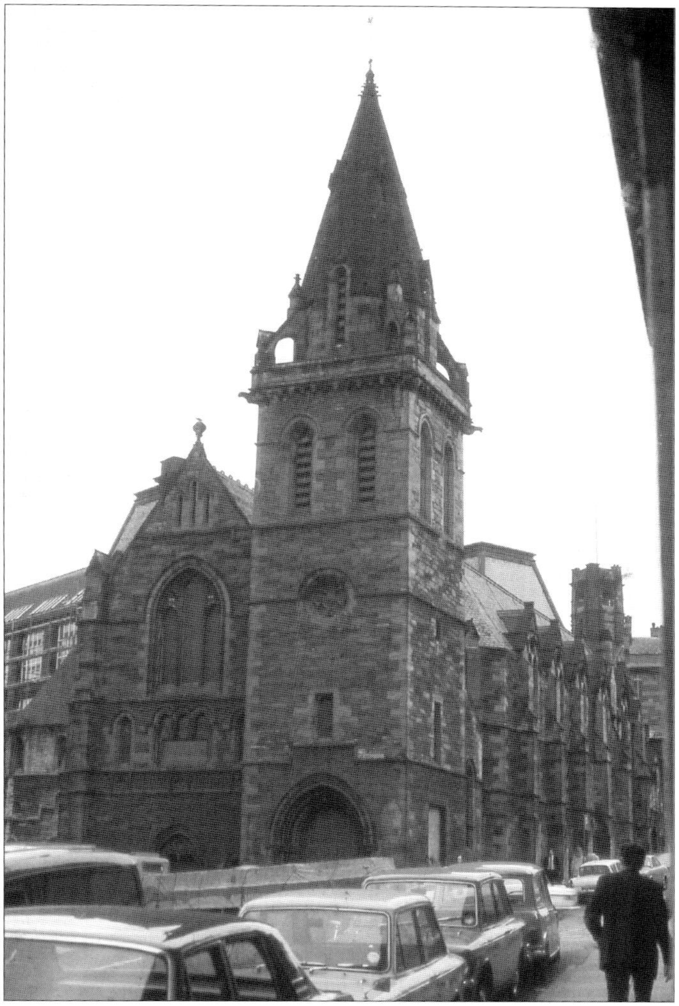

Above left. From King's Stables Road the castle presents a slightly less familiar profile. From left to right the three main buildings are the military hospital, the National War Museum of Scotland, and the New Barracks. The east tower of St Cuthbert's Parish Church is on the left of the photograph, and the gates leading to the former church halls can be seen beyond the three boys. The church halls, now in secular use, were designed by Charles McArthy & Watson in 1893. Off the right-hand side of the picture, King's Stables Road continues eastwards, under the King's Bridge (with Johnston Terrace above) and into the Grassmarket. According to *The Place Names of Edinburgh* by Stuart Harris, the name King's Stables can be traced to the fourteenth century when stables were built nearby to serve Edinburgh Castle. *Malcolm Cant Collection.*

Above right. One of Edinburgh's historically important, but relatively unknown churches stood at the south-east corner of Lady Lawson Street and West Port. Chalmers Church, with its sturdy tower and short steeple supported by flying buttresses, was built in 1884. It replaced a more modest church further down West Port which was opened by Dr Chalmers in 1847 (four years after the Disruption of 1843) as West Port Free – Chalmers Territorial. The old church was sold in 1930, the proceeds of the sale being used to build a hall in 1933 beside the new church. The congregation united with Lauriston Church on 27 April 1958. Both buildings were used until 1965 when the Chalmers building was sold to the Edinburgh College of Art and subsequently demolished.
Courtesy of the family of the late Charles J. Smith.

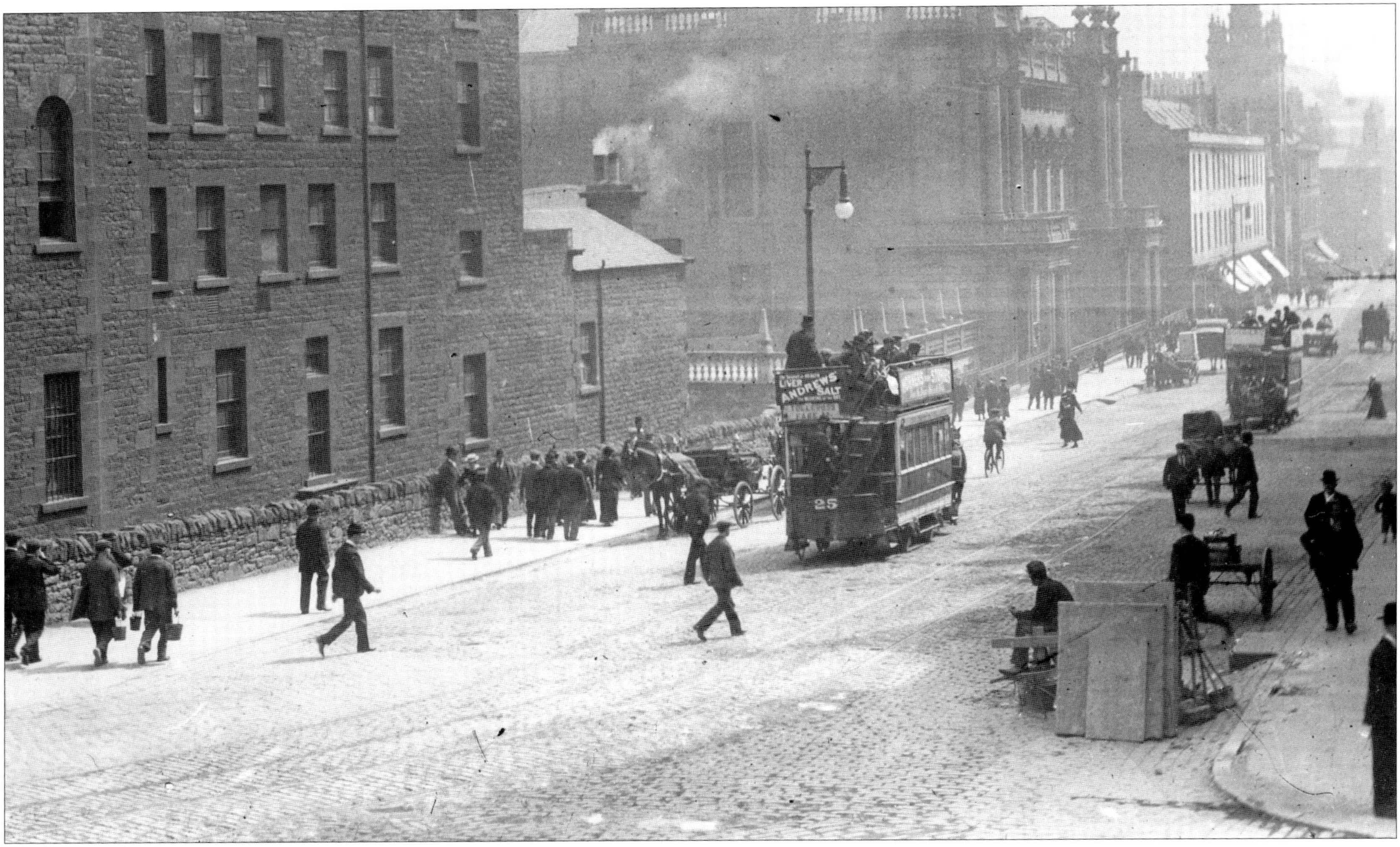

This photograph, looking south along George IV Bridge, appears to have been taken from one of the upper windows of a tenement on the north side of the Lawnmarket, near present-day Deacon Brodie's Tavern. The date of the photograph is between 1895 and 1899. There are two open-topped, horse-drawn trams in the picture, one travelling south and the other coming towards the camera. Tram No. 25 (nearest to the camera) was purchased from Glasgow Tramways & Omnibus Company at the end of 1894, and tram No. 66 (further from the camera) was purchased from the same source in April 1895. On the left of the picture, the rails can be seen to curve round into the High Street. This was because the gradient on the Mound was too great for horse-drawn trams. The rails were rerouted down the Mound when the system was rebuilt on the introduction of cable cars in August 1901.

There is an interesting line of buildings on the left-hand side of George IV Bridge. The site on the corner of George IV Bridge and the High Street is occupied at the present day by the handsome edifice of the former Midlothian County Council headquarters. However, the building in the photograph does not look as though it was designed to face onto a main thoroughfare. It is, in fact, the back of County Hall which was built in 1816 to face towards St Giles Cathedral. When George IV Bridge was constructed from 1827 the rather ugly rear elevation of County Hall was revealed when Libberton Wynd was demolished. The Midlothian County Council building was not begun until 1900. The original County Hall also housed the offices of the Sheriff Clerk and the Procurator Fiscal.

Between the two horse-drawn trams is the pillared façade of the then Sheriff Court which was demolished for the construction of the National Library of Scotland. Further into the picture is the ornate spire of Augustine Congregational Church (now Augustine United Church) built between 1857 and 1861 to seat 1,145.

Courtesy of A. W. Brotchie.

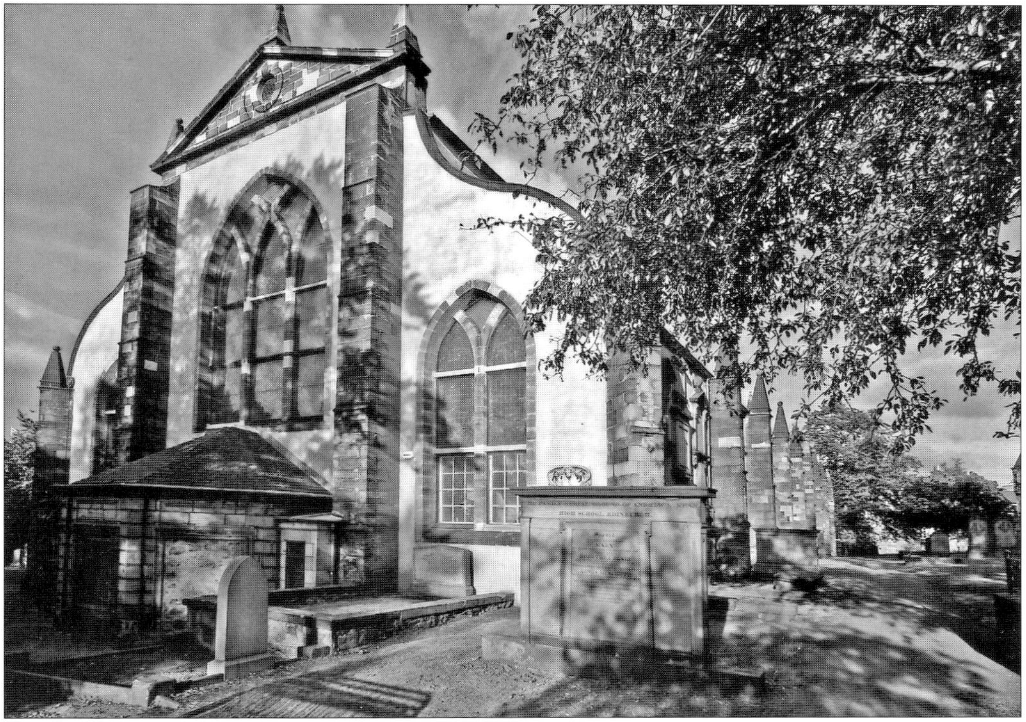

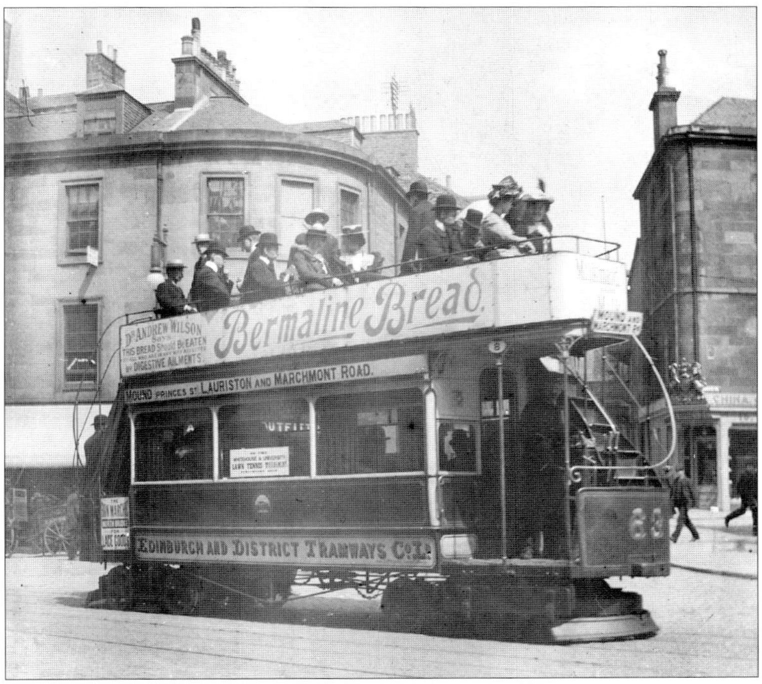

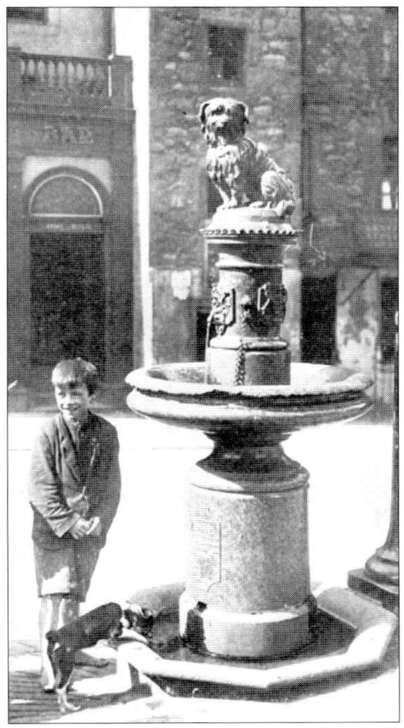

Left. Greyfriars Kirk took its present name, Greyfriars, Tolbooth and Highland, on 28 February 1979, on the union of the congregations of Greyfriars Kirk and Highland Tolbooth St John's in the Lawnmarket. Greyfriars burial ground is older than the church itself. Mary, Queen of Scots gave the land to the city in 1562 to create a new burial ground as the one at St Giles was full. The first Greyfriars Kirk was opened in 1620. Over the years it has featured in several important events, notably the signing (in their own blood) of the National Covenant in 1638 by those opposed to Charles I's decree imposing Episcopal rule on Scotland. *Photograph by Peter Stubbs.*

Lower left. Cable car No. 69, run by Edinburgh & District Tramways Co. Ltd., is photographed at the junction of Lindsay Place, Bristo Port and Bristo Place, sometime between 1901 and 1906 when the Mound to Marchmont service was withdrawn. The advertisements on the side of the car are for Bermaline Bread and Dr Andrew Wilson's various potions for good health. On the extreme right of the picture the 'By Appointment' Royal Coat of Arms is above the doorway of John Donald, China Merchants. *Courtesy of A. W. Brotchie.*

Left. The young lad has brought his pet to drink from the lower trough intended for dogs. The statue of Greyfriars Bobby, on the corner of George IV Bridge and Candlemaker Row, is one of the most visited in Edinburgh. The dog, Bobby, fulfilled the dual role of household pet and guard dog to Constable John Gray and his family who lived in the Grassmarket. After Gray died in 1858, Bobby was looked after by several locals but was given to returning to the place of burial in Greyfriars Kirkyard to stand guard over his master's grave. The bronze statue, by William Brodie in 1872, was unveiled on 15 November 1873. *Malcolm Cant Collection.*

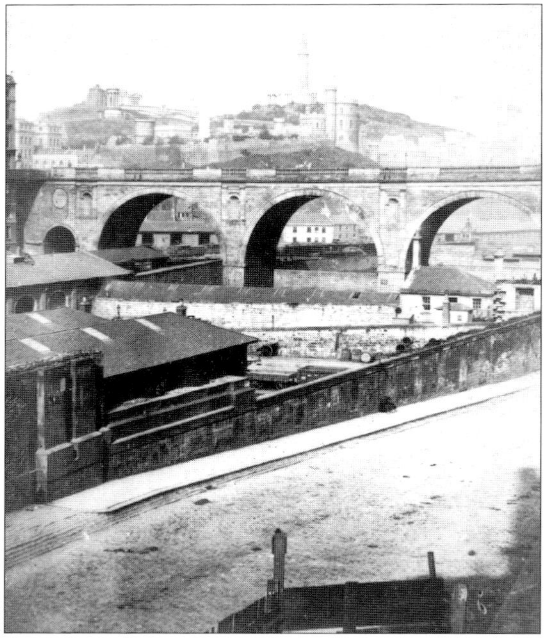

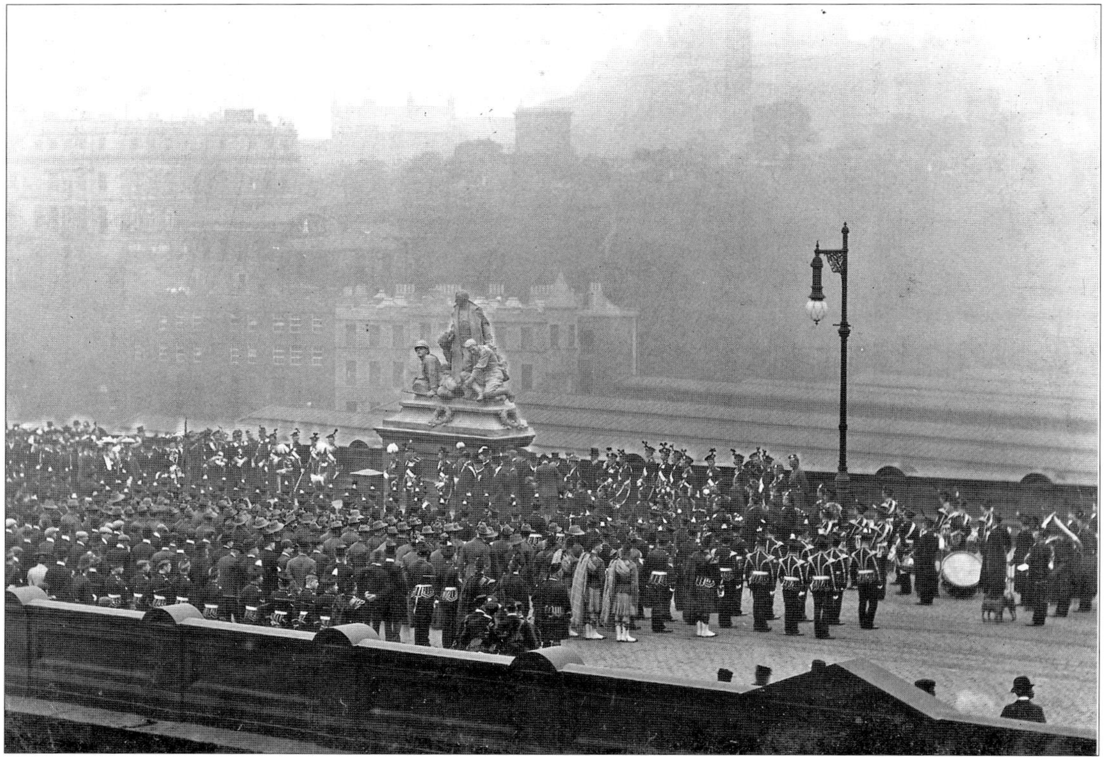

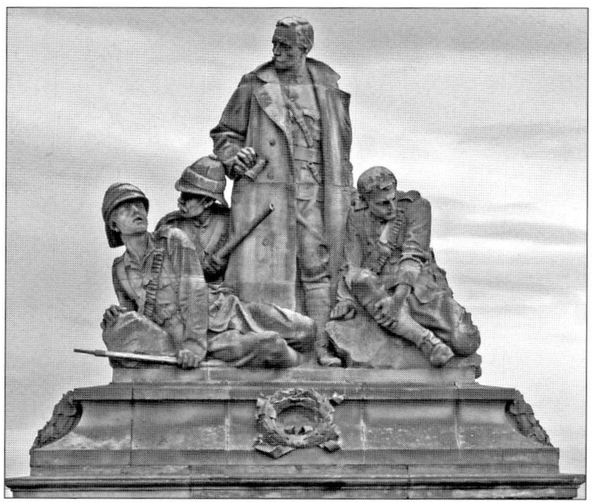

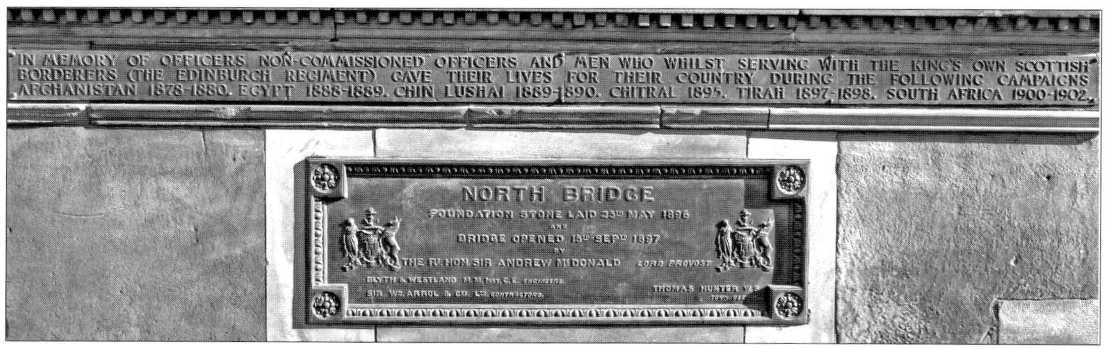

Upper left. The first North Bridge, photographed from the bottom of Cockburn Street, had five stone arches. The foundation stone was laid on 21 October 1763 by Lord Provost George Drummond. Unfortunately, the south arch collapsed in 1769, which delayed the opening until 1772.

Upper right. Officers and men, and civic dignitaries gather on North Bridge for the unveiling of the statue to the officers, non-commissioned officers and men of The King's Own Scottish Borderers who gave their lives between 1878 and 1902 in various military campaigns.

Lower left. The statue, completed by William Birnie Rhind in 1906, depicts a central figure of an officer flanked by three other soldiers. The regiment was raised in 1689 and merged with The Royal Scots on 1 August 2006 to become the 1st Battalion of the new Royal Regiment of Scotland.

Lower right. Below the statue there are details of the various campaigns and also a commemorative plaque for the bridge which was opened on 15 September 1897. *Photographs upper left and upper right, Malcolm Cant Collection. Photographs lower left and lower right by Peter Stubbs.*

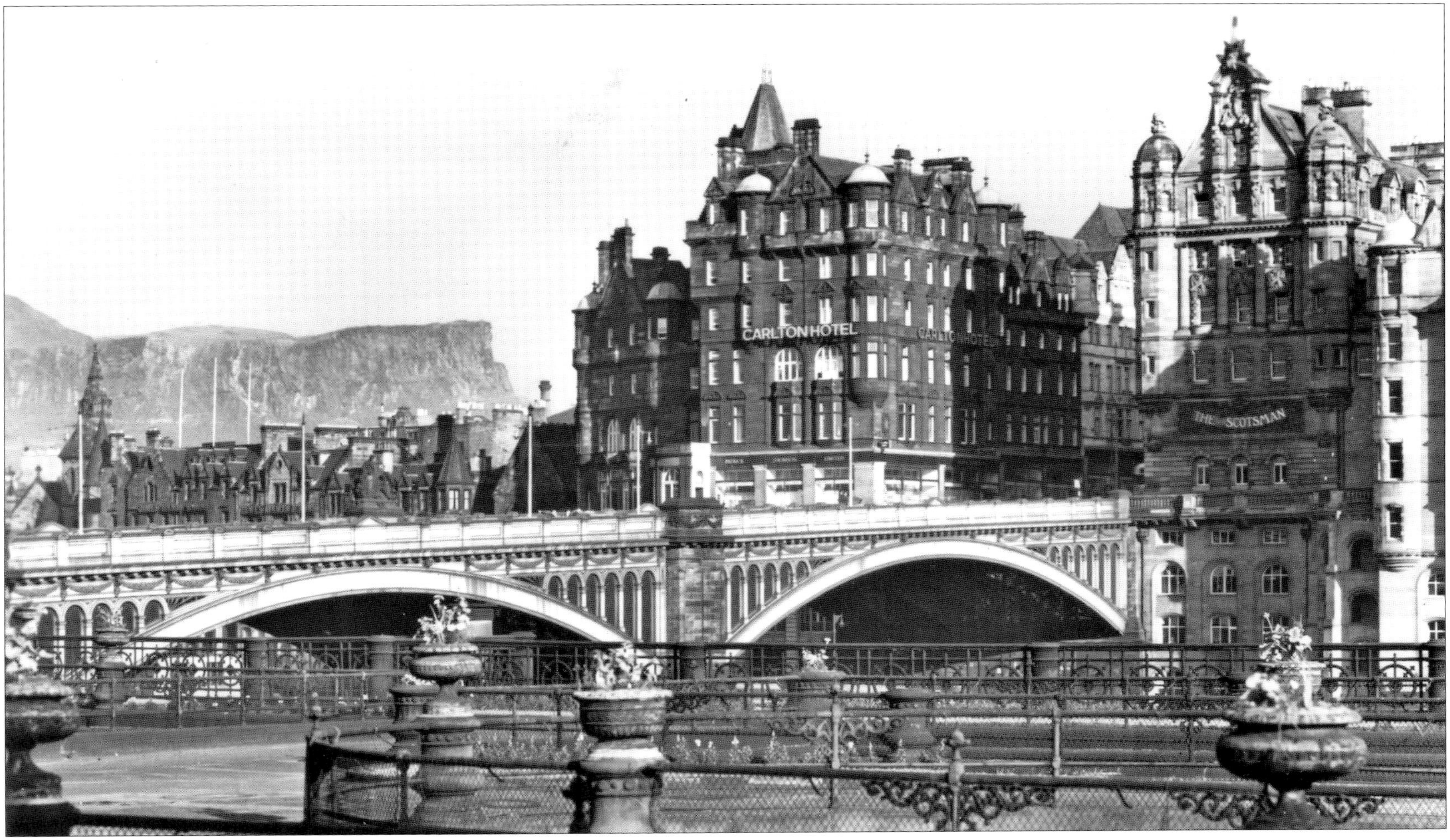

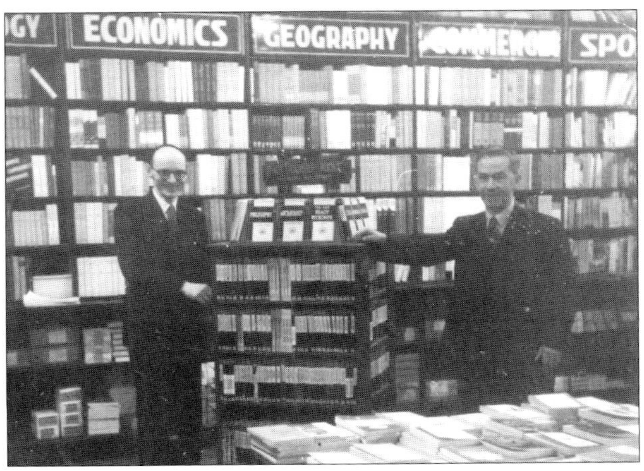

Left. On the left is George Jack and on the right, Peter Watson, at Thins the booksellers in South Bridge in 1957. George Jack began his career with Robert Grant & Son at No. 126 Princes Street in 1934 and moved, with his future wife, Annie Mullan, to Thins in 1956. Later he worked with Oliver & Boyd and also Cambridge University Press. James Thin, the booksellers, were founded in 1848 but after they ceased to trade, the South Bridge premises were taken over by Blackwells in 2004. *Courtesy of Annie Jack.*

Above. The foundation stone for the second North Bridge was laid on 25 May 1896 by Lord Provost McDonald. The North British Railway Company contributed about one third of the cost on condition that the piers were resited to enable them to redesign the layout of Waverley Station. In 1990, extensive work was done to strengthen the parapets to ensure that no vehicle could fall into the station below. This view, from the Waverley Market, shows the Carlton Hotel in the centre, and the equally grand *Scotsman* building on the right, designed by Dunn & Findlay, and built between 1899 and 1902. *Malcolm Cant Collection.*

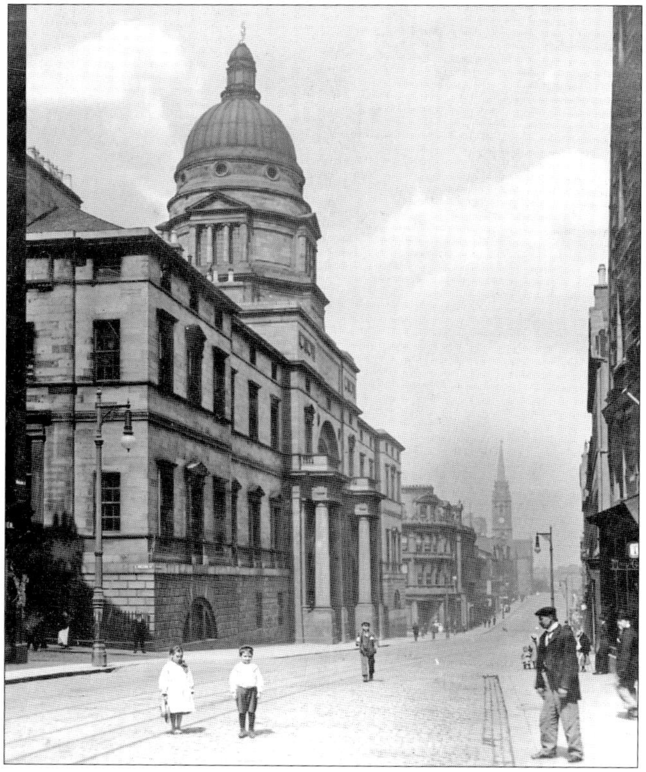

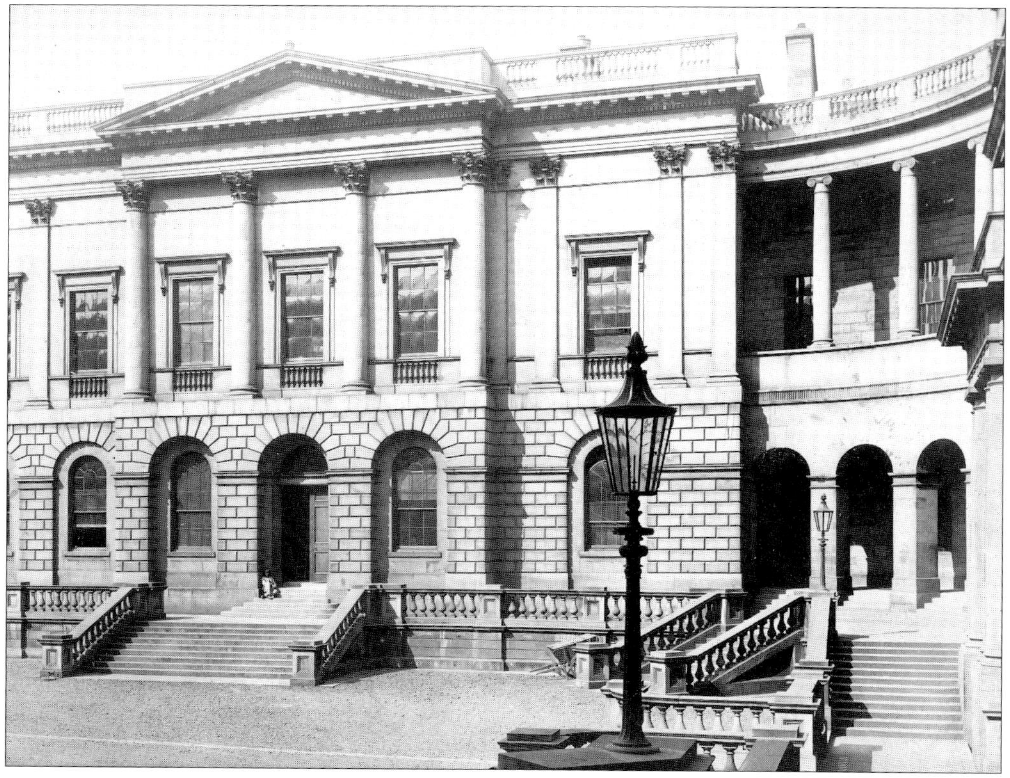

Above. The man on the pavement might be beckoning to the children posing for the camera in the middle of Nicolson Street but there is no traffic to endanger them. The University of Edinburgh was founded in 1583 as the 'Tounis College'. The exterior of the Old Quad, seen here, was designed by Robert Adam and begun in 1789. The dome, designed by R. Rowand Anderson, was added in 1887 and the gilded figure of 'Youth' by John Hutchison in 1888. *Malcolm Cant Collection.*

Above right. Most of the elegant quadrangle was designed by William H. Playfair who replicated, at the three remaining angles, Robert Adam's original curved north-west corner. *Malcolm Cant Collection.*

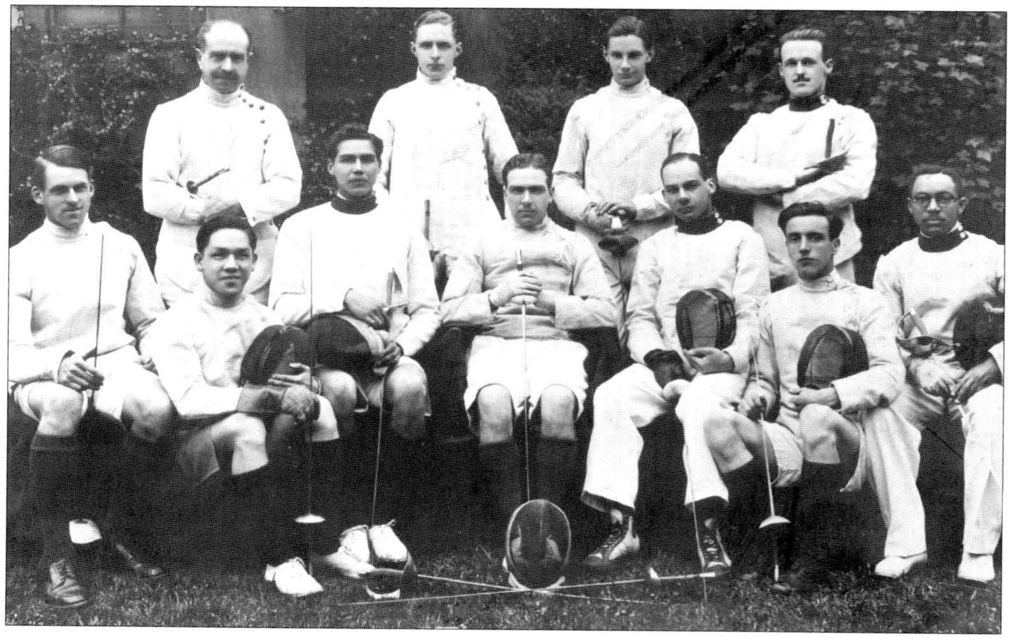

Right. Edinburgh University had the services of a fencing instructor as early as *c.* 1779, and by 1900 the fencing club was run as a subsidiary of the boxing club. However, when this photograph was taken in 1931 the club was fully independent and arranging fixtures with other universities and also the Scottish Fencing Club. *Malcolm Cant Collection.*

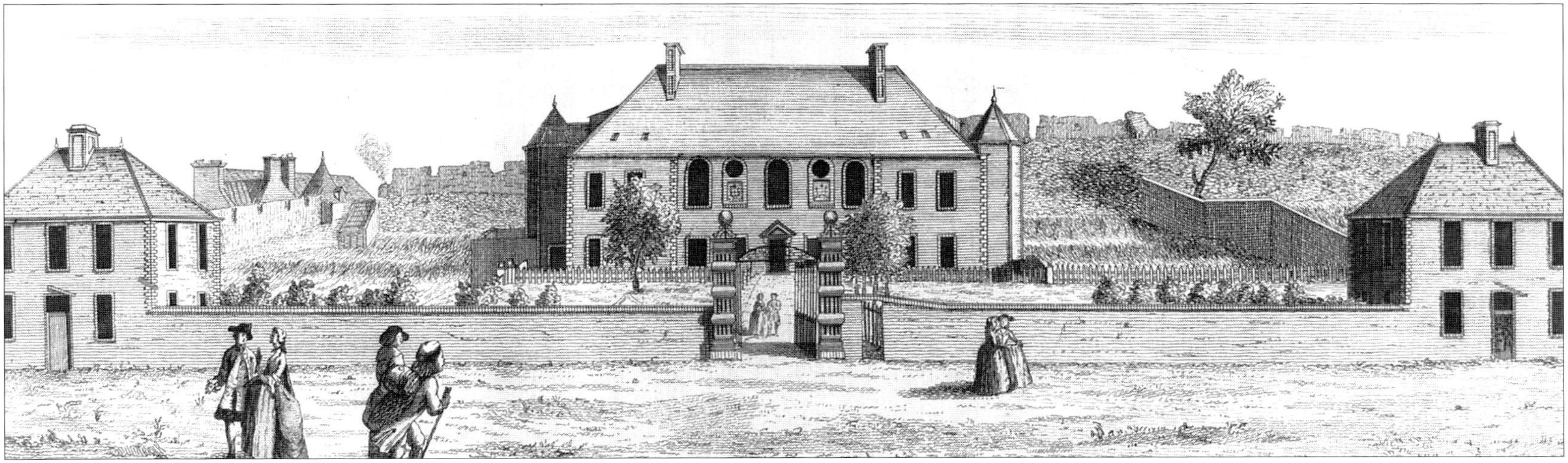

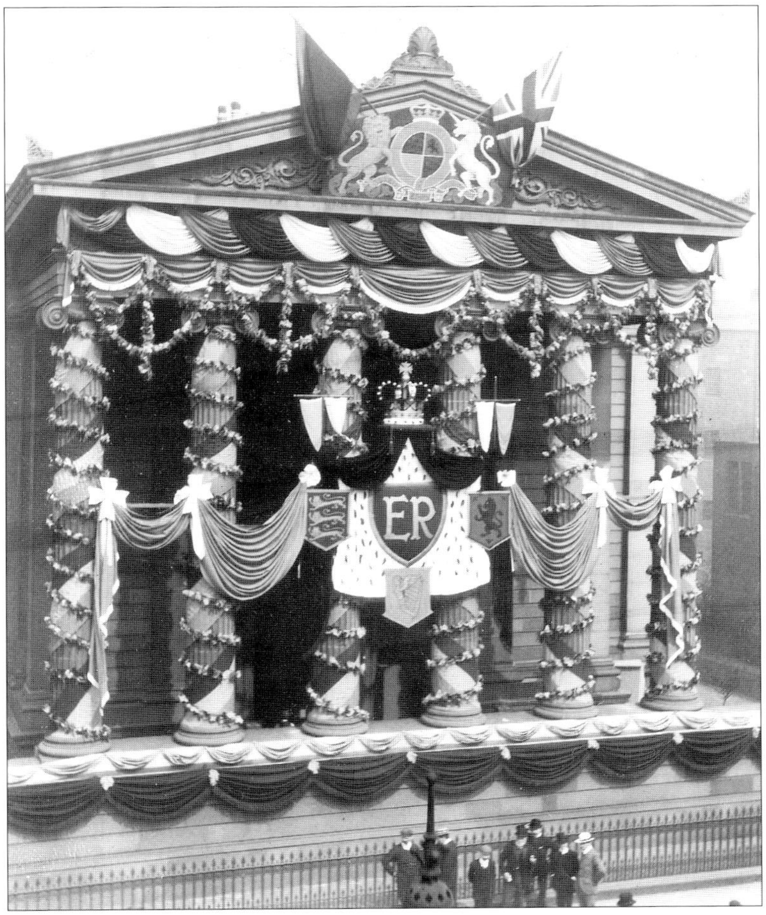

Above. The Royal College of Surgeons of Edinburgh received its Seal of Cause from Edinburgh Town Council in July 1505 which was ratified by James IV in October 1506. The incorporation consisted of the surgeons and the barbers, to which were added the apothecaries in 1657. The royal charter was granted in 1778. Up until 1647 the college did not have a permanent home but met either in the house of the current deacon, or, occasionally, in St Giles Cathedral. In 1647 three rooms were rented in Dickson's Close, off the High Street, for £40 per annum, and then from 1650 accommodation was obtained in Robert Hardie's tenement at the 'foot of the Kirkheugh'. It was not until 1656 that a permanent building was purchased for 3,000 merks, Curryhill House, near the Flodden Wall. After many abortive plans, a decision was taken in 1696 to demolish Curryhill House and replace it with a new building, costing £500, designed by James Smith. During much of the eighteenth century, financial constraints forced the college to let out parts of the building, and even to consider selling it. However, by the 1820s it was clear that the building was no longer suitable and that a new building was needed. The illustration above shows the lay-out of Old Surgeons' Hall, parts of which still remain. *From Maitland's* History of Edinburgh, *published in 1753.*

Left. After considering and rejecting several sites, a decision was taken to build a new college on the site of the Royal Menage, on the east side of Nicolson Street, a few hundred yards to the south of Edinburgh University Old Quad. William H. Playfair, the architect, was selected to draw up plans for a building which would reflect the importance of the college in Edinburgh and beyond. The illustration shows the façade of the Nicolson Street building, opened in 1832, bedecked for the coronation of Edward VII in 1902. A very comprehensive history of the college, *A Famous and Flourishing Society: The History of the Royal College of Surgeons of Edinburgh, 1505–2005*, was written by Helen M. Dingwall. *Courtesy of Robert Murray Stamp Shop.*

Right. Cable car No. 82, on service No. 7, is travelling north on South Bridge en route for Pilrig, probably in the 1920s. The advertisement on the rear of the car is for Baird the Bootmaker. The shops on the left are Peter Allan's, Draper & Milliner, and Goodson's Ltd., Mantle Manufacturers at Nos. 107-8. On the right-hand side of the street is, coincidentally, Baird the Bootmaker at Nos. 14 – 19.

Below. Also on South Bridge, electric tram No. 28 on service No. 19 is travelling southwards past the Tron Church. Service No. 19 went to Tollcross, via Melville Drive, until May 1956. The lorry between the two trams is for Dunbar's aerated waters.

Below right. In the early 1950s, electric tram No. 368 travelling south on South Bridge is bound for Newington Station, probably on service No. 17 which was withdrawn in March 1956. The premises in the background are Bertram Mackay, Printer, John Orr & Co., Drapers, and Macraes, the Furnishers.
All courtesy of A. W. Brotchie.

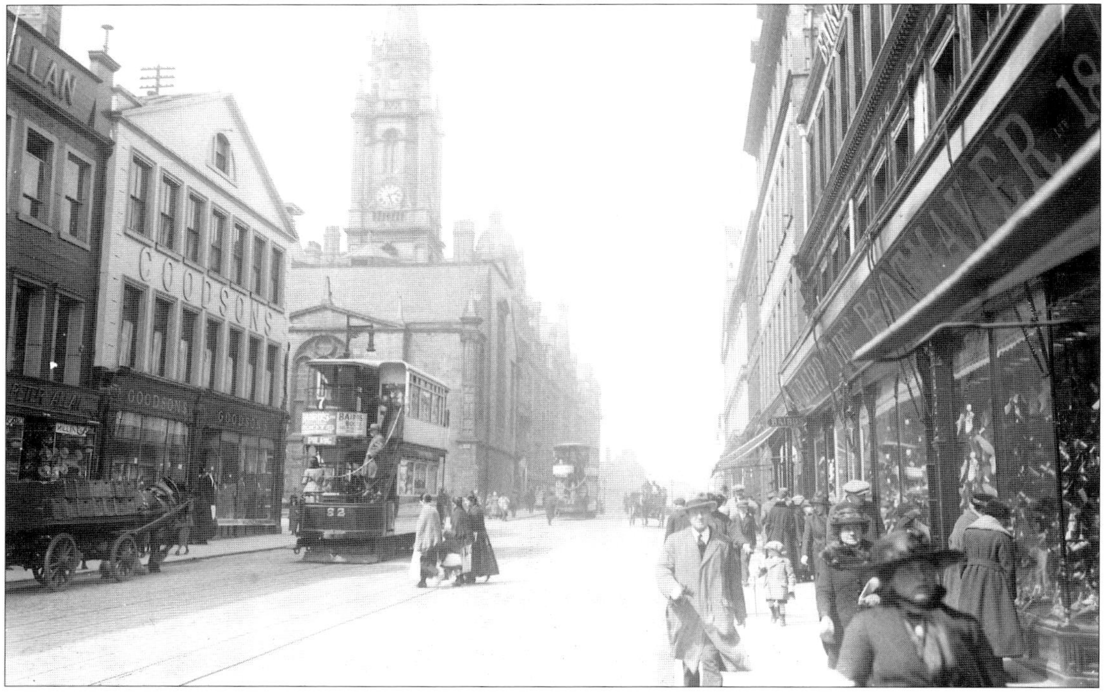

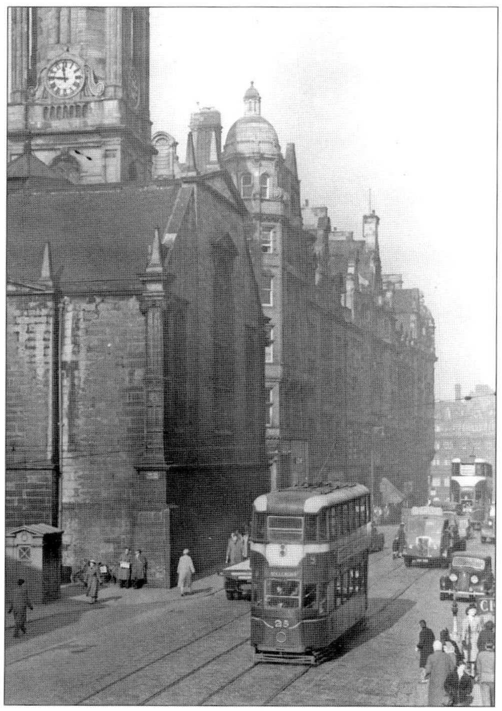

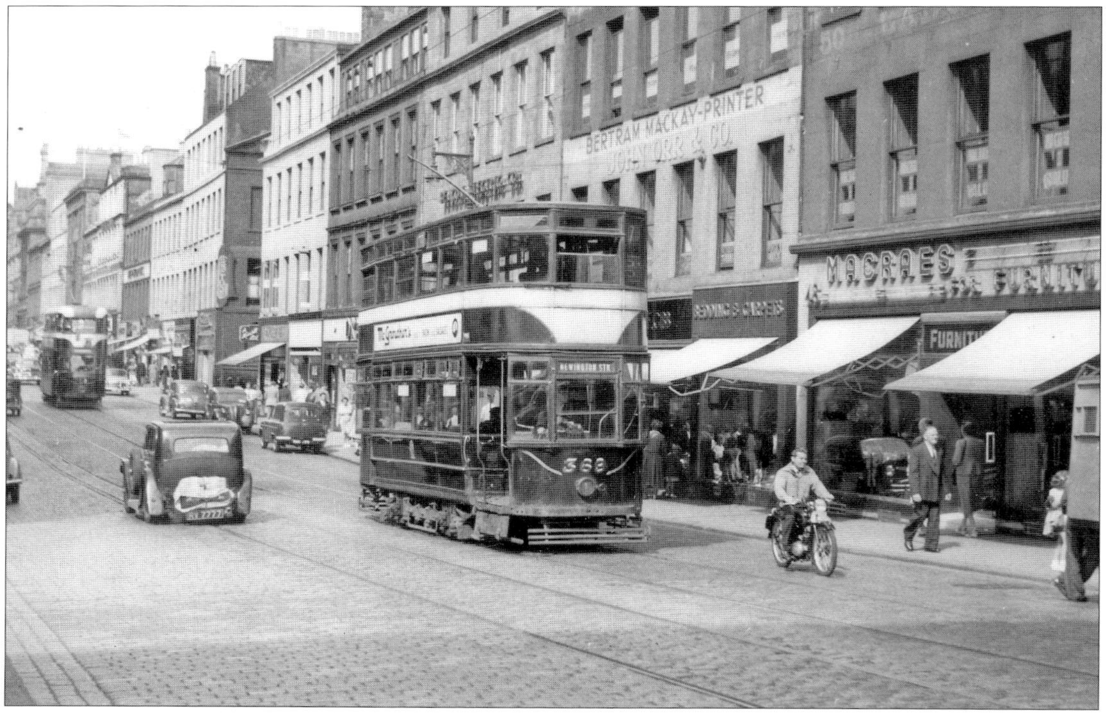

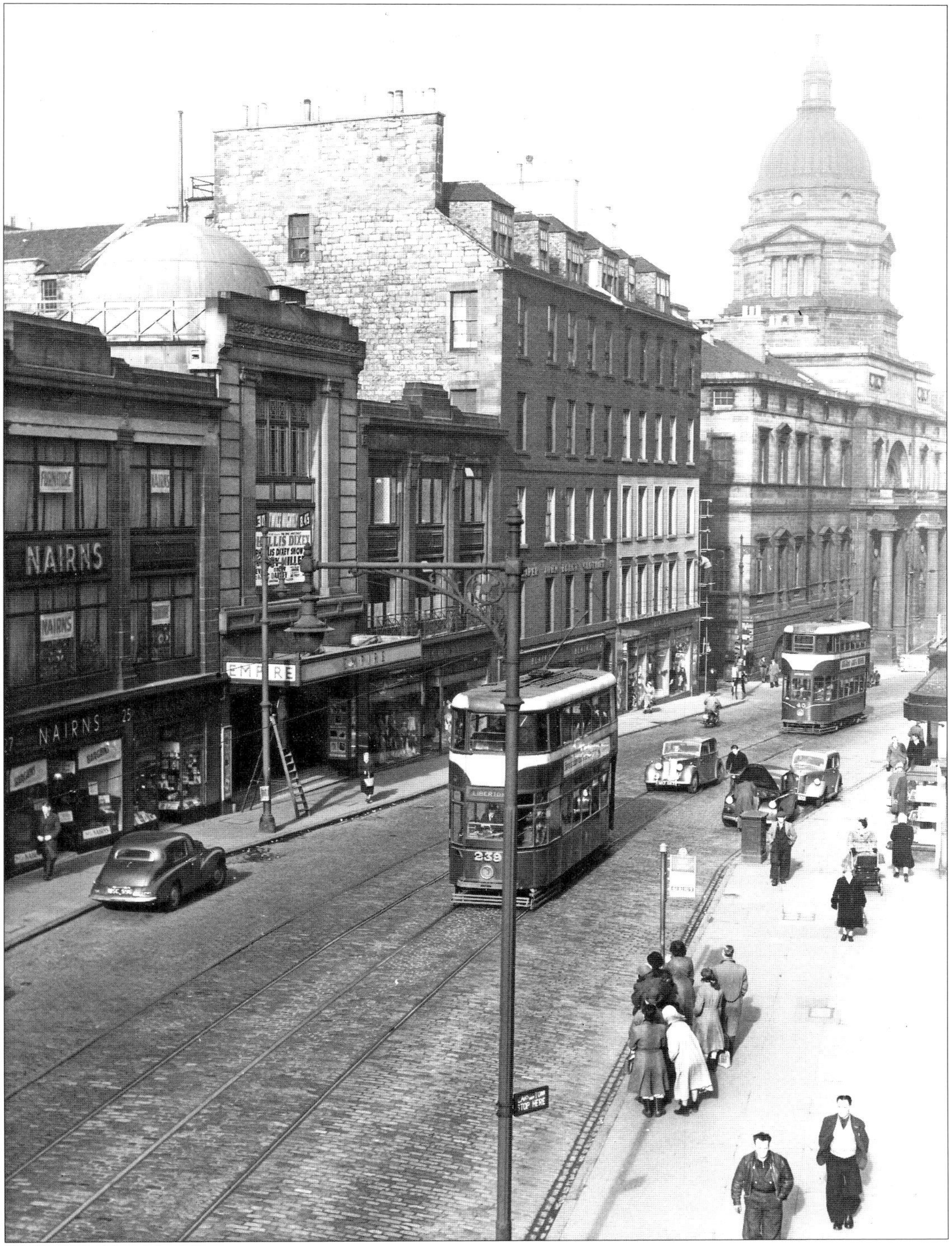

Left. When this photograph was taken of Nicolson Street in the mid-1950s, Edinburgh was in the process of changing from trams to buses. In the foreground the sign on the lamp standard says, CARS FROM TOWN STOP HERE, but people are also standing at the new bus stop nearby. On the left of the picture, the Empire Theatre is advertising the Phyllis Dixey Show, twice nightly, the second performance at 8.45p.m. It was reckoned to be the only 'burlesque' show to come then to the Empire. After the serious fire involving the Great Lafayette in 1911 (see page 64) the Empire Theatre was repaired and then completely rebuilt in 1928. After being used as a bingo hall from 1963 until 1991, the theatre was again revamped and refronted, and opened as the Edinburgh Festival Theatre in 1994.

Below. This busy scene, looking north at the junction of North Bridge and the High Street, dates from 1933. Electric tram No. 63, on service No. 8 bound for Newington Station, is at one of the island stops. Further down North Bridge the tram at an angle is negotiating a temporary section of line, laid to enable work to be done on the westerly track.
Both photographs courtesy of A. W. Brotchie.

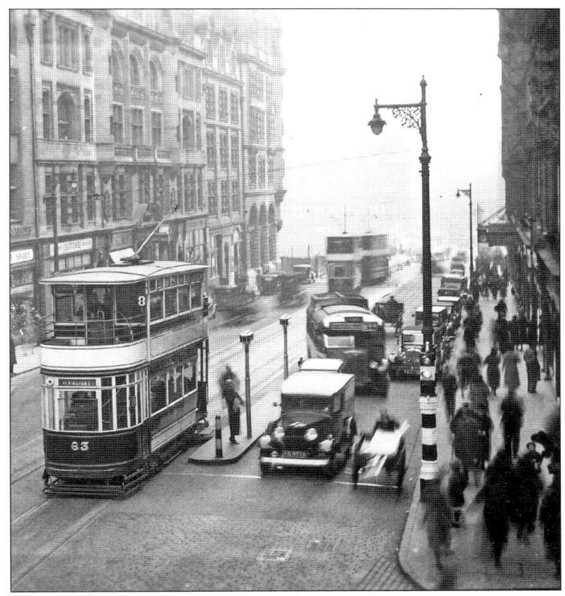

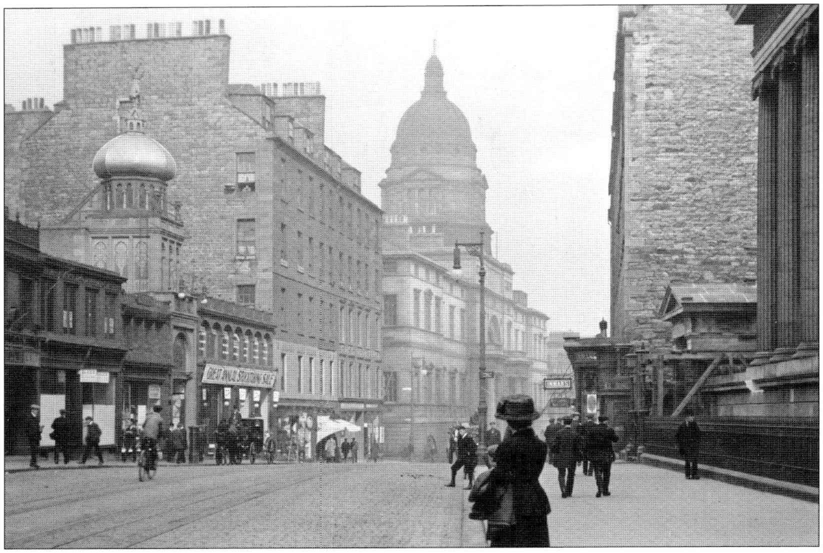

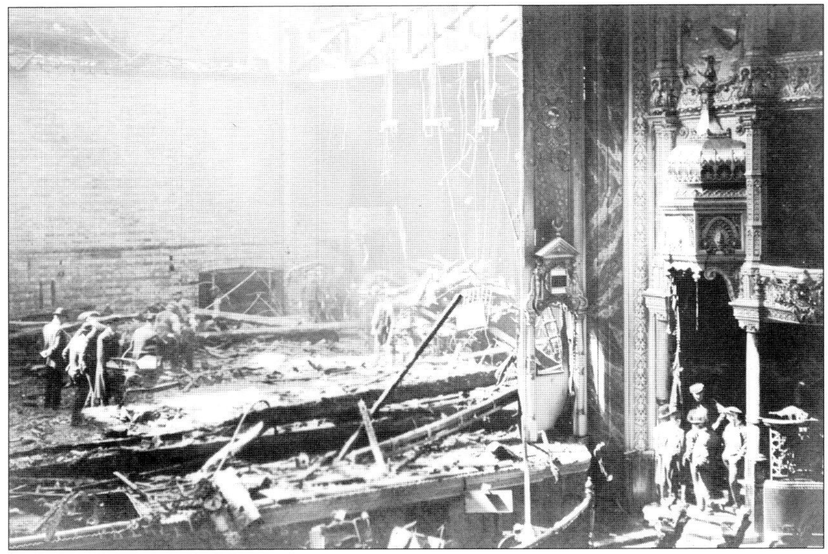

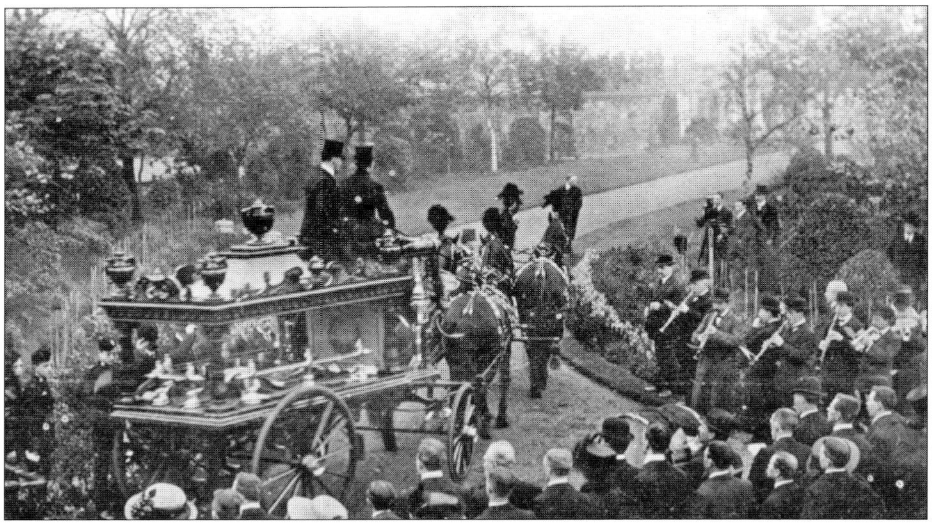

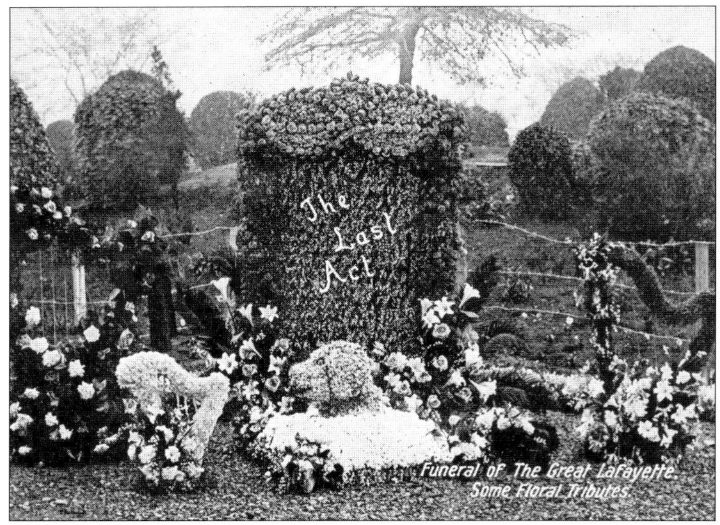

The 1920s photograph (*top left*) shows Moss's pre-1928 Empire Theatre with its distinctive onion dome roof. The earliest theatrical building on the site was the Dunedin Hall, dating from 1839. Unfortunately, on Tuesday 9 May 1911 tragedy struck at the Empire when an act by the illusionist, the Great Lafayette, went wrong and set fire to the stage (*top right*). In all, ten people died, including Lafayette, many other lives being saved by the safety curtain and the assistance of the Royal Scots Territorial Army who just happened to be nearby on evening manoeuvres when the fire broke out. The body of the Great Lafayette was recovered from the debris and taken to Glasgow for cremation prior to his ashes being interred at Piershill Cemetery (*above left*). Just before the interment, when the real body of Lafayette was found under the stage, it was realised that it was Lafayette's stage double, Charles Richards, who had been cremated in Glasgow. A further cruel irony is associated with this tragedy. Lafayette's favourite dog, Beauty, died a few days before the Empire fire. In *Edinburgh Theatres, Cinemas and Circuses*, the author, George Baird, recounts that Lafayette was permitted to have Beauty buried in Piershill Cemetery on the strict understanding that Lafayette would also be buried there when the time came 'no matter in whichever part of the world he might die'. Little did he know that the clock was already ticking. Presumably, the floral tribute in the shape of a dog's head (*above right*) is intended to be Beauty.
All Malcolm Cant Collection.

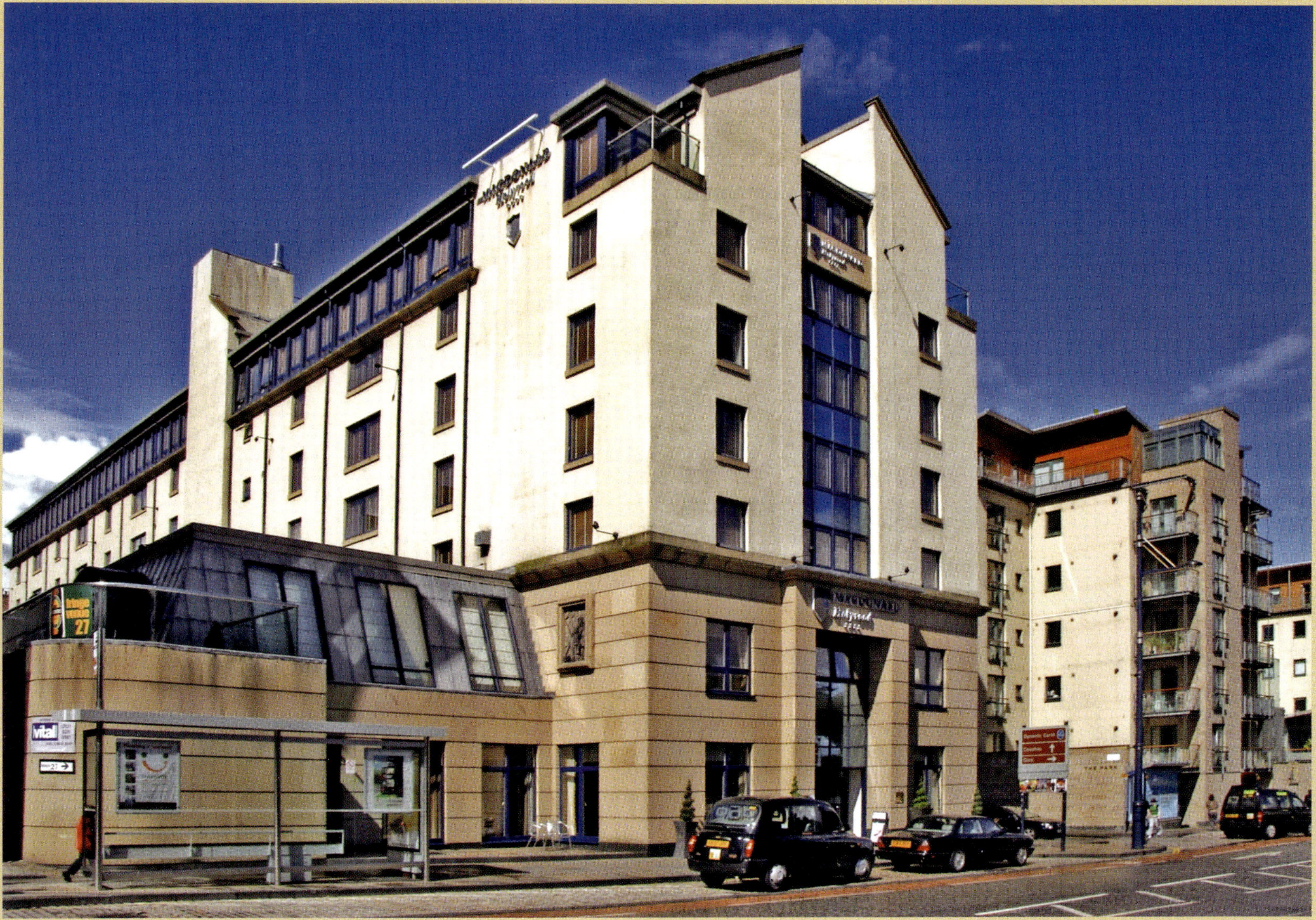

The Macdonald Hotel, at No. 81 Holyrood Road, was designed by H. Roger Legge and opened on 3 October 2000. Morrison Construction Ltd. was the main contractor for the building which has eight floors and 156 rooms. The hotel forms part of the worldwide Macdonald Hotels and Resorts. *Photograph by Peter Stubbs.*

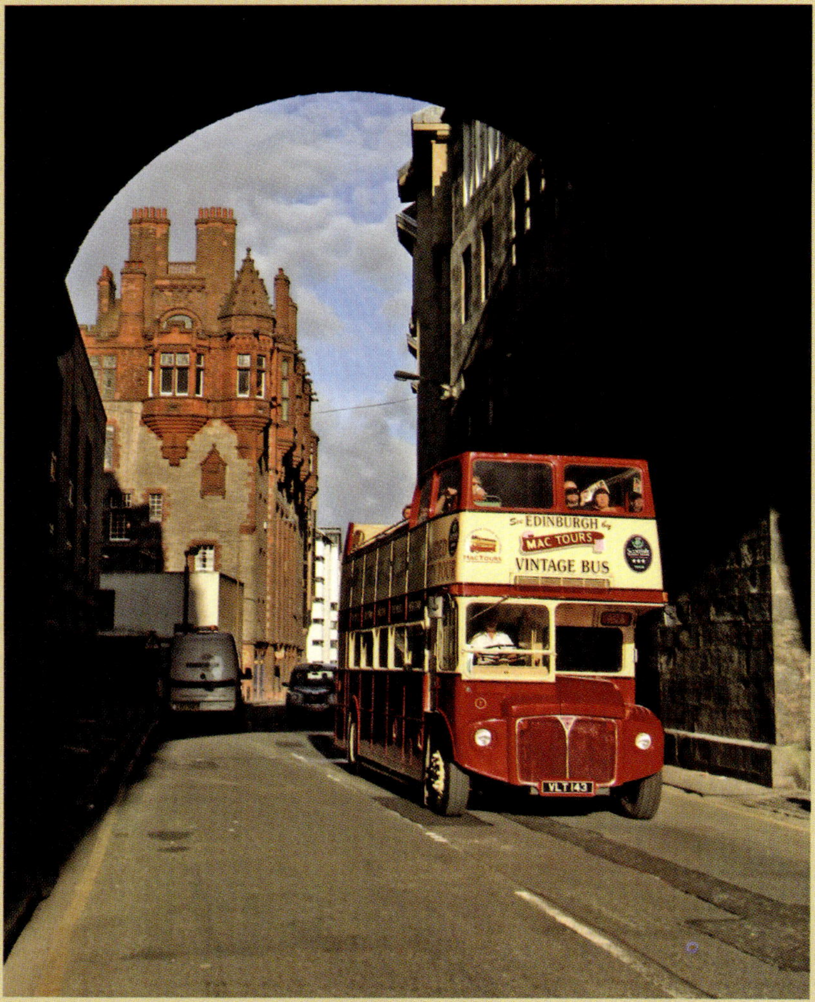

Above. Mac Tours' open-topped bus makes its way westwards in the Cowgate beneath the arch of George IV Bridge. The ornate red sandstone building is the Solicitors' Library.

Right. Also in the Cowgate is the sixteenth-century Magdalen Chapel later converted into the Convening Hall of the Incorporation of Hammermen. The tower was added in 1625. *Photographs by Peter Stubbs.*

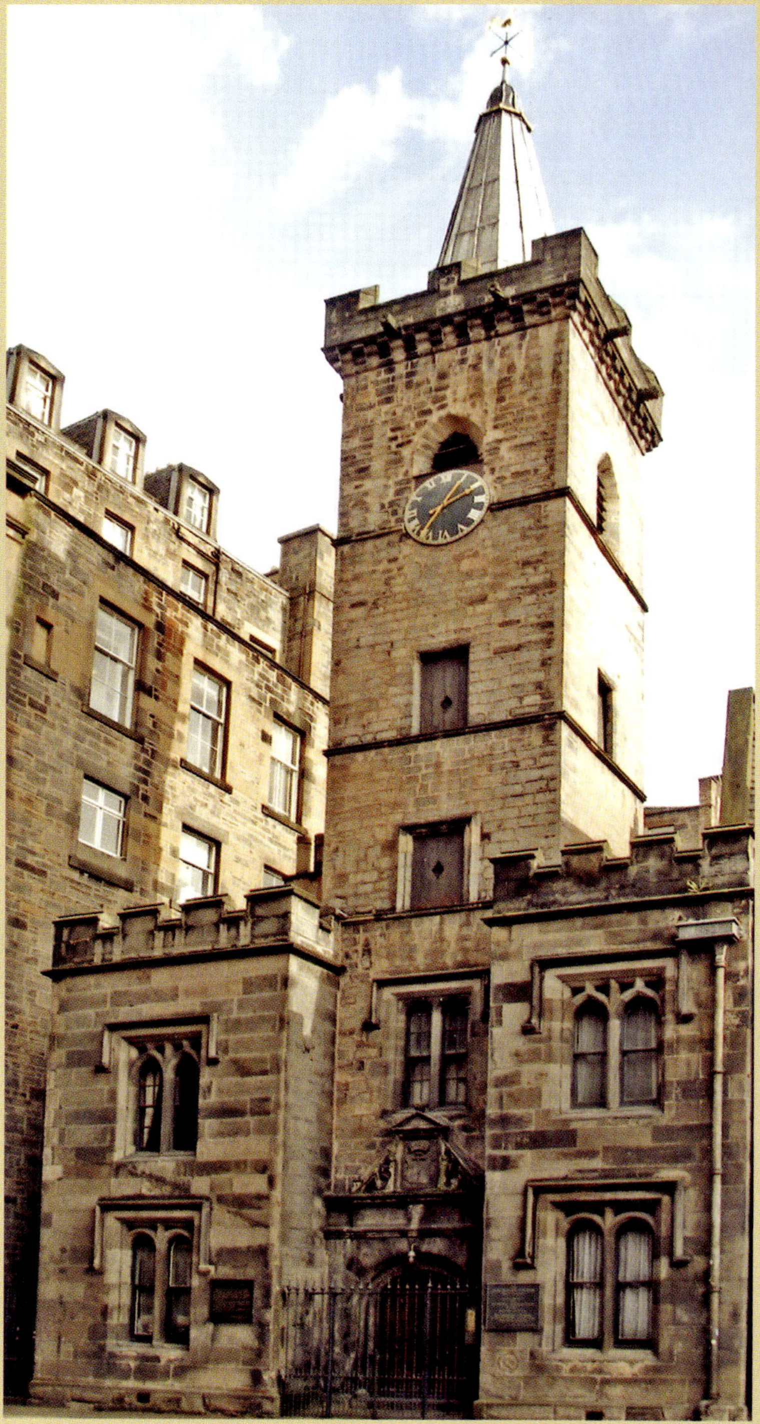

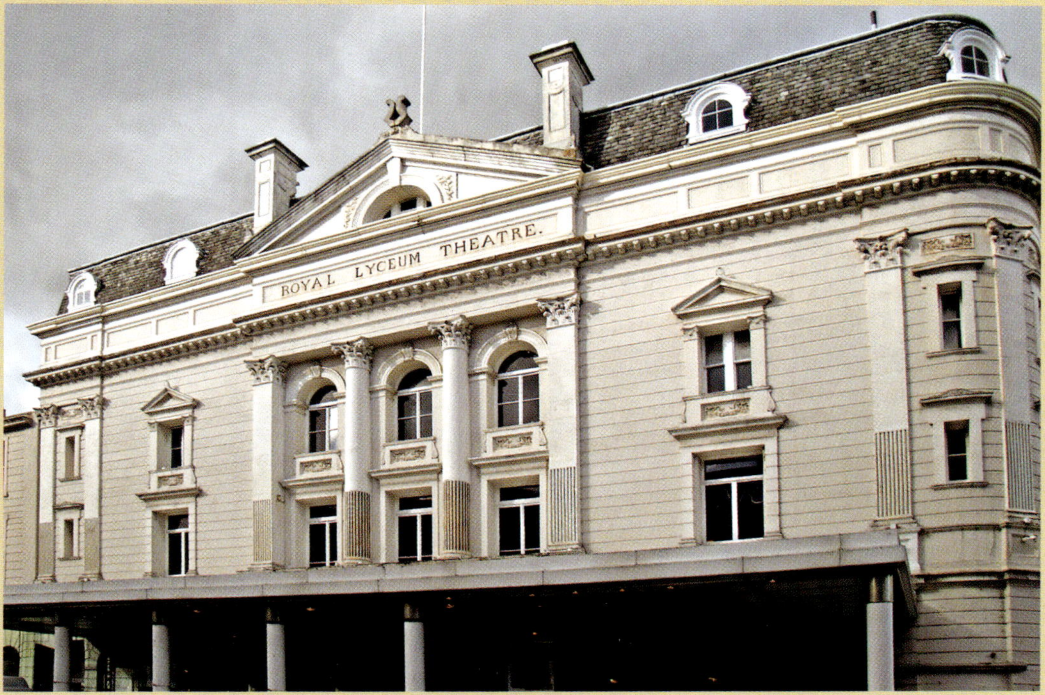

Left. The Royal Lyceum Theatre in Grindlay Street was designed by C. F. Phipps for Howard & Wyndham in 1883, originally to seat 1,950 theatre-goers.

Below left. New Uberior House, part of Princes Exchange, was completed in 2001 for the Bank of Scotland on the north-east side of Earl Grey Street, on a site which had lain derelict for many years. It was designed by PJMP, architects and the main contractor was Skanska Construction.

Below. The Traverse Theatre in Cambridge Street was opened on 3 July 1992 on the site of the former Highland Church. It was designed by the architects, Nicholas Groves Raines of Liberton House. *Photographs by Peter Stubbs.*

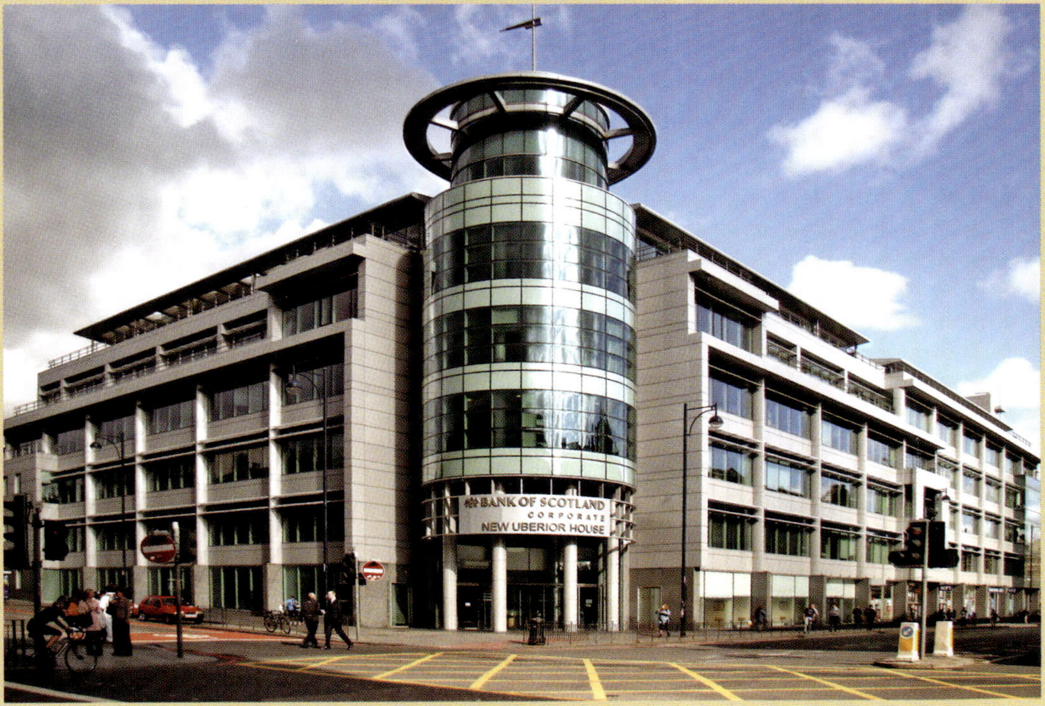

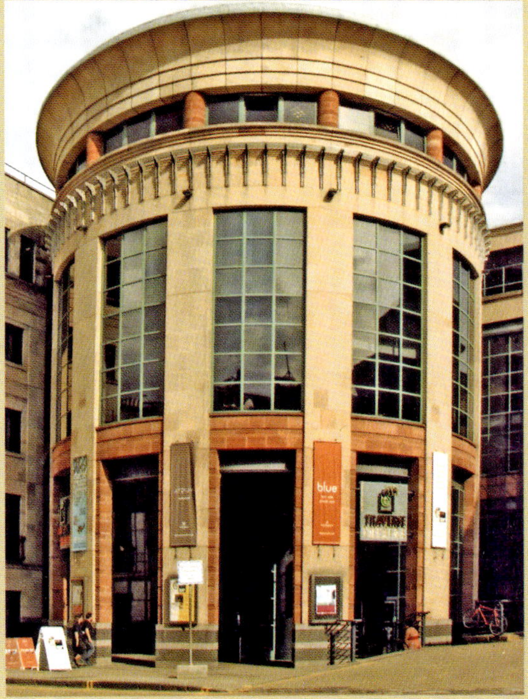

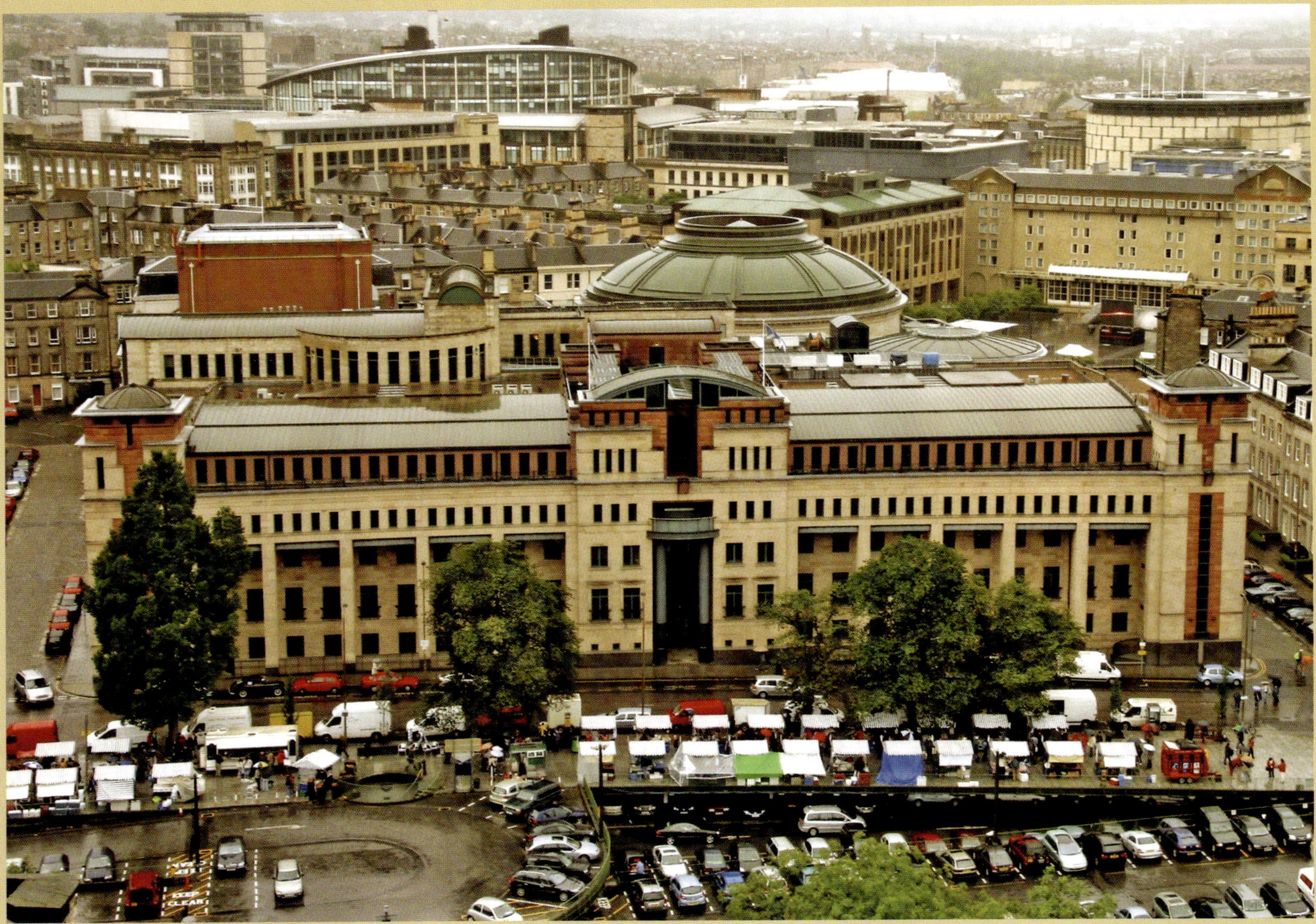

The view westwards from Edinburgh Castle is dominated by the elegant, symmetrical lines of Saltire Court in Castle Terrace. The stalls in the foreground are for the Farmers' Market. The upper part of the picture includes, from left to right: Edinburgh Quay; the Scottish Widows curved building in Morrison Street; the dome of the Usher Hall; the Sheraton Grand Hotel in Festival Square; and the drum-shaped Edinburgh International Conference Centre. *Photograph by Peter Stubbs.*

PART 4

BRISTO

GEORGE SQUARE

LAURISTON PLACE

TOLLCROSS

LOTHIAN ROAD

Part 4 has 36 illustrations covering the area around Bristo, Lauriston and Tollcross. It is therefore peripheral to the Old Town rather than a central part of it. This Introduction has two photographs from the 1950s: firstly, a transport photograph showing the No. 23 tram turning into Lauriston Place from Forrest Road; and, secondly, an almost-aerial view of George Square looking to the north-west to include the old Royal Infirmary and Edinburgh Castle.

After the Introduction, two pages are devoted to Parker's Stores in Charles Street where many Edinburgh people went to buy overalls and other work-related clothing, as well as items of drapery and furniture. In addition to their main shop at Bristo, Parker's had several branches throughout Scotland. The descendants of the Parker family have retained a considerable archive of items relating to the shop, including several photographs taken during the firm's participation in the various fund-raising Infirmary Pageants. There are also more formal photographs taken nearby of the McEwan Hall, George Watson's Ladies' College and the colonial premiers visiting the Students' Union in 1907.

The ancient thoroughfares of Potterrow and Marshall Street were greatly altered, with widespread demolition, in the mid-1960s, to create a piece of concrete roadway which, even today, looks unsure of where it is supposed to be going. Fortunately, the eastern section of Marshall Street was largely unaffected, including the 1937 tenement in which the Tait family ran Dutch House, the china merchants, from 1956 to 2005. The recent discovery of an old photograph of the same corner in the 1920s has led to an interesting story about how this corner of Marshall Street has developed over the years.

Lauriston Place, with the old Royal Infirmary on

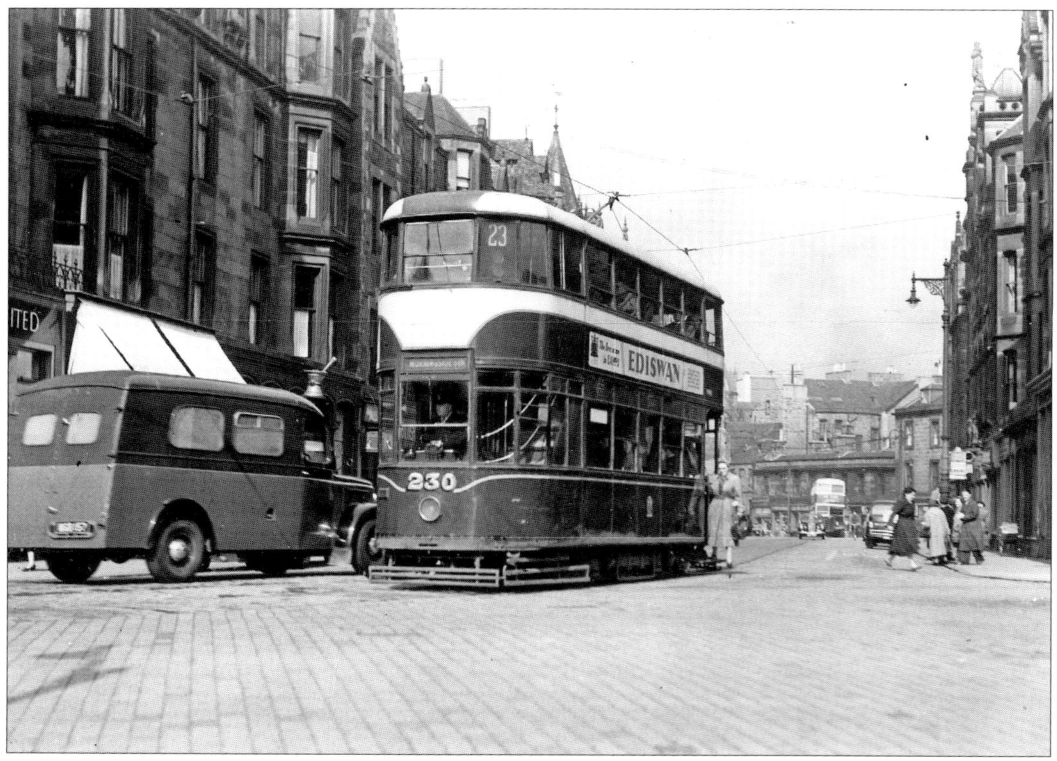

Electric tram No. 230 on service No. 23 en route for Morningside Station slows down at the bend from Forrest Road into Lauriston Place, enabling the lady to alight before the stop outside the old Royal Infirmary. The advertisement on the side of the tram is for Ediswan – 'the first name in lamps'. In the mid-1950s, when this photograph was taken, Forrest Road had two-way traffic and the new Museum of Scotland had not even reached the drawing board. *Courtesy of A. W. Brotchie.*

one side has been a prolific source of images. The general view of the clock-tower and the surgical wards is augmented by four photographs showing the hospital in the early 1900s and 1920s. There are views of the ironing room of the laundry, the principal dispensing room, and the very latest equipment installed in the Radiological Department in 1926. There are also photographs of the royal visit by King George V and Queen Mary, including a special arch constructed from fire-fighting equipment outside Lauriston Fire Station. George Heriot's School, on the other side of Lauriston Place, is also included, particularly the 1932 photograph of Graf Zeppelin flying over the school in one of its peace-time, sight-seeing flights.

Tollcross, first recorded in 1439, is connected to the Old Town by High Riggs which dates from 1387. The photographs assembled are in two groups. Firstly, there is the Methodist Central Hall with emphasis on its dual role as a concert hall. Excerpts from a 1913 programme give many of the artistes and details of the works and songs (with the words) included in the evening's entertainment. The second group of Tollcross photographs relates to transport scenes from the 1950s. These evocative images not only give information about the tramway system but include peripheral information on road signage, street furniture, shops, and the boys of George Heriot's School boarding a tram in Lauriston Place to take them down to their playing fields at Goldenacre.

The final two pages have photographs of Lothian Road. The first is a transport picture, possibly taken on 27 May 1956 on the last day of service No.14. The others are of the Usher Hall, designed by J. Stockdale Harrison of Leicester, and the Highland Church in Cambridge Street which was demolished for the construction of the Traverse Theatre.

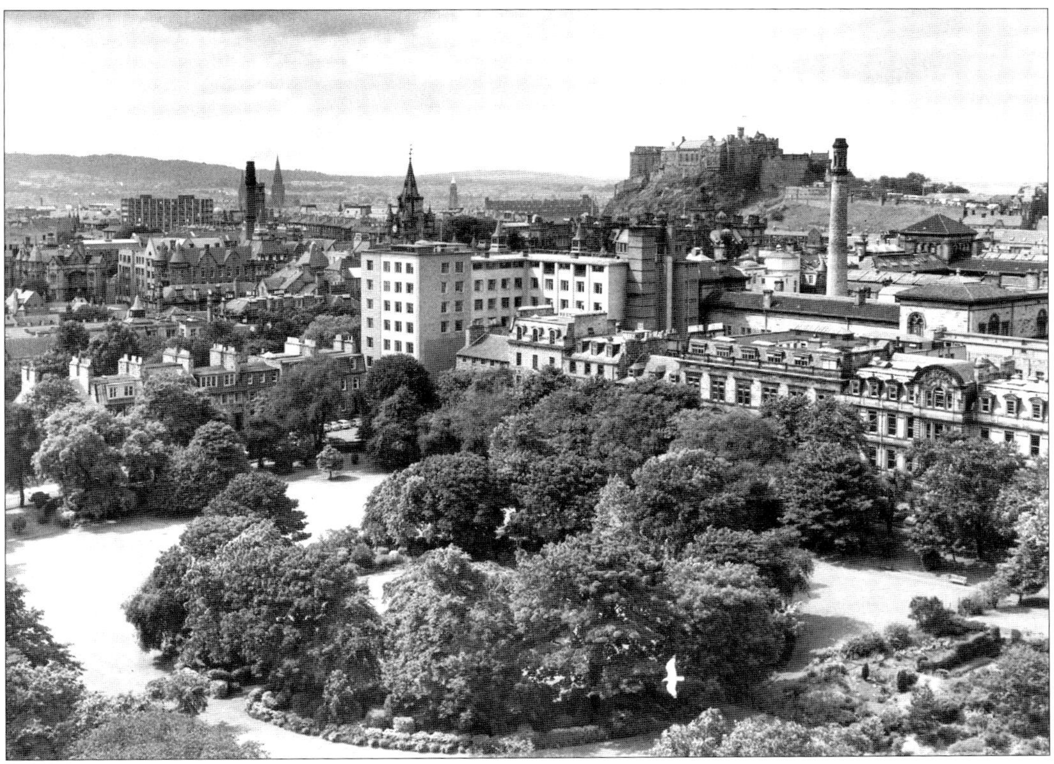

The entire north and south sides, and part of the east side, of George Square have been completely redeveloped (some would say ruined) by twentieth-century development for Edinburgh University. This late 1950s photograph shows, on the left, part of the west side still intact, but with several alterations. The original square was laid out in 1766 by James Brown with terraced houses of uniform size and height on all four sides. *Photograph by John K. Wilkie.*

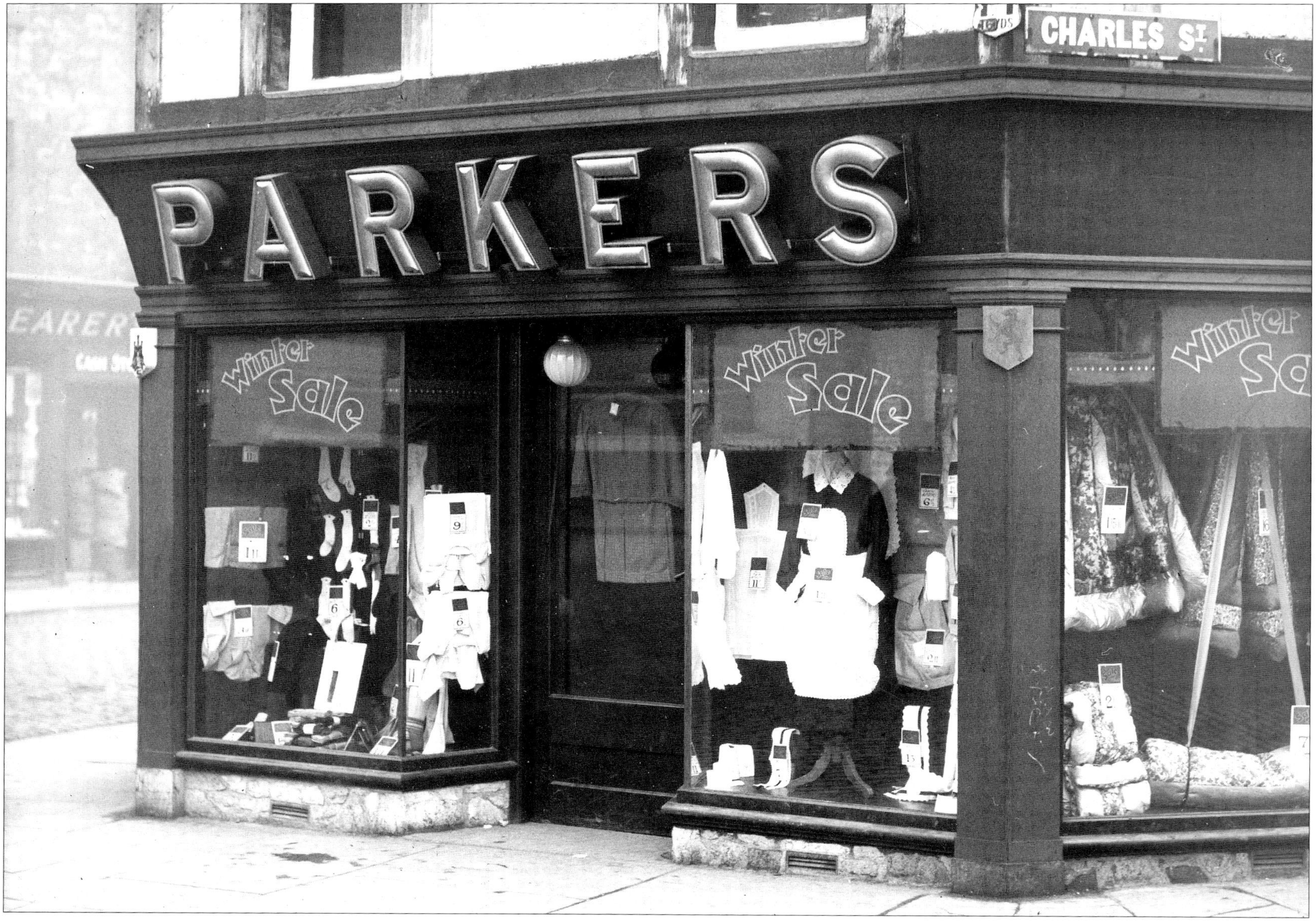

Robert Parker, the founder of Parker's Stores, came to Edinburgh from London shortly after the end of the First World War, in which he had served in the Royal Navy. He probably started off by selling army surplus supplies in the shop (seen here) on the corner of Bristo Street and Charles Street. As the business developed, he was joined by two of his brothers, Fred and George. By 1930 they were firmly established, not only as general drapers, but also as furniture retailers. In addition, they had a Gents' Tailoring Department which offered made-to-measure suits from 30 shillings (£1.50p), and for the large sum of 75 shillings (£3.75p) a 'Real Harris Tweed Suit'. By the 1940s, the business consisted of several separate areas: the Bristo Street complex; branches at Leith, Gorgie, Buckhaven, Methil and Galashiels; a hardware shop in Nicolson Square; and a wholesale business and manufacturing company in Motherwell. Parker's foothold in the Bristo area was threatened in the 1960s by widespread redevelopment by Edinburgh University. By that time, the principal partners in the business were nearing retirement and the opportunity was taken to close the business in the early 1970s.
Courtesy of Pat and Tony Winkle.

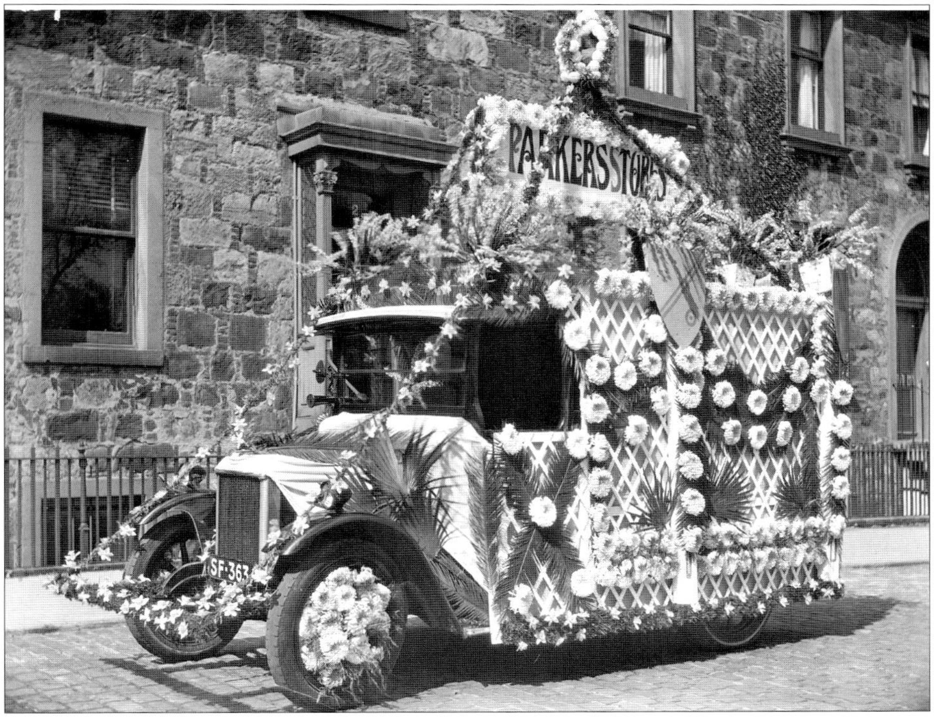

Left. Parker's Stores, in common with many other shops, works and offices, contributed time and money to support the various Infirmary Pageants. The van, bedecked with flowers, is thought to have been photographed in George Square, near to Parker's main store at Bristo.

Below left. The location of this photograph is uncertain but it is definitely of the Royal Infirmary Pageant held on Saturday 28 May 1927. The slogans are: 'Scotland for Ever' and 'Every Copper Helps'. The Royal Infirmary published details of its income and expenditure each year: in the year ending 30 September 1926 the 'ordinary' income was £107,200 and the 'ordinary' expenditure was £129,900, leaving a deficit of £22,700.

Below. The man who advertised Sweet-Orr Overalls formed an integral part of Parker's involvement in the pageant. Parker's was probably best known to a lot of Edinburgh people for their work clothing, such as dungarees and overalls. Their advertisement of the day was headed, 'Sweet-Orr Overalls and Trousers – The Strongest Work Clothes in the World', and continued : 'TUG-OF-WAR TWEED TROUSERS, BIB AND BRACE, BOILER SUITS, JACKETS AND SHIRTS. COMFORT & DURABILITY. MEN!!! YOU SHOULD WEAR THESE OVERALLS. OVERALLS ARE LIKE WORKING MEN – SOME ARE BETTER THAN OTHERS. BEST BY TEST.

All photographs courtesy of Pat and Tony Winkle.

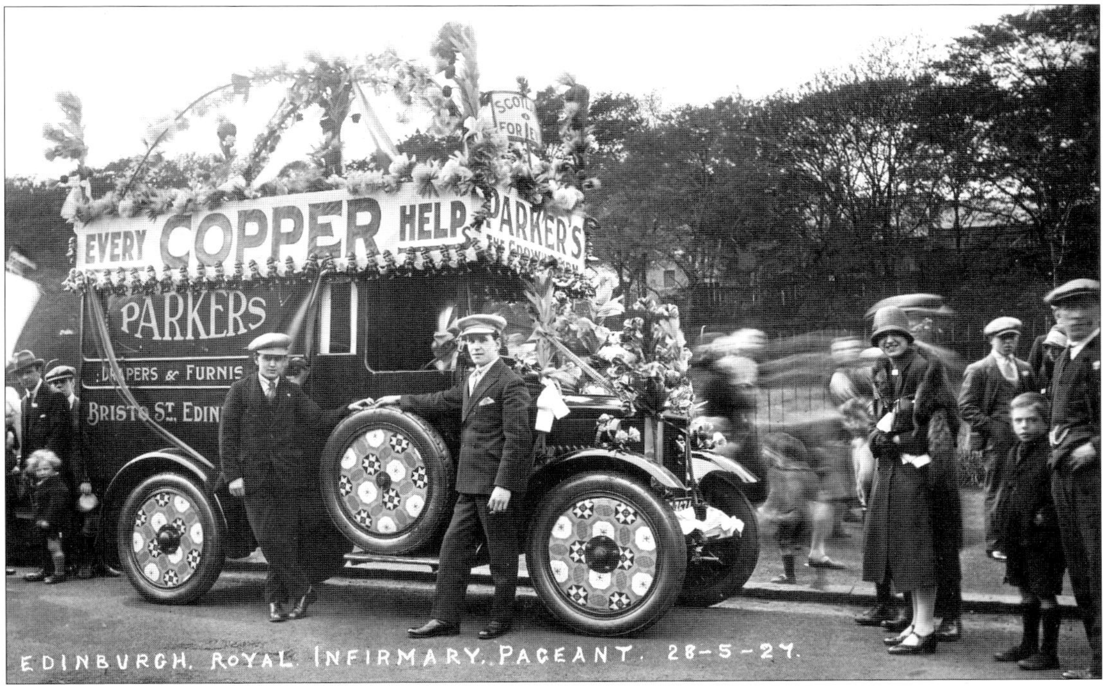

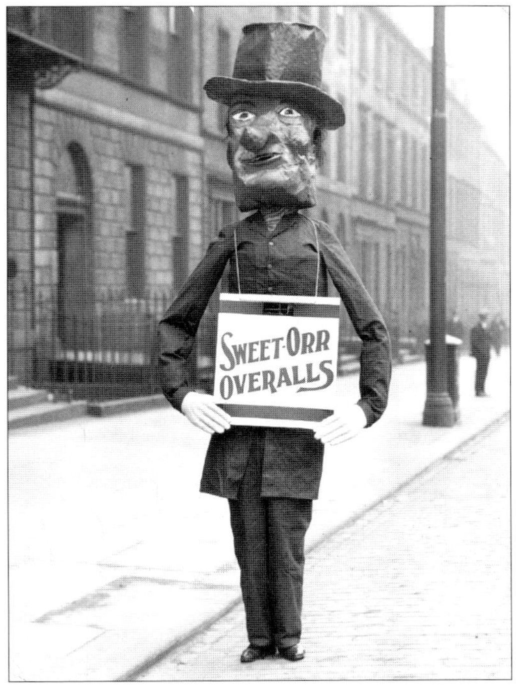

Right. The McEwan Hall in Teviot Place was designed by R. Rowand Anderson in 1874 for Edinburgh University, and built between 1888 and 1897 on what was formerly Park Street. The main contractors were: W. & J. Kirkwood, builders; Barton & Sons, plumbers; Goodwin, Jardine & Co., ironworkers; and Coutts & Cameron, glaziers. The building was named after its sponsor, William McEwan, of the brewing family, who was the MP for Edinburgh Central.
From The Student, *published in 1897.*

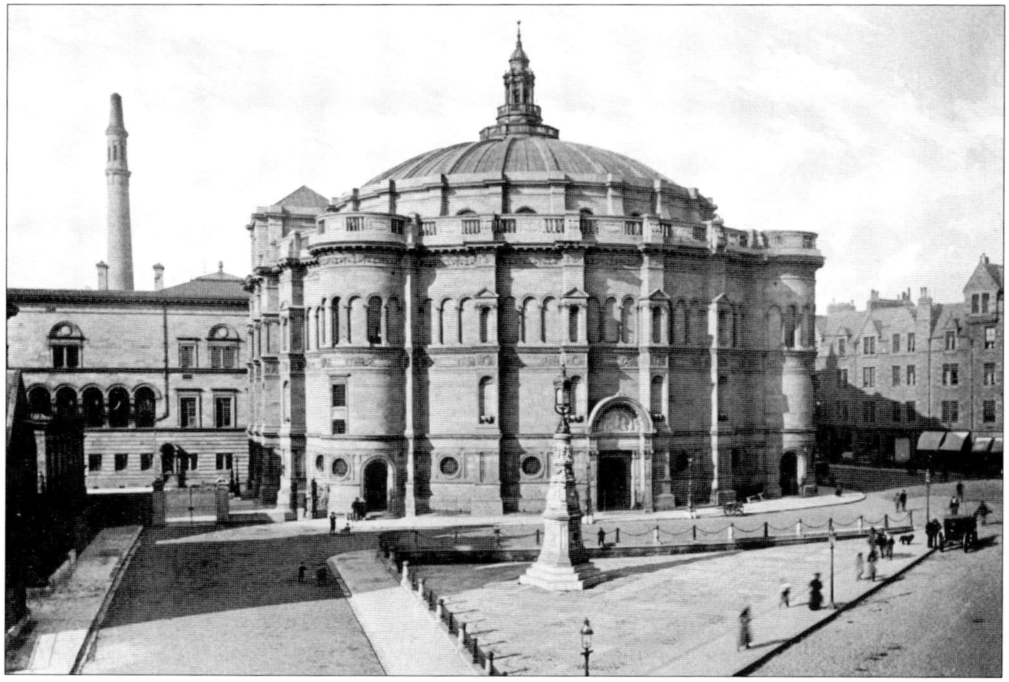

Below. The colonial premiers at Edinburgh University Union on 10 May 1907. Front seat: nearest to the camera, General Louis Botha; furthest from the camera, Dr Jameson. Back seat: nearest to the camera, Mr Deakin; furthest from the camera, Sir Joseph Ward. *Malcolm Cant Collection.*

Lower. King George V was crowned at Westminster Abbey on 22 June 1911. He is seen here at Edinburgh University Union in July of the same year. *Malcolm Cant Collection.*

Right. George Watson's Ladies' College was established in Melville House in George Square in 1871. Over a period of 40 years, extensive redevelopment took place as the school grew in popularity. The architects were MacGibbon & Ross and later George Washington Browne. *Malcolm Cant Collection.*

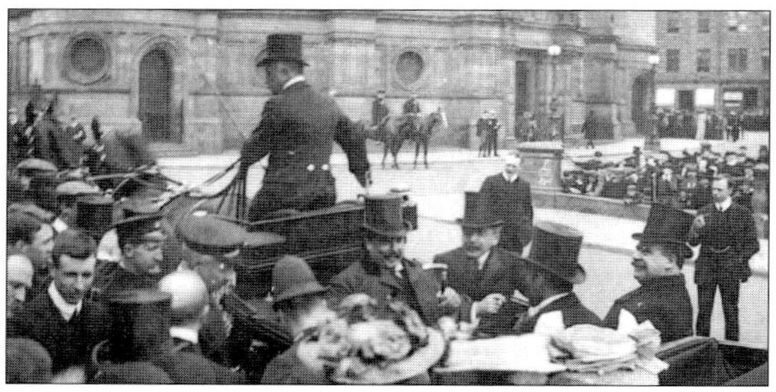

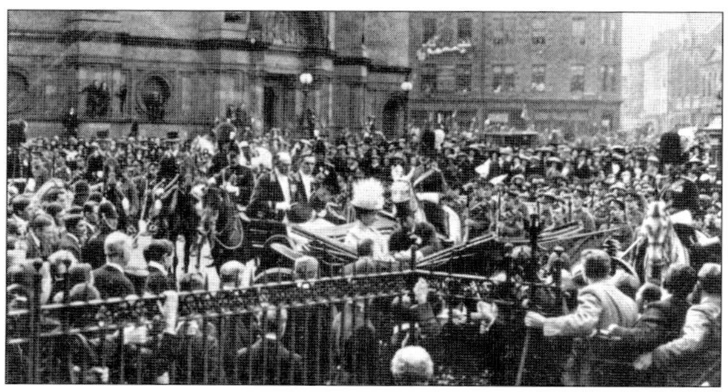

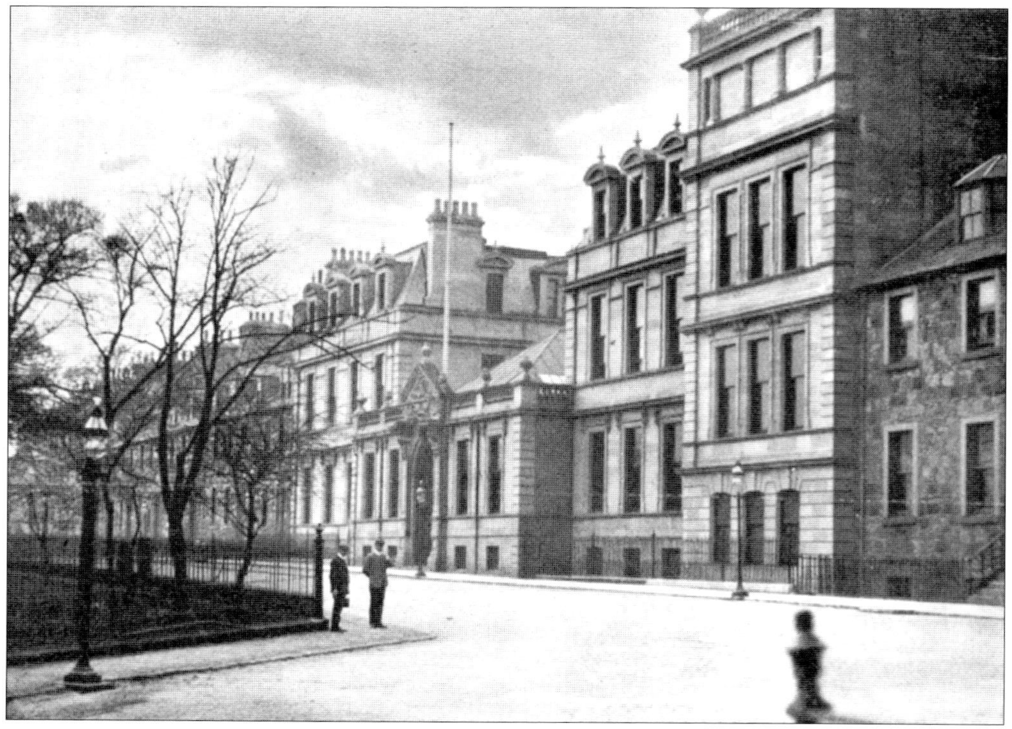

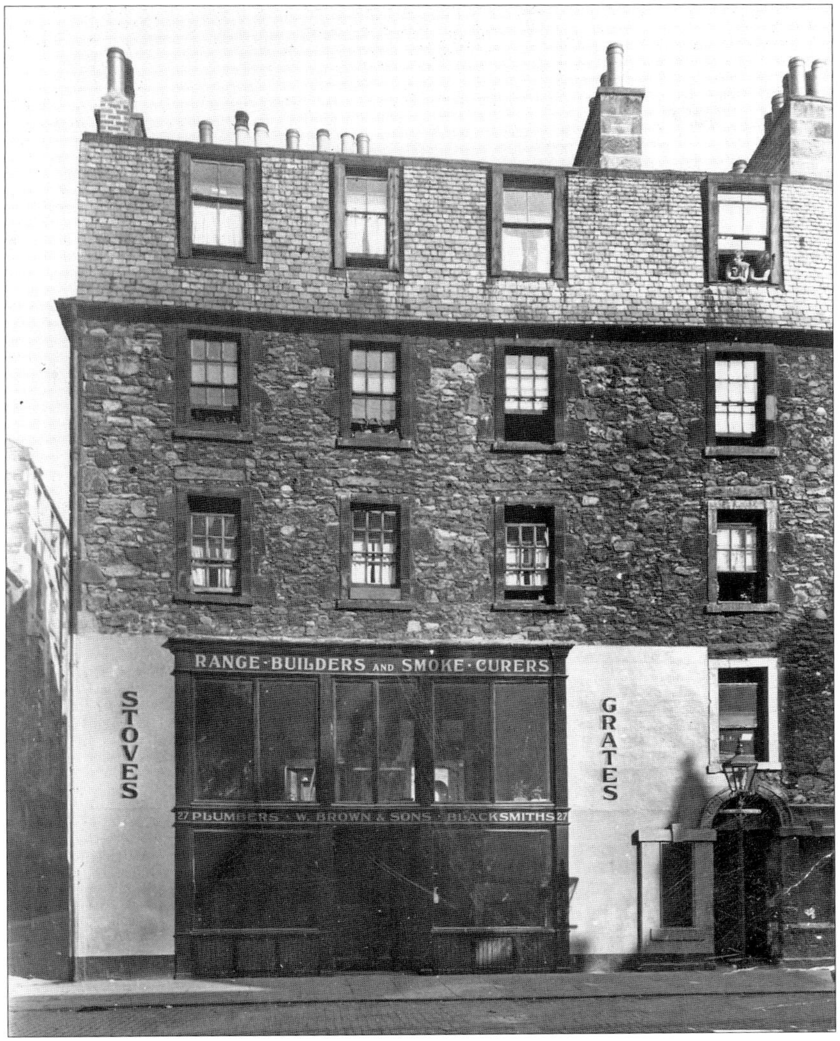

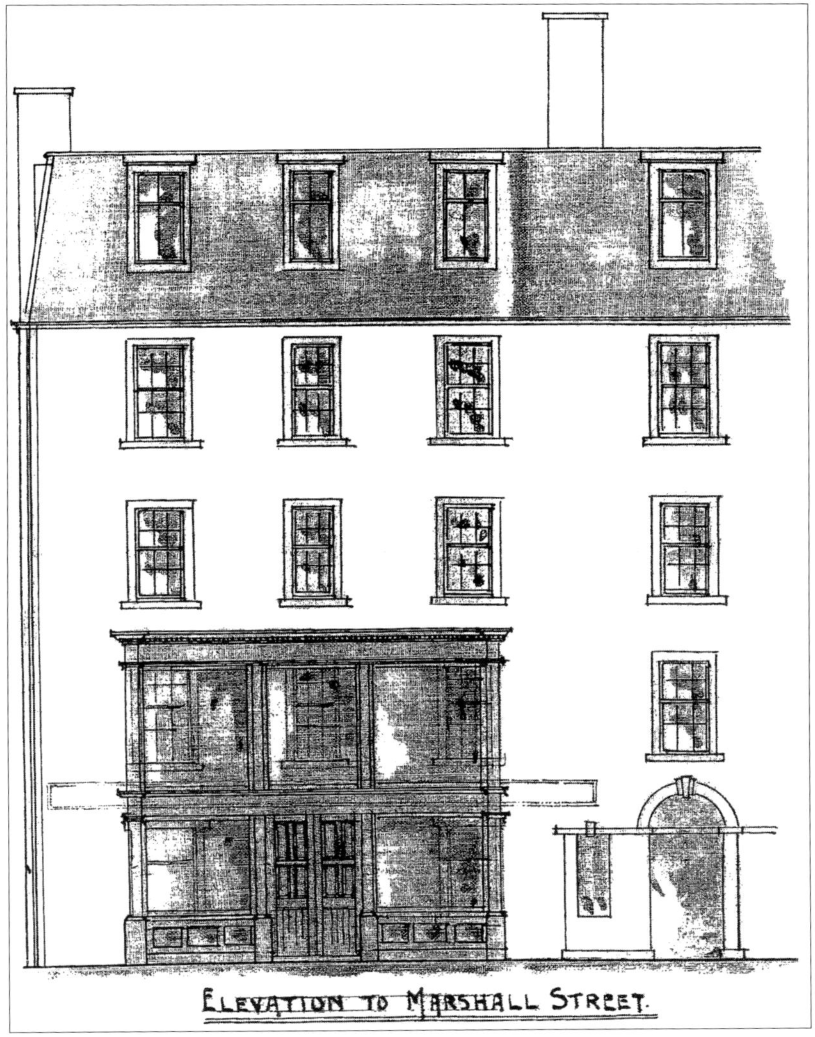

Marshall Street, in Bristo, was proposed in 1866 as part of a general road improvement scheme in an area of old properties to the west of Nicolson Square. It takes its name from John Marshall, a surgeon, who owned property nearby. Originally, Marshall Street ran eastwards from Bristo Street through the junction with Potterrow, and on to Nicolson Square. However, in the mid-1960s the entire western half of Marshall Street was demolished. The photograph (*above left*) shows No. 27 Marshall Street sometime between 1924 and 1937. In 1900, the owner, Hugh Munro of No. 31 Nicolson Square petitioned the Dean of Guild Court for permission to redevelop the roof space into flats. The architect was R. W. Bolster of Gilmore Place and the work went ahead as can be seen in the photograph where two people are at the window of the new flats. In 1911, a new owner, William Brown, the builder and blacksmith, also applied to the Dean of Guild to make alterations to the basement, ground floor and first floor, including a completely new shop front. The architect's drawing (*above right*) shows the new frontage and the earlier conversion of the roof space, neither of which would have met the approval of today's conservationists. In 1937 the property was in such poor condition that Edinburgh Corporation applied to demolish the old tenement and replace it with one similar in size and style. William Brown, the builder, moved back into the basement and ground floor until 1955. In 1956 the premises were bought by George Tait who converted the ground floor into a shop specialising in china and glassware, Dutch House, which became a well-known Edinburgh landmark until 2005 when the family retired from the business. The premises are now occupied as a restaurant.

Photograph courtesy of Malcolm Cant Collection.
Architect's drawing courtesy of Edinburgh City Archives.

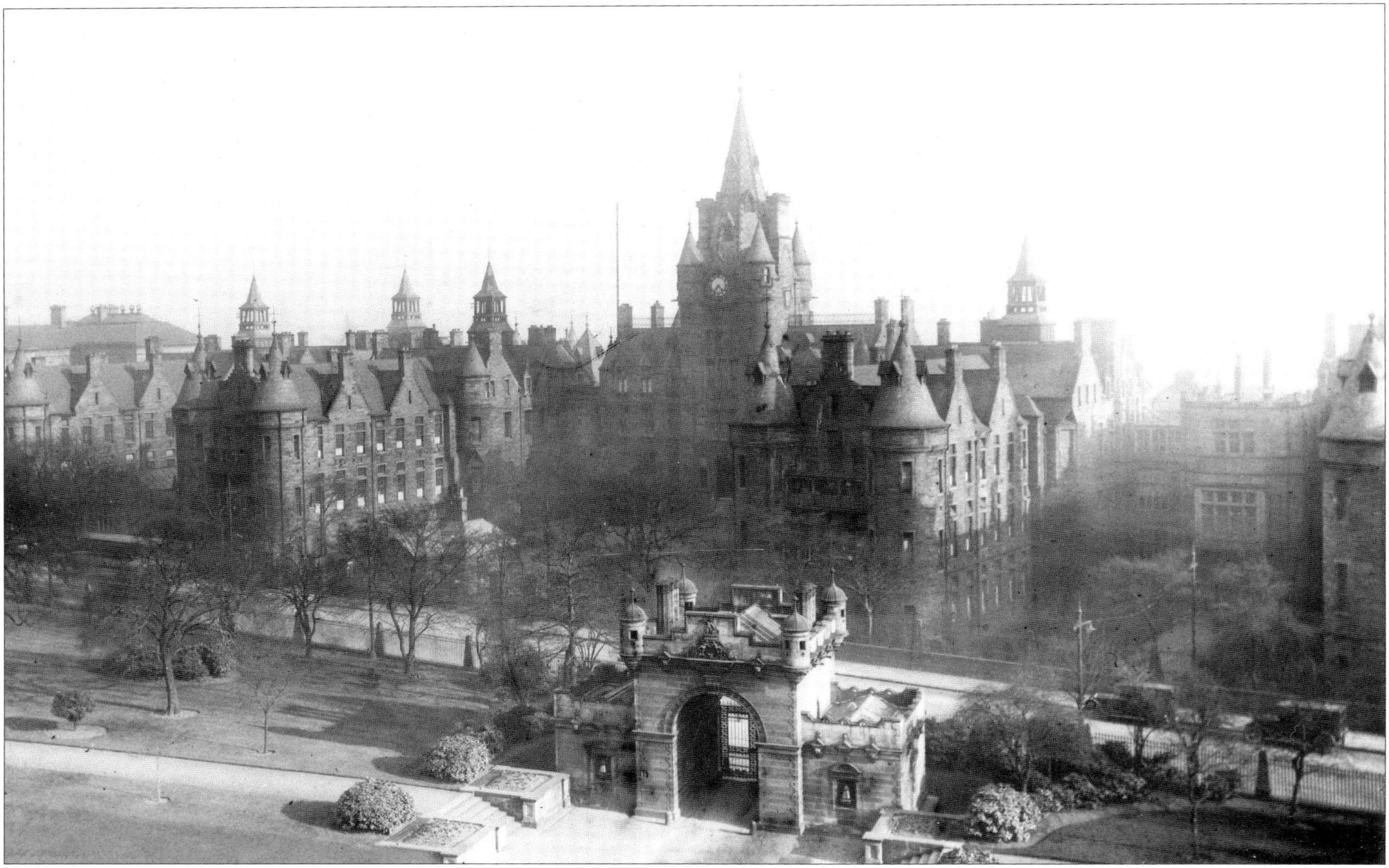

The foreground of the picture shows the 1829 archway gatehouse, with the tiny, flanking lodges, designed by William H. Playfair at the south entrance to George Heriot's School. The archway was intended to be for pedestrian and vehicular access but in response to modern traffic requirements, flanking pedestrian-only gates have recently been constructed from Lauriston Place. The new stonework and the railings are an exact copy of the original. The main school building was constructed from 1628.

The range of buildings with the central clock-tower was designed by David Bryce and begun in 1872 as the (then) new Royal Infirmary of Edinburgh. It replaced two buildings, the old Royal Infirmary, which stood about the position of South Bridge School in Infirmary Street, and the Surgical Hospital, north of Drummond Street. Hardly discernible in the courtyard in front of the clock-tower, the low Italianate lodge, by the architect, John Lessels, does not seem to make quite the same visual impact as the gatehouse to George Heriot's School.

After David Bryce died in 1876, the work on the infirmary was continued by his nephew, John Bryce. The principles of open layout and good ventilation, expounded by Florence Nightingale, were followed and approved by her. The buildings seen in the picture were occupied as the Surgical Hospital. The Medical Hospital and a whole host of other buildings including the Nurses Home (1890) and the Simpson Maternity Pavilion (1935) were built to the south and the west. When Edinburgh's new Royal Infirmary was built at Little France, the Lauriston Place site was sold, and is presently being redeveloped as Quartermile, a most interesting mix of private housing and public spaces. The main downside is the loss of some important historical buildings.
Malcolm Cant Collection.

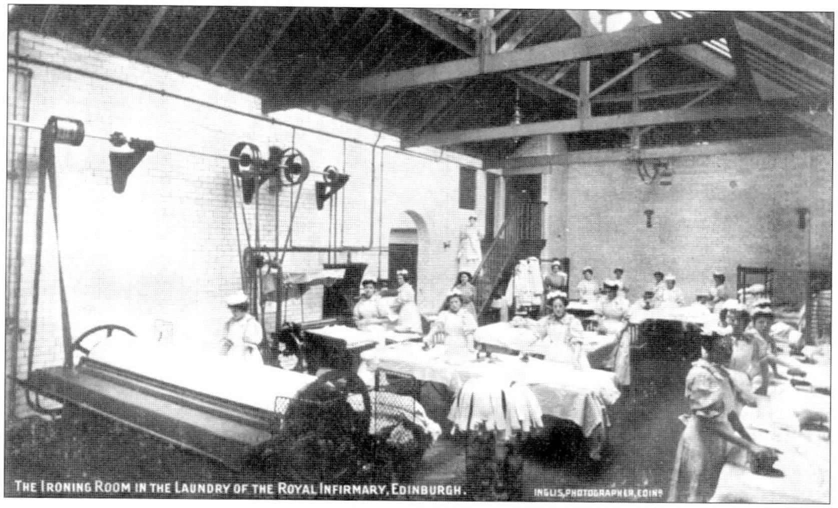

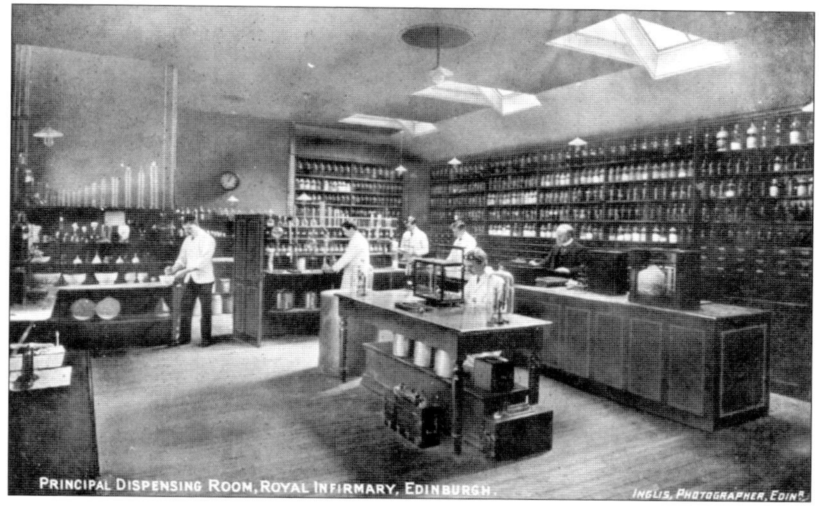

Above left. The ironing room in the laundry of the Royal Infirmary had a fairly large staff in 1908 when this photograph was taken. The large roller and the smaller one are powered by belts from the overhead traction. The sprocket wheel near the centre of the picture has only a very rudimentary guard. Electric irons have not yet been introduced. *Malcolm Cant Collection.*

Above right. In 1909 the principal dispensing room of the Royal Infirmary obviously lacked the huge range of medicines available to pharmacists today. The pharmacy was not only responsible for preparing and issuing medicines but also for the purchase and supply of medical gases and for buying bandages, dressings and surgical instruments. *Malcolm Cant Collection.*

Below left. Ambulance men, nurses and doctors pose for the camera in this undated photograph at the entrance to the Surgical Out-Patient Department which was located on the east side of the hospital, in the narrow roadway off Lauriston Place parallel to Middle Meadow Walk. The ambulance is from the St Andrew's Ambulance Association. *Courtesy of the family of the late Charles J. Smith.*

Below right. In 1926 the Radiological Department of the Royal Infirmary probably housed the most up-to-date equipment available for the treatment of patients. On 9 October 1926 a new radiological department, designed by Thomas Turnbull to meet the requirements of Dr J. Woodburn Morison, the infirmary radiologist, was opened by the Duke of York (later King George VI). *Malcolm Cant Collection.*

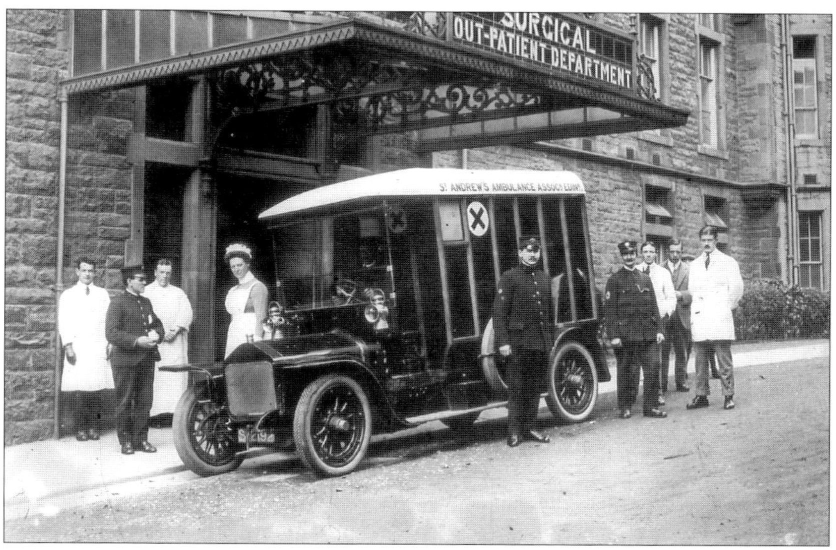

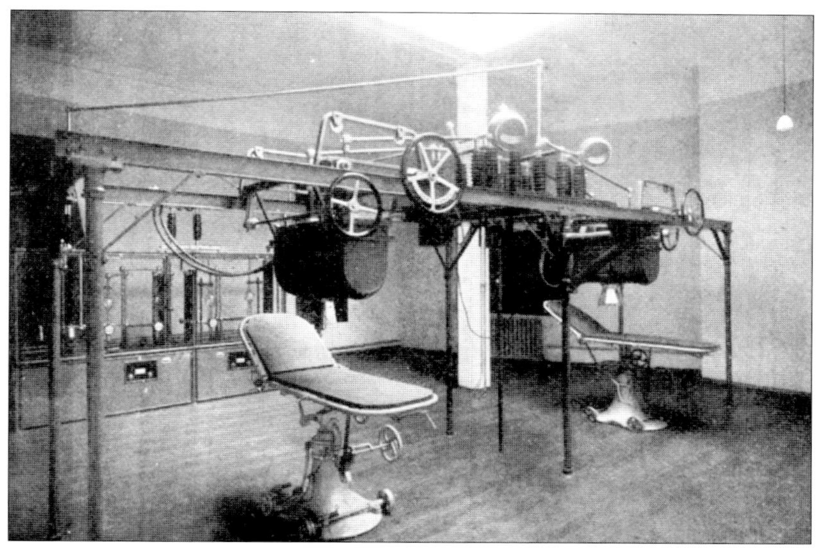

Right. During 1911, the newly crowned King George V undertook several engagements during his Edinburgh tour. He is seen here accompanied by Queen Mary in the royal carriage as it passes along Lauriston Place, near the Vennel. The corner premises are occupied by John Croall & Sons Ltd., funeral directors.

Below right. The royal entourage reaches the gates of the Royal Infirmary of Edinburgh where one of the wards was named after Queen Mary. In the year of the royal visit, the Infirmary made a point of publishing information on its financial position, emphasising that the large number of patients (5,882) from country towns and parishes had cost over £25,000 and that the contributions from the country districts had amounted to only £11,485.

Below. On 19 July 1911, the Edinburgh Fire Brigade rose to the occasion with a grand arch on the processional route, outside Lauriston Fire Station, which was opened in 1900.
All Malcolm Cant Collection.

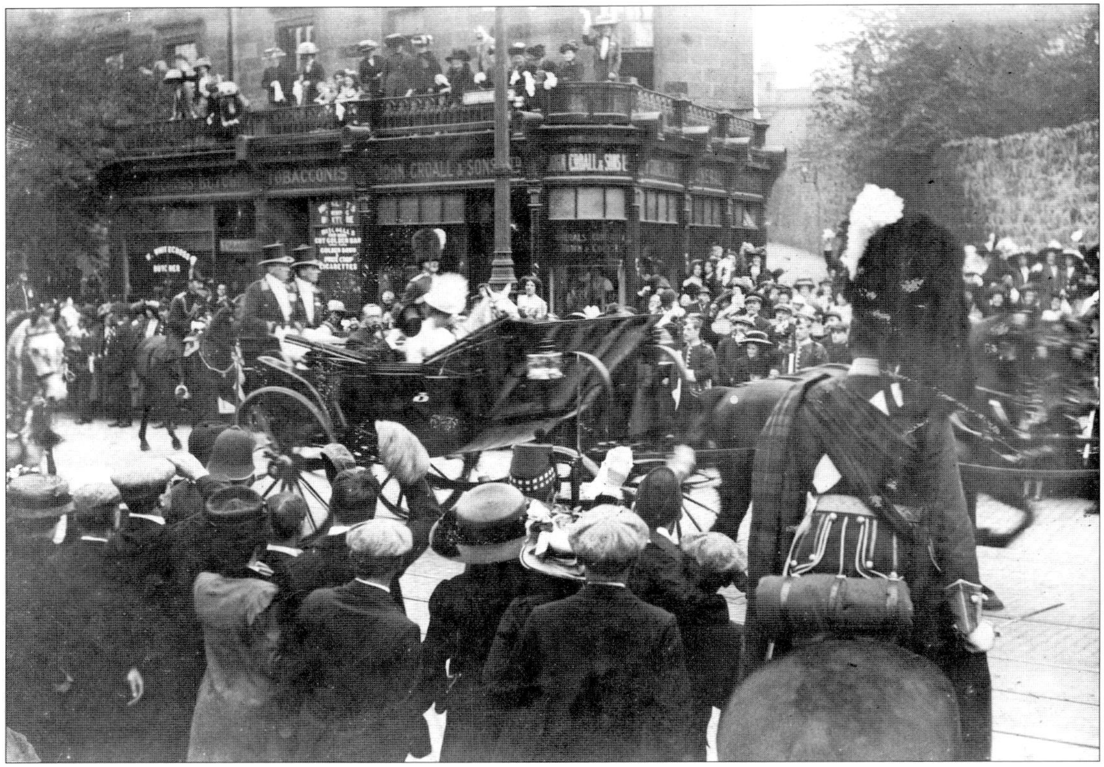

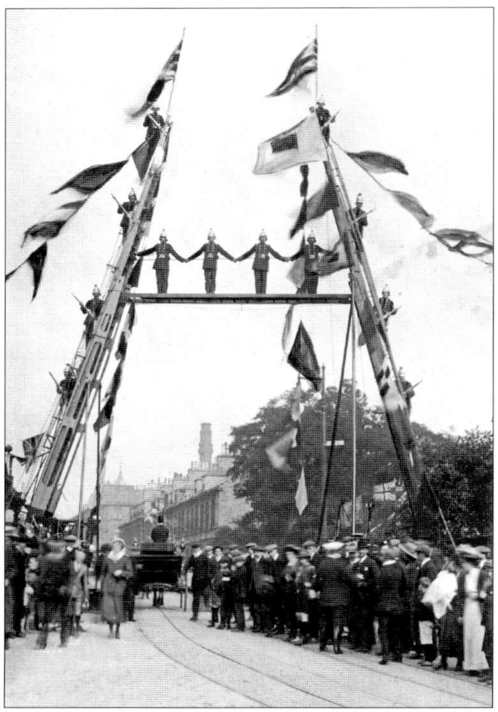

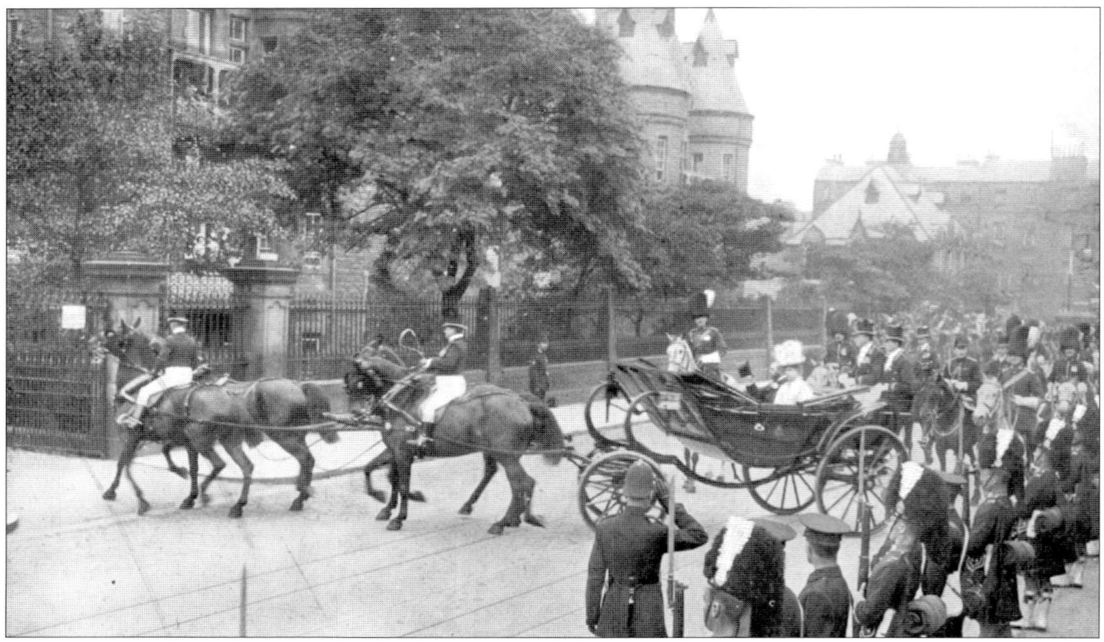

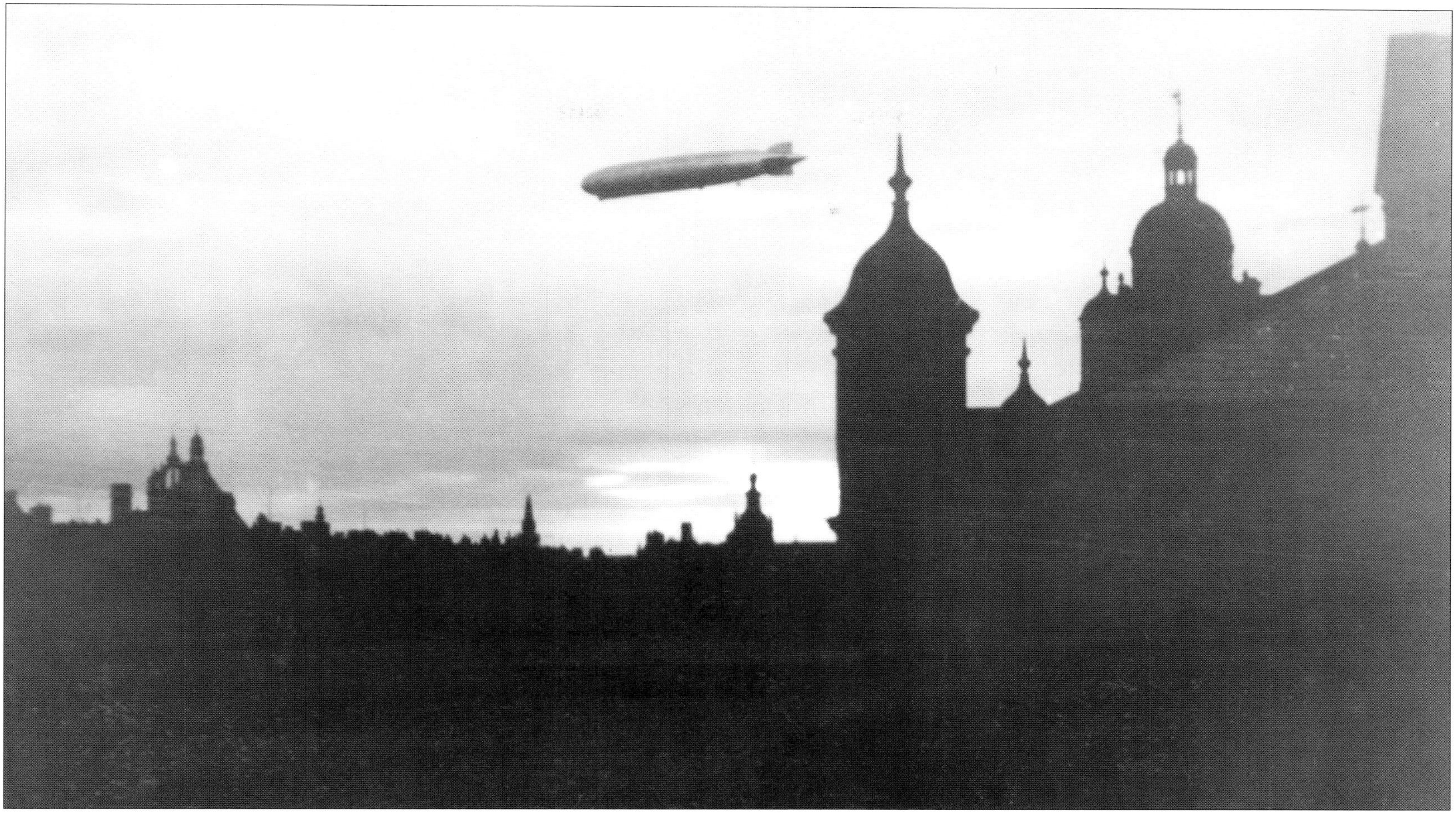

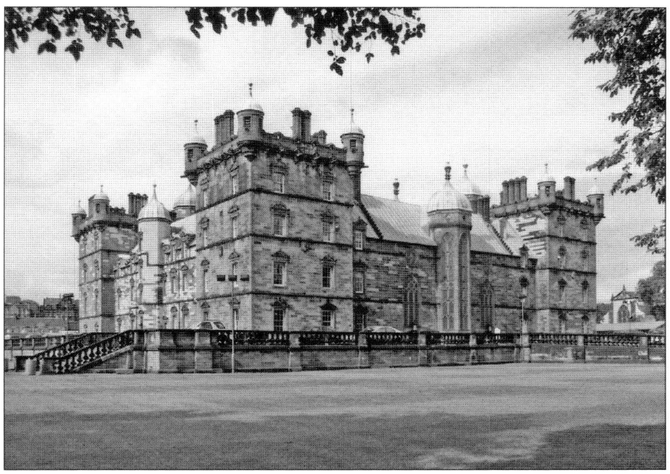

Left. George Heriot's Hospital is now a co-educational primary and secondary school. Work on the building was started in 1628 by William Wallace, Master Mason to the Crown, but it was not finished until about 1650. The money to build it came from George Heriot, royal goldsmith and banker, who left the sum of nearly £24,000 to build a charity school for the upbringing and education of 'puire fatherless bairnes, friemens sones of that Toune of Edinburgh'. Owing to various delays in the building work, the first boys were not admitted until 1659. *Photograph by Peter Stubbs.*

Above. Graf Zeppelin is seen flying over the north section of George Heriot's School with the outline of the Old Town in the background. The unidentified photographer recorded the picture as having been taken at 5.30 a.m. on 3 July 1932. Zeppelins had, of course, been over Edinburgh in bombing raids during the First World War (1914-18) but on this occasion flight No. 254 was definitely on a sight-seeing trip only. According to *Graf Zeppelin Flights to England* by John Duggan and published by the Zeppelin Study Group in 1998, the route of flight No. 254 included Edinburgh between 05.10 and 05.16 on 3 July 1932. *Malcolm Cant Collection.*

Right. The Central Hall in Earl Grey Street has been the home of the Methodist Church since it was built in 1901 to designs by the architects, Dunn & Findlay. The entrance in West Tollcross, flanked by Ionic columns, opens directly onto a flight of stairs leading to the hall above which has a curved and ribbed ceiling. Most of the ground floor facing Earl Grey Street was constructed as retail units, their rents helping to defray the cost of erecting the building.

Since the hall was opened, it has been a popular venue for a wide variety of lectures, films, shows and concerts, many of them not directly associated with the Methodist Church. The first 'moving pictures' show, Fraser's and Elrick's Royal Cinematograph, was held on Saturday 21 September 1901, with tickets being available from Fleming's Stores on the corner of Earl Grey Street. *Malcolm Cant Collection.*

Below right. This photograph by A. Swan Watson of Bruntsfield Place shows the elegant double staircase which leads to the crush hall above. The hall was designed for a total seating capacity of 2,000: 1,200 in the area, 700 in the gallery, and 100 on the platform. *Malcolm Cant Collection.*

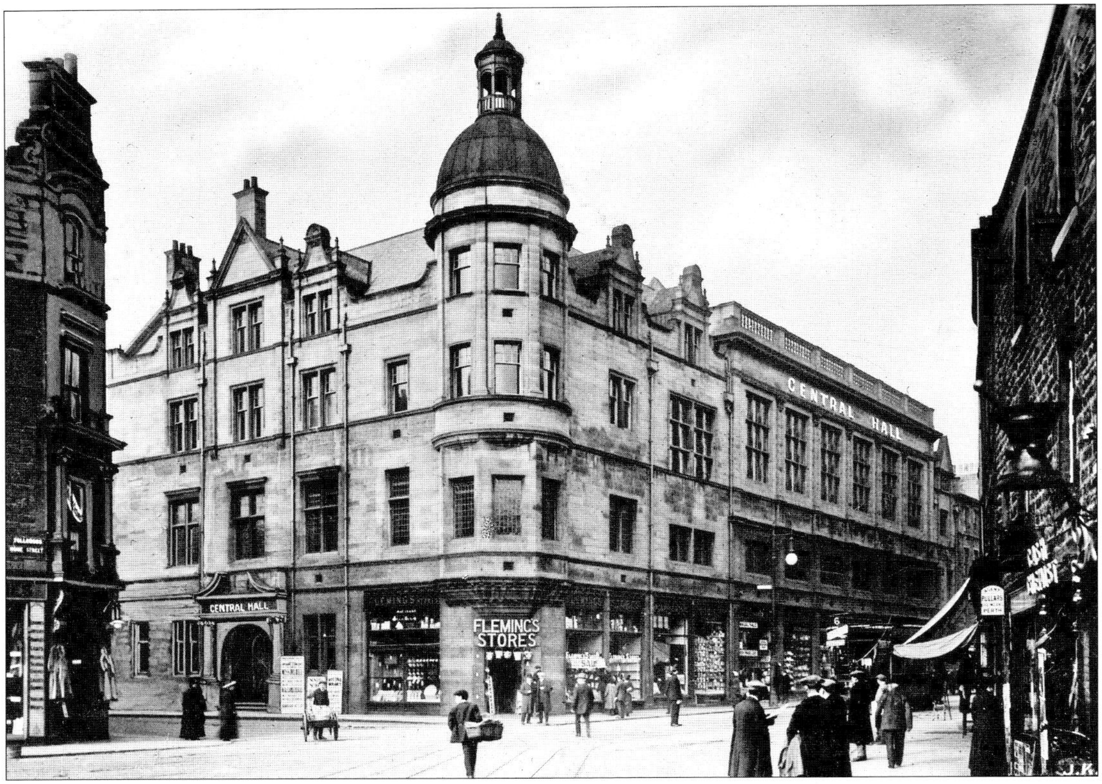

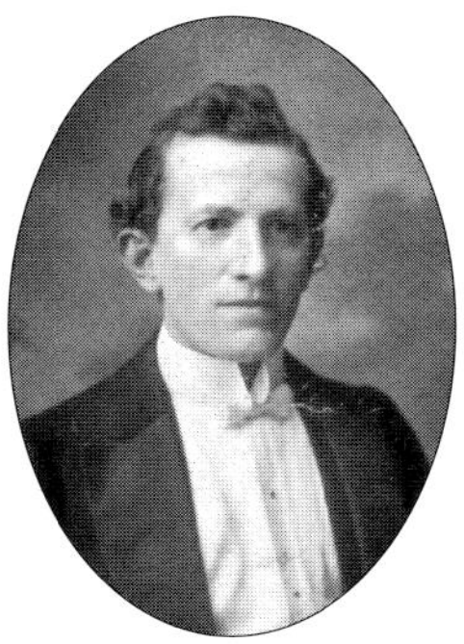

The concert on 4 October 1913 was preceded by a half-hour organ recital by T. Badenoch Caie. His repertoire included works by Bach, Hailing and Schubert, followed by a selection from 'Rob Roy'.

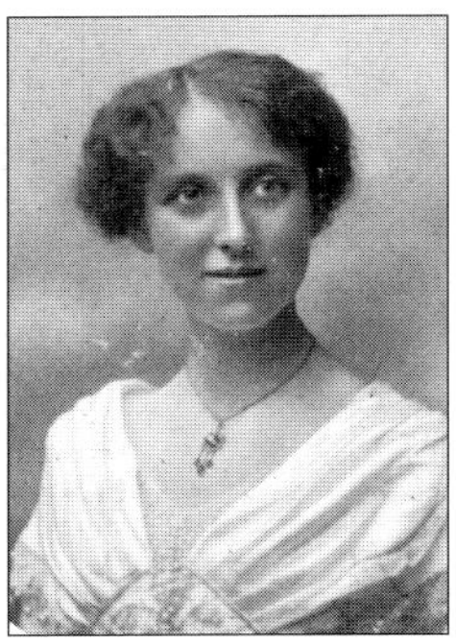

Miss Alice Cleugh, soprano, began with a song 'April Morn' by Batten, the concluding couplet being: 'Once again carol forth your joyous strain, Tell me now, will my love come again?'

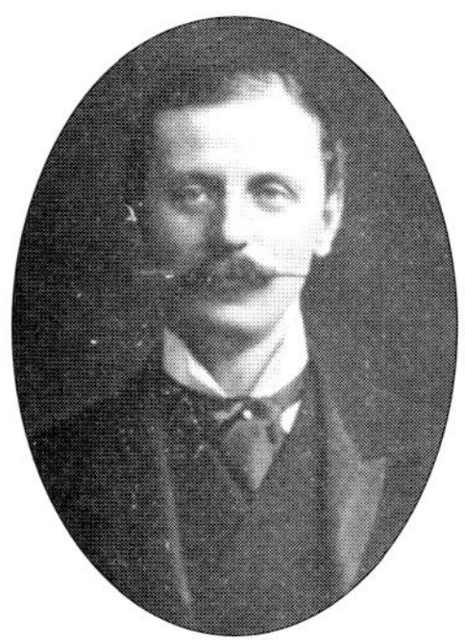

Mr George Campbell, baritone, was billed No. 2 on the programme with 'Eleanore': 'Oh take me to thy bosom fair; Oh, cover me with thy golden hair.'

All three portraits courtesy of Gordon McKean.

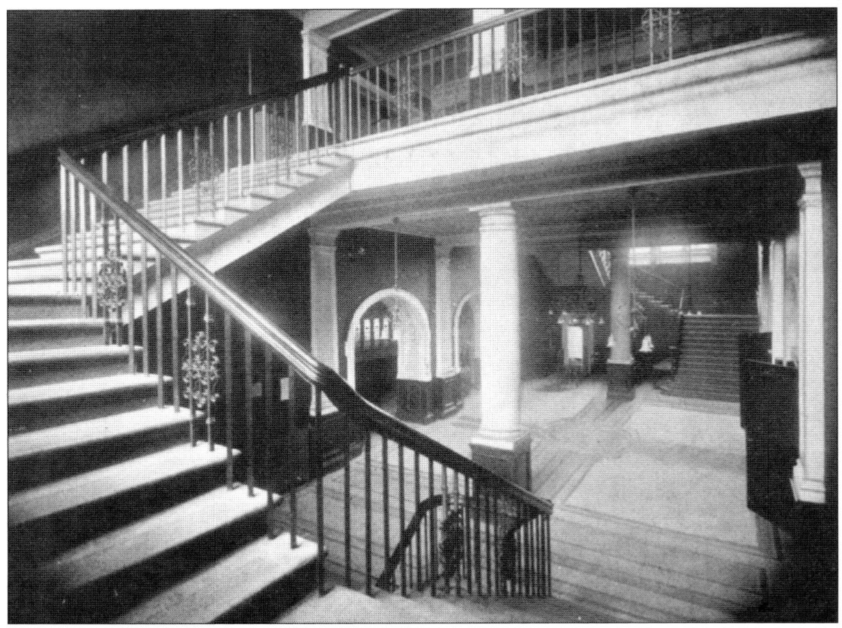

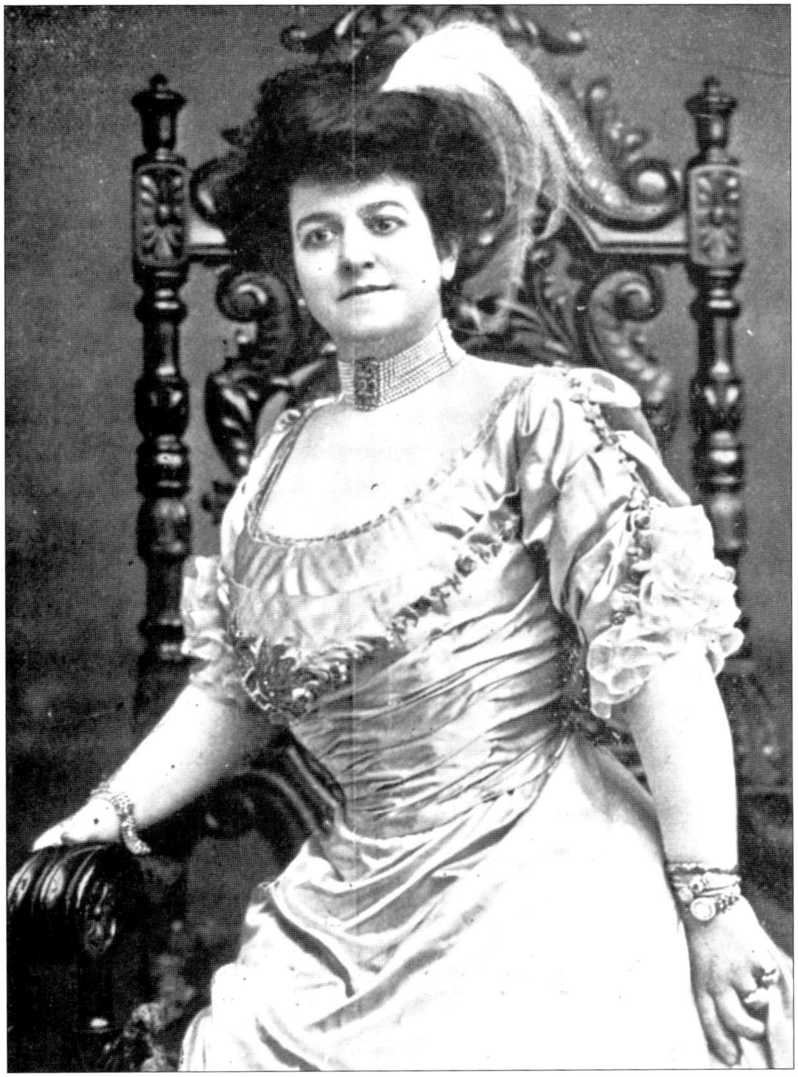

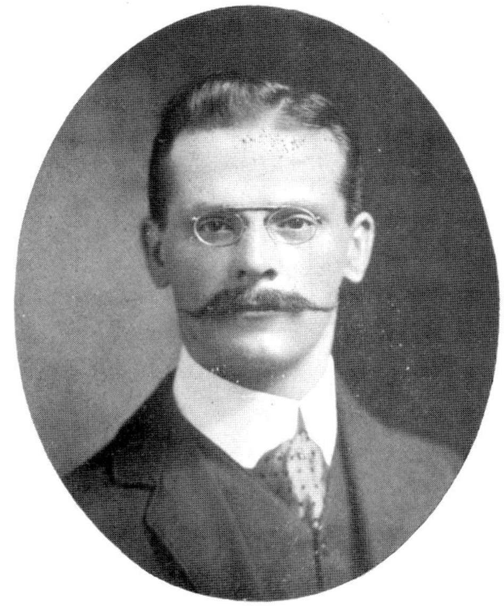

Manager: Mr Martin Hobkirk

SATURDAY POPULAR CONCERTS

11th October, at 7-30 p.m.

Madame Anna Shergold

Soprano

Of the Queen's Hall, London, and Clara Butt Tour

Miss Madge Macdonald = Elocutionist

Mr Charles Capper = Whistler

London and Provincial Concerts

Mr Gordon Brown = = = Baritone

Mr Martin Hobkirk, Pianist & Accompanist

Cinematograph Exhibition

(SERIES OF FOUR INTERESTING FILMS)

ADMISSION - - 6d and 3d

Front Balcony, Reserved and Numbered, 1s

Tickets at Fleming's Stores, Earl Grey Street

Above. The photograph of Mademoiselle Zelie de Lussan, the famous prima donna, adorns the front page of the programme of the Grand Opening Concert for the winter season at the Central Hall, Tollcross, beginning at 7.30 p.m. on Saturday 4 October 1913. The supporting cast included a host of other artistes: Miss Alice Cleugh, soprano; Mr Wilson Thornton, tenor; Mr George Campbell, baritone; Mr James Winram, violinist; Mr T. Badenoch Caie, organist; and Mr Martin Hobkirk, pianist.

Right. The back page of the same 1913 programme carried a picture of Mr Martin Hobkirk and a note of forthcoming attractions in the regular Saturday night concerts. *Both photographs courtesy of Gordon McKean.*

Right. The photograph is of the Tollcross junction, looking towards High Riggs and Lauriston Place, *c.* 1954. The clock has been moved on various occasions in the past to accommodate changes in road layout. The police box in the centre still has on its roof an air-raid siren used during the Second World War. The group of people are waiting for the next tram as the one in the picture says 'Tollcross' and is about to be reversed into the depot in West Tollcross, once the trolley has been turned round.

Lower left. The tram in Lauriston Place has PRIVATE on the destination board as it is on special operations, on this occasion to take boys from George Heriot's School to their playing fields at Goldenacre. The 1955 Trojan van, LWS 382, is an Edinburgh Corporation Transport control vehicle fitted with a radio mast. Some of the old shop fronts, now demolished, can be seen between the tram and the Trojan van.

Lower right. Electric tram No. 238 on service No. 23 is coming down Lauriston Place towards Tollcross, en route for Morningside Station. The shops on the right are: A. Marshall, the butcher; Fay's, the ladies' hairdresser; and Robert Bros., the fishmongers. The large van to the left of the tram belongs to Stuart Ward, the house furnishers of Lauriston Place.
All photographs courtesy of A. W. Brotchie.

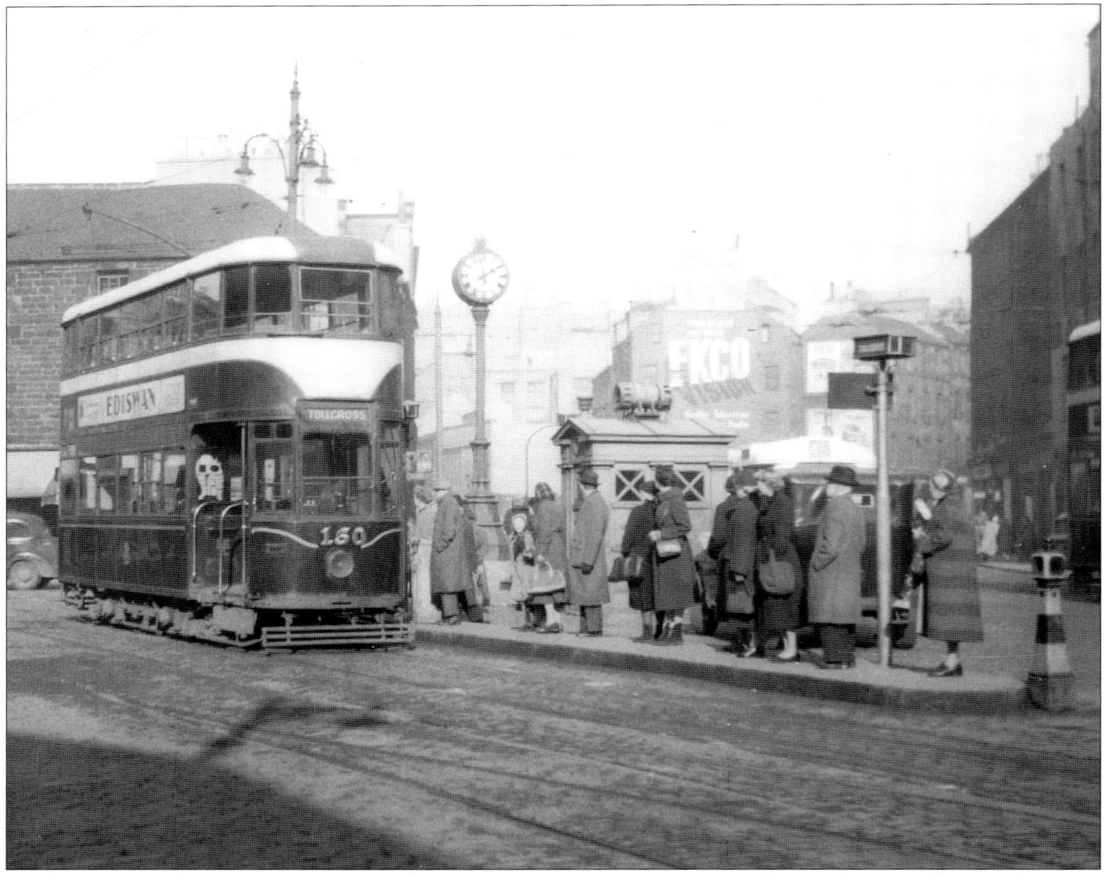

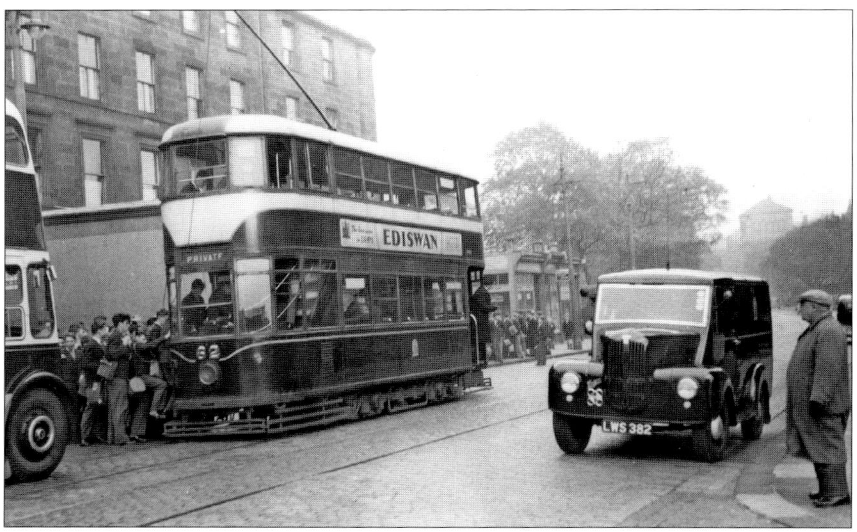

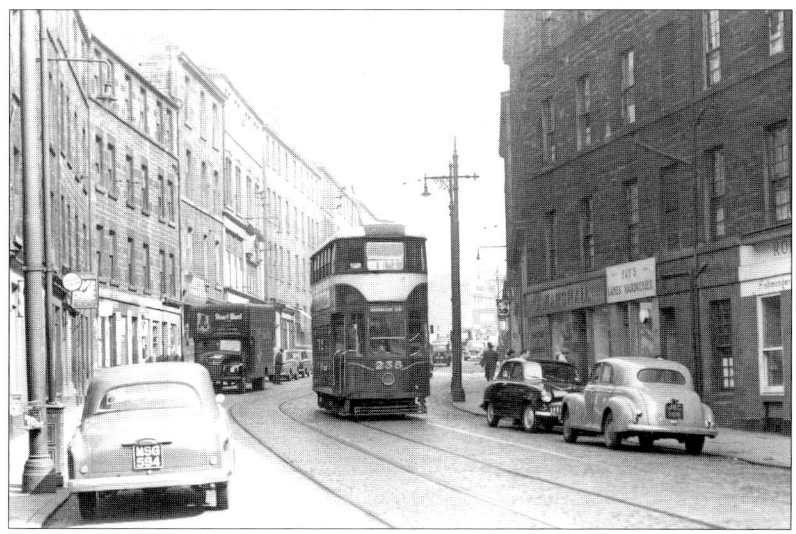

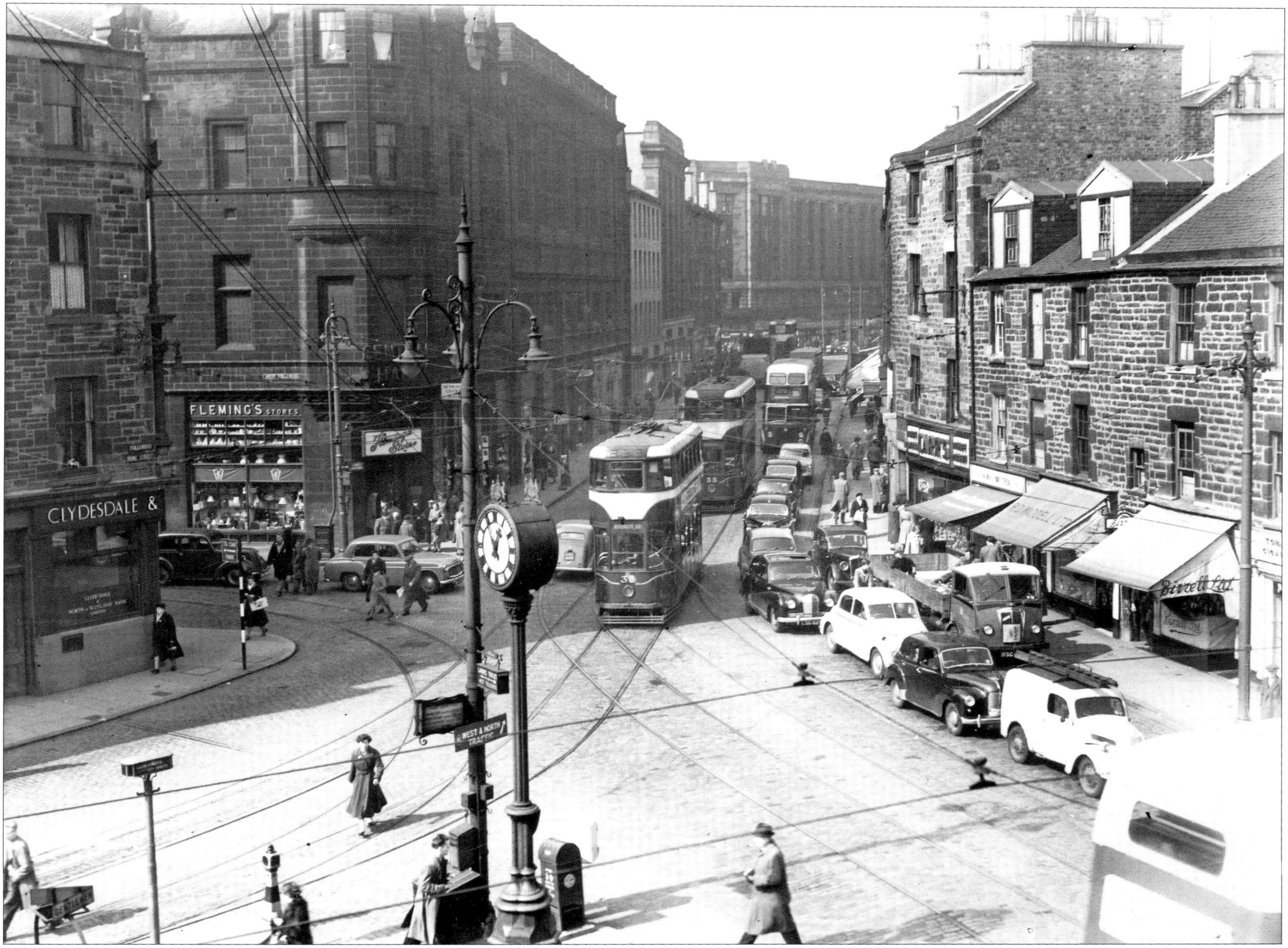

In this mid-1950s photograph, Earl Grey Street is only half its present width but has to contend with two-way traffic. Traffic was able to emerge, with difficulty, from West Tollcross where Fleming's Stores occupied the corner of the Methodist Central Hall building. The street furniture is very typical of the period: ornate lamp standards; a tiny road sign with an arrow for 'West & North Traffic'; and the city's answer to the litter problem – a small receptacle beside the lamp standard with the words, 'In your hands rests the cleanliness of Edinburgh'. On the right of the picture, the shops include Carr's Shoes and Birrell, the confectioner. The long line of traffic coming out of Earl Grey Street includes the No.15 bus which replaced the No.15 tram on 20 September 1954. Although the tramway system was being run down, the Tollcross depot was still in use, as can be seen from the single track running from West Tollcross. *Courtesy of A. W. Brotchie.*

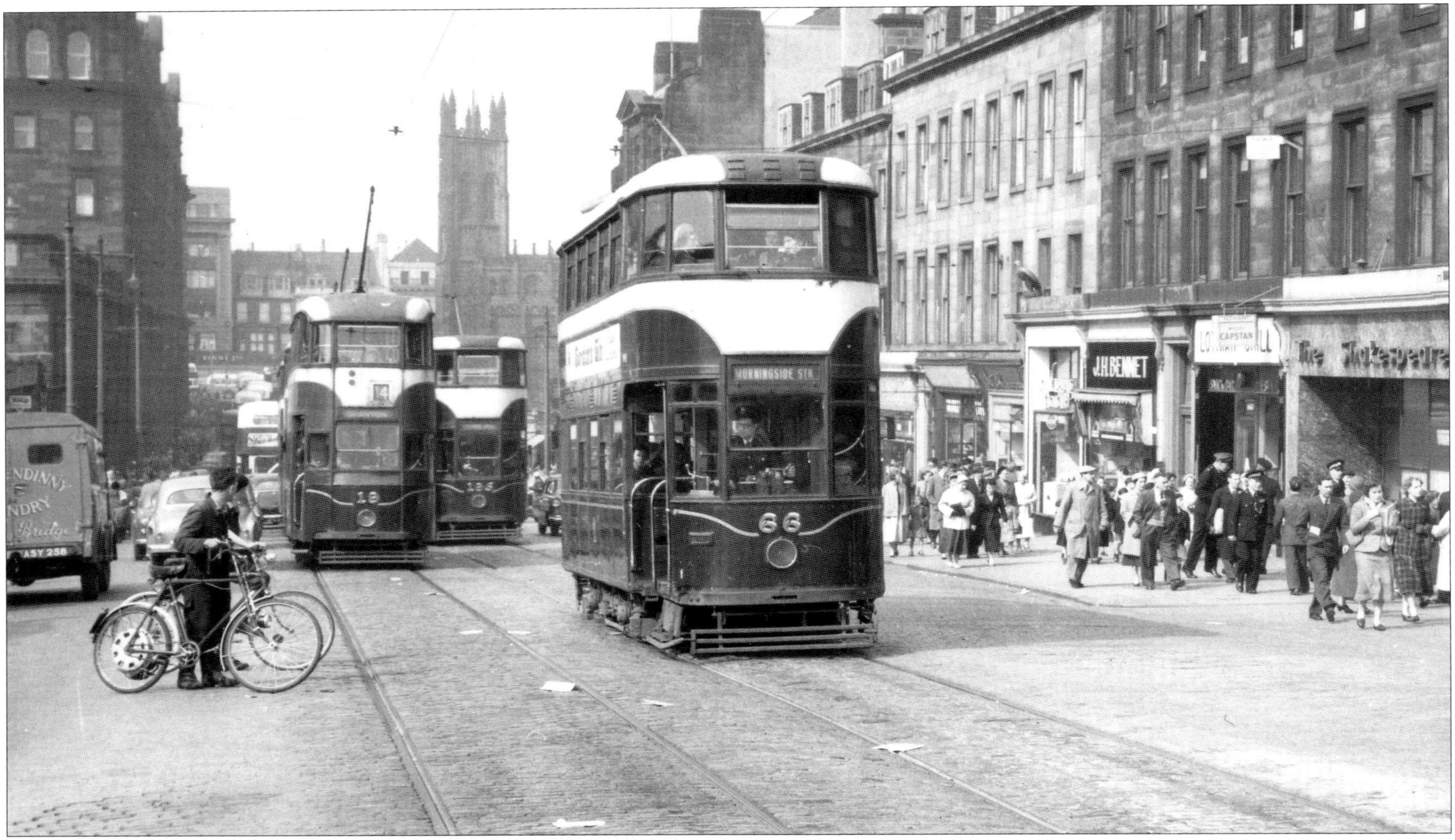

Above. The driver of the leading tram appears to be indicating to the young cyclists to cross. It is probably on service No.15, 'short working' to Morningside Station only. The bicycle nearest to the camera, which is fitted with a 2-stroke engine on the rear wheel, was possibly bought from J. R. Alexander & Co. Ltd., motor and cycle agents, of Nos. 10-14 Lothian Road. The van to the left of the cyclists is for the Auchendinny Laundry at Milton Bridge. The shops on the right include the Shakespeare Bar and J. H. Bennet for gramophone records, radio and television. The right-hand pavement is very busy, there are four policemen in the crowd and the roadway has a lot of discarded paper, which might suggest the aftermath of some event. The photograph might have been taken on 27 May 1956, being the last day of service No. 14, seen on the left going down Lothian Road. *Courtesy of A. W. Brotchie.*

Right. The Edinburgh Highland Church in Cambridge Street was built in 1851 and opened as Lothian Road Gaelic Free. The architect was Patrick Wilson. In 1956 the church formed a union with Tolbooth-St John's in Castlehill. The Cambridge Street building was later demolished for the construction of the Traverse Theatre. *Malcolm Cant Collection.*

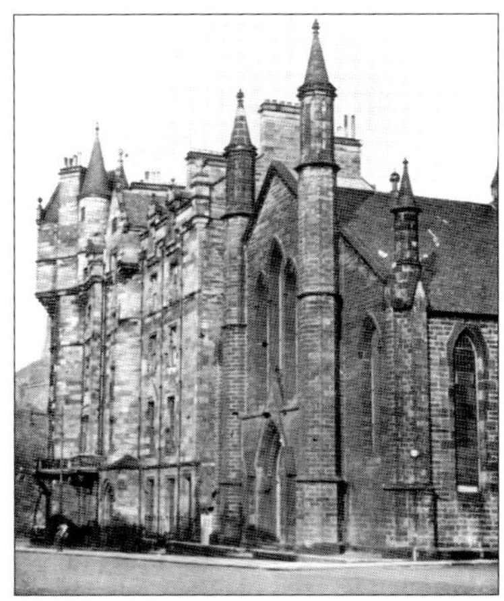

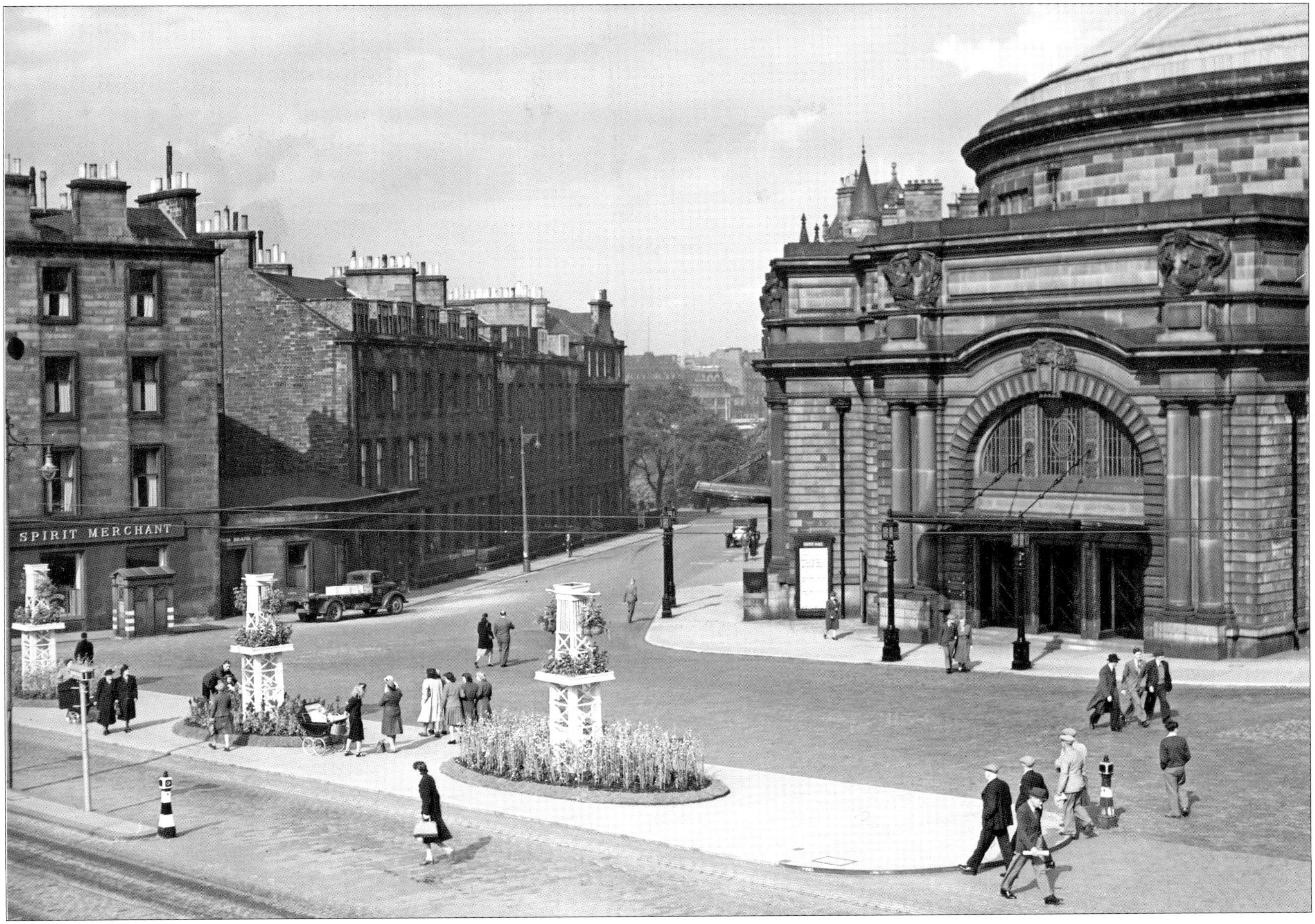

In this mid-1950s photograph, Lothian Road has been brightened up during the Edinburgh International Festival by the presence of temporary flower beds opposite the Usher Hall. The turf retaining the soil was merely laid directly on to the pavement. The photograph was taken before 1956 when Edinburgh's tram system was discontinued. The present Bell Tower was erected in about the position of the central floral display.

The foundation stones for the Usher Hall were laid by King George V and Queen Mary on 19 July 1911. A very elaborate ceremony was arranged with two identical stones in front of a large, open-fronted marquee for the royal guests and their entourage, guarded by the Royal Company of Archers and watched by a huge crowd of civic dignitaries. The architect was J. Stockdale Harrison of Leicester who won an open competition to design the hall, sponsored by Andrew Usher, the brewer, to the tune of £100,000.

Photograph by Norward Inglis.

INDEX